THE GLOSSARY OF
INFORMATION
ARCHITECTURE

Compiled & Edited By:
Vimal Gupta
Manasi Pathak

Rhythm

Independent
Publication

THE GLOSSARY OF INFORMATION ARCHITECTURE

Compiled & Edited By:
Vimal Gupta
Manasi Pathak

ISBN:9798862257151

9798862257151

Published by:

Rhythm Independent Publication,

Jinkethimmanahalli, Varanasi, Bengaluru, Karnataka, India - 560036

For all types of correspondence, send your mails to the provided address above.

The information presented herein has been collated from a diverse range of sources, comprehensive perspective on the subject matter.

A/B Tasty

A/B Tasty is an information architecture (IA) tool designed to help optimize and improve the user experience of websites through the use of A/B testing. A/B testing, also known as split testing, is a method of comparing two versions of a webpage or user interface to determine which one performs better in terms of achieving a desired outcome. It involves splitting your audience into two groups and showing each group a different version of your webpage. By comparing the performance metrics of each version, such as conversion rates or click-through rates, you can identify which version is more effective. A/B Tasty provides a platform for creating and managing A/B tests in a user-friendly manner. It includes features such as a visual editor for creating variations of webpages, advanced targeting options to show different versions to specific segments of your audience, and robust analytics to measure the impact of each variation. The tool also offers multivariate testing, which allows you to test multiple elements of a webpage simultaneously to determine the optimal combination. In addition to A/B testing, A/B Tasty also supports other types of experiments, such as personalization and split URL testing. Personalization involves dynamically adapting the content of a webpage based on specific user characteristics or behaviors, while split URL testing allows you to test different versions of an entire webpage on separate URLs. Overall, A/B Tasty is a powerful IA tool that enables website owners and marketers to make data-driven decisions about website design, layout, and content. By continuously testing and optimizing different variations of webpages, organizations can improve the user experience, increase conversions, and ultimately achieve their business goals.

Accessibility Auditing

An accessibility audit in the context of Information Architecture (IA) refers to the formal evaluation and assessment of a website or digital product to determine its level of accessibility for individuals with disabilities. The goal of an accessibility audit is to identify and address any barriers or obstacles that may prevent users with disabilities from effectively accessing and using the website or product. During an accessibility audit, various aspects of the IA are examined including the design, layout, navigation, and content of the website or product. Auditors review the implementation of accessibility standards and guidelines such as the Web Content Accessibility Guidelines (WCAG) to ensure compliance and to identify any deviations or areas of improvement.

Accessibility Compliance

Accessibility compliance in the context of Information Architecture (IA) refers to the practice of designing and implementing systems and digital experiences that are usable and accessible to all individuals, including those with disabilities. It involves adhering to specific guidelines and standards to ensure that information and interactive elements are perceptible, operable, understandable, and robust for all users. Perceptibility addresses the need for content to be presented in multiple formats to accommodate various disabilities. This includes providing alternatives to non-text content, such as images or multimedia, through captions, transcripts, or audio descriptions. It also involves using high contrast colors, clear typography, and appropriate font sizes to facilitate readability for people with visual impairments. Operability focuses on the ease with which users can navigate and interact with the digital experience. It encompasses considerations such as intuitive navigation menus, keyboard accessibility, and compatibility with assistive technologies like screen readers or speech recognition software. By ensuring that users can easily move through the content and perform actions, accessibility compliance enhances usability for individuals with motor impairments or those who rely on alternative input methods. Understanding refers to the clarity and simplicity of the content and interactive elements within the digital experience. It involves using plain and concise language, avoiding jargon, and providing clear instructions or error messages. Accessibility compliance in this regard facilitates comprehension for individuals with cognitive disabilities or limited literacy skills.

Robustness addresses the ability of the digital experience to adapt and withstand variations in user agents or assistive technologies. This includes using standard code and technologies, ensuring compatibility with different web browsers, and providing fallback options for non-supported features. By being robust, accessibility compliance ensures that the digital experience can be accessed by as many users as possible, regardless of the tools or technologies they use.

Accessibility Testing

Accessibility testing in the context of Information Architecture (IA) refers to the process of evaluating how easily individuals with disabilities can access and interact with a digital product or website. It is an essential component of designing and creating inclusive and user-friendly digital experiences. The goal of accessibility testing is to identify any barriers or limitations that may prevent individuals with disabilities from fully utilizing the digital product or website. This can include individuals with visual, auditory, cognitive, or motor impairments, as well as those with temporary disabilities or situational limitations. During accessibility testing, various techniques are employed to assess the product's compliance with accessibility guidelines and standards, such as the Web Content Accessibility Guidelines (WCAG). These techniques may involve both automated testing tools and manual evaluation, relying on assistive technologies like screen readers, keyboard navigation, or voice recognition software. The testing process typically involves examining multiple aspects of the digital product or website, including its visual design, structure, navigation, content, and functionality. It aims to ensure that individuals with disabilities can perceive, understand, navigate, and interact with the information and features effectively. Accessibility testing also involves addressing the concept of "equivalent access." It focuses on providing individuals with disabilities the same level of access and functionality as those without disabilities, removing any unnecessary barriers or limitations that may hinder their experience. By conducting accessibility testing, IA professionals can identify accessibility issues and implement corrective measures to enhance the overall usability and inclusivity of the digital product or website. This ensures that individuals with disabilities can access and engage with the content and services provided, promoting equal opportunities and user satisfaction.

Adalo

Adalo is a powerful platform that enables users to create custom mobile apps without the need for coding, allowing them to design and develop their own applications using a visual interface. In the context of Information Architecture (IA), Adalo offers a range of tools and features that help users in organizing and structuring information within their applications. With Adalo's IA capabilities, users can define the structure and hierarchy of their app's navigation menus, screens, and content. This allows for a seamless and intuitive user experience, as users can easily navigate through the app and find the information they are looking for. Adalo provides a user-friendly interface that simplifies the process of creating and managing consistent navigation patterns, ensuring that users can effortlessly move between different sections and screens of the app.

Adobe Fireworks

Adobe Fireworks is a software application that is widely used in Information Architecture (IA) for creating and editing visual designs and user interfaces for websites and applications. It is specifically designed to optimize the workflow of web designers and developers, allowing them to quickly and efficiently create, prototype, and refine their designs. With its powerful set of tools and features, Adobe Fireworks enables IA professionals to create wireframes, mockups, and interactive prototypes that help visualize the structure and layout of a website or application. It provides an intuitive and user-friendly interface, allowing IA experts to easily translate their ideas into visually appealing designs.

Adobe XD

Adobe XD is a software tool specifically designed for creating and prototyping user interfaces and experiences. It is widely used in the field of Information Architecture (IA) to assist in the creation and organization of digital content. IA is the practice of structuring and organizing information to enhance user understanding and interaction with a system or application. It focuses on strategic planning and designing the underlying structure and organization of content to ensure easy navigation and a seamless user experience. With Adobe XD, designers and IA professionals can visually design and prototype websites, web applications, mobile apps, and other digital products. The tool allows for the creation of wireframes, interactive prototypes, and highly detailed designs that help stakeholders and team members understand the layout, navigation, and flow of information within a system.

Affinity Diagram

An affinity diagram is a technique used in Information Architecture (IA) to organize and categorize large amounts of information or data into meaningful groups or clusters. It helps to identify patterns, connections, and relationships among various pieces of information, enabling IA practitioners to gain insights and make informed decisions. The affinity diagram process typically involves the following steps: - Brainstorming: Individuals or groups generate ideas, concepts, or data points related to a specific topic or problem. These ideas are usually written on sticky notes or index cards. - Sorting: The collected sticky notes or index cards are then grouped and sorted based on their similarities or common themes. This can be done by physically moving and arranging the cards on a wall or using digital tools. - Labeling: Each group or cluster is assigned a descriptive label that represents the common theme or category. This helps to provide an overarching structure and organization to the information. - Iteration and refinement: The process can be iterative, with participants continuously reviewing and refining the groupings and labels based on additional insights or perspectives. The affinity diagram technique leverages the natural cognitive ability of humans to identify patterns and relationships. By organizing information into clusters, it becomes easier to see connections and identify potential gaps or overlaps. This can be particularly useful when dealing with complex or multidimensional data sets. Information architects use affinity diagrams to facilitate the uncovering of user needs, goals, and preferences, which are essential for designing effective IA systems. It helps to make sense of large amounts of information and provides a visual representation of the relationships, allowing for clearer communication and collaboration among stakeholders. Overall, the affinity diagram is a valuable tool in the IA toolbox, enabling practitioners to make sense of complex information, discover insights, and create meaningful structures for effective information organization and retrieval.

Affordance

Affordance in the context of Information Architecture (IA) refers to the perceived or actual functionality or possibilities of an element or object within a digital interface. It is the visual or structural cues that suggest how an element can be used or interacted with. Affordances help users understand the potential actions they can take and guide their behavior within a digital system. They provide important clues that communicate both the purpose and functionality of an element, helping users to make effective and efficient decisions about how to interact with the interface.

Affordances

Affordances, in the context of Information Architecture (IA), refer to the potential actions or interactions that can be inferred by users based on the design and appearance of an object or interface. They provide cues to users about how they can interact with a system, guiding them towards the intended functionality and helping them make informed decisions. In IA, affordances play a crucial role in shaping the user experience and influencing usability. They guide users in exploring and understanding the structure and organization of information within a digital environment. By understanding and leveraging affordances, designers can create intuitive and user-friendly interfaces that facilitate seamless navigation and information retrieval.

Amplitude

Amplitude refers to the breadth and range of information within an Information Architecture (IA) system. It encompasses the overall scope and extent of the content, data, and functionality that is included within the IA. In the context of IA, amplitude is a crucial consideration for designing and managing digital systems. It plays a vital role in shaping the user experience and ensuring that the IA system meets the needs of its intended users. The amplitude of an IA system is determined by the various components it encompasses, including the number and types of information resources, the breadth of topics covered, and the diversity of functionalities provided. This includes the range of content types, such as text, images, videos, and interactive elements, as well as the depth of information provided within each content type. Amplitude also takes into account the organization and structure of the IA system. This involves how the information is categorized, classified, and interconnected, in order to facilitate effective navigation and retrieval for users. It considers the hierarchy and relationships between different information elements and ensures that the IA system can accommodate future growth and expansion. Striking the right balance of amplitude is crucial in IA design. Too narrow an amplitude can limit the system's usefulness and relevance, leaving users without access to the necessary information and functionality. Conversely, excessive amplitude can result in information overload and make it challenging for users to find and navigate the relevant content. Designers and architects need to consider the target audience and their specific information needs when determining the amplitude of an IA system. By understanding the users' goals, tasks, and preferences, they can ensure that the IA system provides the right level of breadth and depth, enabling users to locate and utilize the information effectively.

Antetype

Antetype is a software tool used in Information Architecture (IA) to create interactive, high-fidelity prototypes for digital products. It is specifically designed to facilitate the design and testing of user interfaces, navigation structures, and content organization. Antetype provides a range of features that support the IA process, including a comprehensive set of pre-built UI components, customizable widget libraries, and an intuitive drag-and-drop interface. These features allow IA professionals to quickly and efficiently design and iterate on the layout and structure of a website or application.

Anti-Pattern

An Anti-Pattern refers to a recurring design or practice that initially seems like a solution but ultimately leads to negative consequences and inefficiencies within a system, process, or methodology. In the context of Information Architecture (IA), an Anti-Pattern signifies the use of suboptimal or counterproductive techniques in organizing and presenting information, hindering users' ability to find, comprehend, and navigate the content effectively. One example of an IA Anti-Pattern is the "Mega Menu" approach. Mega menus typically employ an expansive dropdown interface on websites, aiming to display a large number of navigational options at once. Despite the intention of providing users with more choices and easy access to various sections, mega menus often lead to confusion, cognitive overload, and difficulty in quickly locating desired information. Another common IA Anti-Pattern is the excessive use of Deep Nested Menus. This occurs when hierarchical menu structures become overly complex, with numerous levels of submenus nested within one another. Deep nested menus tend to overwhelm users by hiding important content layers deep within the navigation structure, making it arduous to navigate back and forth or comprehend the overall information architecture. Furthermore, the "Everything is Important" Anti-Pattern represents a flawed approach to prioritization and content hierarchy. This phenomenon occurs when every element on a website or application is presented with equal visual weight and prominence, leading to visual clutter and a lack of visual cues for users to distinguish important information from less crucial details. As a result, users struggle to focus on key content, leading to a compromised user experience.

Apptimize

Apptimize is a platform that offers A/B testing and multivariate testing solutions for mobile apps. It allows information architects to optimize their app's user experience by testing different variations of elements such as layouts, features, and content to determine which version performs better in terms of user engagement and conversions. With Apptimize, information architects can create multiple variants of their mobile app's interface and deploy them to different segments of their user base. Through these tests, they can analyze and measure the impact of each variation on user behavior, interactions, and conversions. These insights help information architects make data-driven decisions to improve the overall user experience and achieve their desired goals, such as increasing user engagement, retention, and conversion rates.

Augmented Reality (AR) IA

4

Augmented Reality (AR) in the context of Information Architecture (IA) refers to the integration of virtual elements into the real world environment through the use of technology. IA, on the other hand, focuses on organizing and structuring information to facilitate user interaction and navigation within a digital platform. AR IA combines the principles and techniques of both augmented reality and information architecture to create meaningful and immersive experiences for users. It involves the incorporation of virtual content, such as 3D models, animations, and interactive elements, into the physical world in a way that seamlessly blends with the user's surroundings. This integration allows users to interact with and manipulate digital information in a more intuitive and natural manner. The goal of AR IA is to enhance the user's understanding and interaction with the information presented. By overlaying digital content onto the physical world, AR IA provides users with additional context, guidance, and feedback, leading to improved comprehension and navigation. It enables users to visualize and explore complex data, concepts, or processes in a more tangible and accessible way. AR IA involves a systematic approach to structuring and organizing virtual content within the augmented environment. It requires careful consideration of the information hierarchy, navigation patterns, and user interactions to ensure a seamless and user-friendly experience. The IA aspect of AR IA focuses on designing clear and logical pathways for users to access and interact with the augmented content. This involves the use of information organization techniques, such as categorization, labeling, and grouping, to facilitate efficient and effective information retrieval and manipulation. In summary, Augmented Reality in the context of Information Architecture combines the principles of both augmented reality and information architecture to create immersive and meaningful experiences for users. It involves the integration of virtual content into the real world environment to enhance user understanding and interaction with information. AR IA requires careful organization and structuring of information within the augmented environment to facilitate seamless navigation and manipulation. By blending digital and physical elements, AR IA provides users with a more intuitive and accessible way to interact with digital information.

Augmented Reality (AR)

Augmented Reality (AR) is a technological concept used in Information Architecture (IA) that involves the integration of digital information with the physical environment, resulting in a mixed reality experience. AR aims to enhance and enrich the user's perception of reality by overlaying computer-generated content onto their view of the real world. This is achieved using a combination of sensors, cameras, and displays, allowing users to see and interact with virtual objects as if they were physically present in their surroundings.

Avocode

Avocode is a software tool designed for collaboration among designers and developers in the context of Information Architecture (IA). It facilitates efficient design hand-off by allowing designers to upload their files in various formats, such as Sketch, Adobe XD, and Figma, which can then be inspected, coded, and version-controlled by developers. The primary purpose of Avocode in the realm of IA is to bridge the gap between design and development teams, enabling seamless communication and collaboration throughout the entire design process. It serves as a central hub where designers can store and share their design files, while developers can access, analyze, and extract necessary information from these files to implement the design in code.

Axure Cloud

Axure Cloud is a cloud-based platform designed for the creation, sharing, and collaboration of interactive prototypes and design documentation within the field of Information Architecture (IA). As an information architect, one of the fundamental tasks is to visually communicate the structure and organization of information within a system or website. Axure Cloud serves as a valuable tool in this process by allowing IA professionals to efficiently create and share interactive prototypes that accurately represent the hierarchical relationships and navigation paths of the information.

Axure RP

Axure RP is a software tool used for creating interactive wireframes, prototypes, and specifications for websites and applications. In the context of Information Architecture (IA), Axure RP is a powerful tool that enables IA professionals to visually design and communicate the structure and organization of information within a website or application. It provides a platform for IA practitioners to create wireframes and prototypes that showcase the navigation, content layout, and interaction patterns of a digital product. Axure RP allows IA professionals to define and refine the taxonomy and hierarchy of a website or application by creating visual representations of the information structure. Through its drag-and-drop interface, IA practitioners can easily create and modify sitemaps, flowcharts, and user flow diagrams to represent the organization of content and the relationships between different sections and pages. With Axure RP, IA professionals can also define and annotate the content and functionality of different components or elements within the wireframes or prototypes. This helps to articulate the purpose and behavior of various interactive elements, such as menus, buttons, forms, and navigation bars, within the overall information structure. Furthermore, Axure RP offers features for user testing and feedback gathering. IA professionals can create interactive prototypes with simulated user interactions and collect feedback on the usability and effectiveness of the information architecture. This allows for iterative refinements based on user insights and helps ensure that the final product aligns with the intended user experience and IA goals. In summary, Axure RP is a specialized software tool that facilitates the creation of visual representations of information architecture, enabling IA professionals to design, communicate, and refine the structure and organization of websites and applications.

Axure Share

Axure Share is a web-based platform that facilitates the collaboration and sharing of Axure RP prototypes and design specifications within a team or with clients. It is a tool used in the practice of Information Architecture (IA) to streamline the process of gathering feedback, conducting user testing, and iterating on designs. With Axure Share, designers can upload their Axure RP files and create interactive prototypes that can be easily accessed and viewed by stakeholders. This allows team members to provide feedback and comments directly on the prototypes, eliminating the need for lengthy email chains or physical meetings. The platform also supports version control, ensuring that everyone is working on the most up-to-date design. The ability to share design specifications is another valuable feature of Axure Share. Designers can easily generate documentation that outlines the details of the design, including colors, fonts, interactions, and other specifications. This ensures consistency in the implementation of the design and helps developers understand the intended behavior of the interface. Axure Share also supports user testing and usability studies. Designers can create multiple versions of a prototype and distribute them to different user groups for testing purposes. The platform provides tools for collecting and analyzing user feedback, allowing designers to make informed decisions based on user preferences and behaviors. In the context of Information Architecture, Axure Share plays a crucial role in facilitating collaboration among IA professionals, designers, developers, and stakeholders. It helps align everyone involved in the design process and ensures a shared understanding of the project's goals and requirements. By providing a centralized platform for communication and feedback, Axure Share enhances the efficiency and effectiveness of the IA process. Overall, Axure Share is an essential tool for IA professionals, as it streamlines the collaboration and sharing of prototypes and design specifications. It improves the communication and feedback process, facilitates user testing and usability studies, and ultimately helps create successful and user-friendly digital products.

Balsamiq Cloud

Balsamiq Cloud is an online platform for creating and collaborating on wireframe designs. It is specifically designed to support the practice of Information Architecture (IA), which involves organizing and structuring information to enhance usability, findability, and overall user experience. As an IA tool, Balsamiq Cloud provides a user-friendly interface that allows designers and stakeholders to quickly sketch out and iterate on wireframe designs. Wireframes are simplified visual representations of web pages or application screens that focus on the layout, structure, and functionality of the user interface.

Balsamiq

Balsamiq is a wireframing tool designed to help information architects visually represent and conceptualize the structure and functionality of a digital product or website. It is used to create low-fidelity prototypes that mimic the basic layout and interactions of the final product, allowing designers and stakeholders to quickly iterate and gather feedback. As an information architecture tool, Balsamiq aids in the creation of user-centered designs by providing a platform to effectively communicate and validate design decisions. It allows IA professionals to organize and present information hierarchically, showcasing the relationships between different content elements and navigation paths.

Beaver Builder

Beaver Builder is a drag-and-drop page builder plugin for WordPress that allows users to customize the design and layout of their website without the need for coding or technical skills. It provides a user-friendly interface and a set of intuitive tools that enable users to create and edit website pages in a visual and interactive way. From an Information Architecture (IA) perspective, Beaver Builder plays a significant role in enhancing the overall user experience and usability of a website. By allowing users to easily modify the layout and structure of their web pages, it empowers them to organize and present information in a more intuitive and user-friendly manner.

Bluemap

A Bluemap is an essential tool in Information Architecture (IA) used to create visual representations of the structure and organization of a website or application. It is a diagrammatic representation that illustrates the hierarchical relationships between pages, sections, and content elements within a digital product. The purpose of a Bluemap is to provide a clear and concise overview of the IA, allowing designers, developers, and stakeholders to understand and navigate the complexity of information within the system. It serves as a blueprint or roadmap for the design and development process, facilitating communication and collaboration among team members.

Booster For WooCommerce

Booster for WooCommerce is a plugin developed specifically for the WooCommerce platform which enhances the functionality and performance of online stores powered by WooCommerce. Created by Pluggabl LLC, Booster for WooCommerce aims to optimize the shopping experience for both store admins and customers by providing a wide range of features and tools. As an information architecture (IA) component, Booster for WooCommerce plays a crucial role in organizing and structuring the content and functionality of an online store. It helps establish a solid foundation for the user interface (UI) and user experience (UX) design by ensuring intuitive navigation and clear communication of information. By implementing Booster for WooCommerce, online store owners and developers can benefit from its rich set of features, including product price and currency management, product add-ons, discount rules, custom fields, cart customization, and many others. These features enable store admins to seamlessly manage their products, pricing, and promotional activities, ultimately resulting in improved efficiency and increased sales. From an IA perspective, Booster for WooCommerce contributes to the organization and categorization of product-related information. It allows for the creation of custom product fields, enabling store admins to add specific attributes to their products, such as size, color, or material. This helps users easily find and filter products based on their preferences, leading to a more personalized and targeted shopping experience. Moreover, with Booster for WooCommerce, online stores can implement dynamic pricing strategies by setting up discount rules based on various criteria, such as product quantity, customer role, or purchase history. This customization capability ensures that customers receive fair pricing, encourages repeat purchases, and enhances customer loyalty. In conclusion, Booster for WooCommerce is an essential element of the information architecture of WooCommerce-powered online stores. It provides a comprehensive set of features that enhance the functionality and usability of online stores, facilitating efficient product management, personalized shopping experiences, and dynamic pricing strategies.

Bottom-Up Card Sorting

Bottom-Up Card Sorting is a method used in Information Architecture (IA) to organize and categorize large amounts of information or content. It is a user-centered approach that involves the participation of users in the process of structuring information and creating meaningful categories. In Bottom-Up Card Sorting, users are provided with a set of cards, each representing a piece of information or content, and they are asked to group these cards into categories that make sense to them. Unlike Top-Down Card Sorting where predefined categories are given to users, Bottom-Up Card Sorting allows users to define their own categories based on their own mental models and understanding of the content.

Breadcrumb Navigation

Breadcrumb Navigation is a user interface element commonly used in Information Architecture (IA) to provide users with a clear and visually displayed path of their current location within a website or application. It allows users to easily understand their current position within the overall structure of the website or application, and provides them with a convenient way to navigate back to previously visited pages. The term "Breadcrumb Navigation" is derived from the Hansel and Gretel fairy tale, where the characters used breadcrumbs to mark their path through the forest. Similarly, in the context of IA, breadcrumb navigation serves as a trail of clickable links that represent the hierarchical path a user has taken to arrive at the current page. The breadcrumb navigation typically appears near the top of a webpage or application interface, either horizontally or vertically, depending on the design. It consists of a sequence of links separated by a delimiter, usually an arrow or a slash. Each link represents a level of the website or application's hierarchy, starting from the homepage or the highest level and ending with the current page. The purpose of breadcrumb navigation is to enhance the user experience by providing a clear and intuitive way for users to navigate within a website or application. It enables users to quickly understand the relationship between different pages, and allows them to easily backtrack or jump to higher-level pages. From an information architecture standpoint, breadcrumb navigation helps users understand the structure and organization of the content within the website or application. It provides a visual representation of the hierarchical relationships between pages, helping users to better comprehend the overall information space. In summary, breadcrumb navigation is a user interface element used in information architecture to provide users with a clear and visual representation of their current location within a website or application. It enhances the user experience by enabling easy navigation and helping users understand the structure and organization of the content.

Breadcrumbs

Breadcrumbs are a navigational aid commonly used in website design and information architecture (IA) to provide users with a way to understand their current location within a website's structure and easily navigate back to higher-level categories or pages. They typically appear at the top of a webpage, just below the header or primary navigation, and consist of a series of links or labels that represent the hierarchical path to the current page. In their simplest form, breadcrumbs consist of a single link or label that represents the homepage or main landing page of the website. As users navigate deeper into the site, additional links or labels are added to the breadcrumb trail to represent the categories, sub-categories, or pages above the current page. Each link or label in the breadcrumb trail is separated by a delimiter, such as a forward slash (/) or a right angle bracket (>), which helps visually distinguish the links. The primary purpose of breadcrumbs is to improve the usability and user experience of a website by providing users with a clear understanding of their current location within the site's structure. This is particularly useful for larger websites with complex structures or deep hierarchical levels. Breadcrumbs help users orient themselves, maintain a sense of context, and easily navigate back to higher-level categories or pages without relying solely on the browser's back button or the website's primary navigation. Breadcrumbs can also provide additional benefits for search engine optimization (SEO) and usability. From an SEO perspective, breadcrumbs can enhance the website's internal linking structure, providing search engines with more information about the hierarchy and relationships between pages. This can potentially improve the visibility and ranking of individual pages in search engine results. From a usability standpoint, breadcrumbs can reduce cognitive load by providing a visual representation of the user's location, making it easier for them to backtrack or explore related content.

Brick

A brick in the context of Information Architecture (IA) refers to a small unit of information that serves as a building block for organizing and structuring content within a digital system. It represents a discrete piece of content that can be categorized, labeled, and interconnected with other bricks to form a cohesive and navigable information space. Bricks in IA are typically designed to be modular and reusable, allowing for flexible content creation and organization. They can take various forms, such as text documents, images, videos, audio files, or interactive elements, depending on the nature of the information being represented.

Brizy

Information Architecture (IA) in the context of web design refers to the organization and structure of information within a website or application. It involves designing a logical and intuitive navigation system and categorizing content in a way that allows users to easily find and access the information they need. IA focuses on creating a clear and coherent structure for the content, ensuring that it is organized in a hierarchical manner. This involves grouping related information together and separating different types of content. The goal of IA is to make the user experience seamless and efficient, enabling users to quickly locate the information they are looking for.

Bubble

In the context of Information Architecture (IA), a bubble refers to a visual representation of a specific area or topic within a larger system or website. It signifies the presence of content, functionality, or information that is contained within a defined boundary or context. A bubble is typically used to organize and categorize content in a hierarchical manner, allowing users to navigate and access information more efficiently. It helps to create a clear and logical structure for organizing complex sets of data, making it easier for users to understand and find relevant information.

Cacoo

Cacoo is a cloud-based software tool used for creating and sharing diagrams, specifically in the context of Information Architecture (IA). It allows users to visually represent and communicate complex information through various types of diagrams such as flowcharts, wireframes, mind maps, and org charts. As an integral part of IA, Cacoo provides a platform for creating clear and insightful diagrams that aid in the organization, structure, and navigation of information systems. The software offers a wide range of pre-built templates and shapes specifically designed for IA purposes, enabling users to intuitively represent the relationships and hierarchies within a system or website.

Card Sorting

Card sorting is a method used in the field of Information Architecture (IA) to organize and categorize information in a way that reflects the mental models and thinking processes of target users or participants. It is primarily used as a user-centered design technique to gain insights into how users perceive and group information. In card sorting, participants are given a set of cards, each representing a discrete piece of information or content element. The participants are then asked to sort these cards into groups or categories based on their own understanding and associations. This process helps to uncover users' mental models, thought processes, and natural groupings of information.

Chalkmark

Chalkmark is an online usability testing tool that is commonly used in the field of Information Architecture (IA). It allows researchers to gather feedback on the effectiveness and efficiency of a website's navigation and organization. With Chalkmark, researchers can create tasks for participants to complete, such as finding specific information or completing a specific action on a website. Participants then interact with a prototype or a live website, and their mouse movements and clicks are recorded. Chalkmark captures this data and provides researchers with visual representations, such as heatmaps and clickmaps, to understand how participants navigate through the website. This tool enables researchers to gain insights into how users interpret and use the information architecture of a website. It helps to identify any potential usability issues, such as confusing navigation or unclear information hierarchy. Researchers can analyze the data collected through Chalkmark to make data-driven decisions about the website's IA, and make improvements accordingly. Chalkmark offers features that aid in the analysis of the gathered data. Researchers can filter and segment the data by participant demographics or other variables of interest, allowing for a deeper understanding of user behavior. Additionally, researchers can compare different iterations of a website's IA to evaluate the impact of changes. In conclusion, Chalkmark is a valuable tool in the field of Information Architecture. It provides researchers with the means to conduct usability testing, gather data on user interactions, and analyze the effectiveness of a website's IA. By utilizing Chalkmark, researchers can identify and address usability issues, improving the overall user experience of a website.

Clickable Prototypes

Clickable prototypes are interactive representations of a proposed design or user interface (UI) that allow users to simulate how the final product will function and navigate. They are a crucial component in the Information Architecture (IA) design process as they help designers, stakeholders, and users understand and evaluate the proposed content organization and navigation structure. A clickable prototype is typically created using HTML, CSS, and JavaScript, as these languages allow for interactivity and simulate user actions such as clicking, hovering, and scrolling. The prototype aims to replicate the actual user experience, allowing users to engage with the design by interacting with buttons, links, menus, and other UI elements. By providing users with the ability to click through the prototype, designers can gather valuable feedback on the proposed IA. Users can test the navigation flow, discover potential usability issues, and verify if the content organization meets their expectations and needs. This helps designers iterate and refine the IA before moving into the development phase. The construction of a clickable prototype involves careful consideration of the content hierarchy and navigation structure. Designers should prioritize easy access to key information, ensure intuitive navigation paths, and anticipate user behavior to create a seamless user experience. Clickable prototypes can be created at different fidelity levels. Low-fidelity prototypes are quick sketches or wireframes that focus on the structural layout and basic interaction. They are ideal for early concept validation and gathering initial feedback. High-fidelity prototypes, on the other hand, provide a more realistic representation of the final design, including visual details, and are best suited for user testing before development. In conclusion, clickable prototypes in the context of Information Architecture are interactive representations of proposed designs or UIs. They enable users to simulate the intended user experience, gather feedback, and refine the content organization and navigation structure. By allowing users to click through and interact with the prototype, designers can validate the IA design and provide stakeholders with a tangible understanding of the proposed solution.

Closed Card Sorting

Closed Card Sorting is a method used in Information Architecture (IA) to organize and categorize information based on user input. It involves the sorting and grouping of content into predefined categories or labels, known as closed categories, that have been predetermined by the IA practitioner or researcher. This method is called "closed" because the categories are already defined and users are not allowed to create their own categories. In a Closed Card Sorting activity, participants are given a set of cards, each representing a piece of content or information. The cards typically contain a short description or title, but may also include additional details or attributes if necessary. The participants' task is to sort and group these cards into the predefined categories provided. The process typically begins with a brief introduction to the purpose of the activity and an overview of the predefined categories. Participants are then given the set of cards and are asked to sort them into the categories they believe best fit. They can rearrange the cards as many times as they wish until they are satisfied with their categorization. Once the participants have completed their sorting, the IA practitioner or researcher collects the categorized cards and analyzes them to identify common patterns, inconsistencies, or challenges. The data collected through Closed Card Sorting can be used to inform the organization and structure of the information architecture, such as the navigation menus, sitemaps, or content hierarchies. Closed Card Sorting has several advantages. Firstly, it provides a structured approach to organizing content, ensuring that information is placed within the predefined categories. This can be particularly useful when designing websites or applications with specific predefined information architectures. Secondly, it allows for the collection of quantitative data, as the frequency of cards appearing in specific categories can be measured. Lastly, Closed Card Sorting can be relatively quick and inexpensive to conduct, making it an accessible method for IA practitioners and researchers. In conclusion, Closed Card Sorting is a method used in Information Architecture to categorize and organize content into predefined categories. Participants are given a set of cards and asked to sort them into these categories, providing valuable insights for designing effective information architectures.

Cloudcraft

Cloudcraft is an online tool used for designing and visualizing cloud architecture in the field of Information Architecture (IA). It allows users to create diagrams and models that represent the structure and components of a cloud-based system. These diagrams help in understanding the layout and functionality of the system, making it easier to communicate and collaborate with stakeholders. The main purpose of Cloudcraft is to provide a platform for designing, planning, and documenting cloud infrastructure. It offers a wide range of pre-defined icons and templates that can be used to represent various cloud services, servers, databases, networking components, and more. Users can drag and drop these icons onto the canvas to create a visual representation of their cloud environment. One of the key features of Cloudcraft is its ability to auto-generate accurate and up-to-date cloud diagrams based on real-time data from cloud providers such as AWS (Amazon Web Services). It can fetch information about resources, relationships, and configurations from the actual infrastructure and reflect them in the diagram. This ensures that the diagram remains synchronized with the cloud environment, eliminating the need for manual updates. Cloudcraft also supports collaboration and sharing of cloud diagrams. Multiple users can work together on a single diagram, making it ideal for teams working on cloud projects. It provides features like version history, commenting, and real-time editing, allowing users to collaborate effectively and exchange feedback. In addition to designing cloud architecture, Cloudcraft offers features for cost estimation and optimization. It can calculate the cost of resources and services deployed in the cloud environment, helping users make informed decisions regarding cost management and optimization. This feature is particularly useful for organizations looking to optimize their cloud spending. In conclusion, Cloudcraft is a web-based tool that assists in the design, visualization, and documentation of cloud architecture. It simplifies the process of creating cloud diagrams, promotes collaboration among team members, and provides cost estimation capabilities. Its integration with cloud providers ensures accurate and up-to-date representations of cloud environments, making it a valuable tool in the field of Information Architecture.

Coggle

Information Architecture (IA) refers to the practice of organizing and structuring information to facilitate effective navigation, retrieval, and understanding. It involves the design and construction of information environments that support the needs and behaviors of users. IA is concerned with the organization, labeling, and prioritization of information to create intuitive and user-friendly systems. It aims to enhance the findability, comprehensibility, and usability of information by creating logical and coherent structures.

Cognitive Load

Cognitive load refers to the amount of mental effort or resources required by an individual to process and understand information. In the context of Information Architecture (IA), cognitive load is a crucial factor to consider when designing and organizing digital content and interfaces. In order to minimize cognitive load, IA aims to present information in a clear, concise, and organized manner. This involves categorizing information into logical groups, providing meaningful labels and navigation elements, and reducing unnecessary complexity or distractions.

Cognitive Walkthrough

A cognitive walkthrough is a method used in Information Architecture (IA) to evaluate the usability and effectiveness of a website or application from a user's perspective. It involves analyzing and assessing how well users can accomplish tasks and achieve goals within the system, without any prior knowledge or assistance. During a cognitive walkthrough, an evaluator simulates specific user scenarios and steps through the interface, considering the user's thought process and decision-making at each stage. The primary objective is to identify any potential obstacles or shortcomings in the design that may hinder user engagement or lead to confusion. The process typically involves the following steps: 1. Define the user personas and their goals: Identify the target audience and the specific tasks they are likely to perform on the website or application. This helps frame the evaluation process and ensure it aligns with the intended user experience. 2. Create user scenarios: Develop a set of realistic scenarios that align with the identified personas and goals. These scenarios will be used to guide the evaluator's actions during the walkthrough. 3. Step through the interface: The evaluator systematically goes through each step of the user scenarios, interacting with the interface as a user would. They consider the visual hierarchy, information organization, and navigational structure of the system. 4. Evaluate task completion: For each step in the user scenarios, the evaluator assesses how easily the user can accomplish the intended task. They consider factors such as the clarity of instructions, the visibility of call-to-action elements, and the feedback provided after task completion. 5. Identify issues and propose improvements: Any usability issues or challenges encountered during the walkthrough are documented. These can include confusing labels, unclear directions, or cumbersome navigation. The evaluator then suggests potential improvements or design changes to address these issues. The cognitive walkthrough provides valuable insights into the user experience and helps identify areas for improvement in an information architecture design. By considering the user's perspective in each step of the evaluation, it enables designers and developers to create interfaces that are intuitive, efficient, and user-friendly. A cognitive walkthrough is an essential evaluation technique in Information Architecture, helping to ensure that the design meets the needs and expectations of the intended user audience.

Cohere Technologies

Cohere Technologies is a company that specializes in the development of innovative solutions for wireless communication systems. In the context of Information Architecture (IA), Cohere Technologies can be understood as a crucial player in the design and implementation of efficient and reliable networks. Information Architecture (IA) refers to the structure and organization of information within a system, which includes the design and arrangement of data, content, and functionality. It encompasses the methods and strategies used to categorize, label, and organize information to facilitate efficient navigation and usability. In this context, Cohere Technologies plays a vital role in IA by providing advanced wireless communication solutions that enable seamless connectivity and enhance the overall performance of information systems. Their expertise lies in developing innovative technologies that optimize the transmission and reception of data, improving the reliability, speed, and coverage of wireless networks. By leveraging Cohere Technologies' solutions, information architects can ensure that the underlying communication infrastructure is robust and capable of supporting the intended information system. This allows for the seamless transmission of data, enabling users to navigate through the system efficiently and access the information they need without delays or disruptions. Furthermore, Cohere Technologies' wireless communication solutions can enhance the overall user experience by providing high-speed connections, increased network capacity, and improved reliability. This directly contributes to the usability and accessibility of the information system, ultimately leading to enhanced user satisfaction. Overall, Cohere Technologies' expertise in developing and implementing advanced wireless communication solutions makes them a valuable partner in the field of Information Architecture. Their technologies contribute to the overall efficiency, reliability, and usability of information systems, ensuring seamless connectivity and an optimal user experience.

Concept Mapping Tools

A concept mapping tool is a software application or a visual representation method used in the field of Information Architecture (IA). It is designed to organize and connect various pieces of information or ideas based on their relationships, creating a visual map or diagram that helps in understanding complex subjects or concepts. In the context of IA, concept mapping tools are used to structure and organize information in a way that is logical and intuitive for users. These tools allow IA professionals to create visual representations of the connections and relationships between different concepts, helping to define the structure and hierarchy of information within a system or website.

Concept Testing

Concept testing, in the context of Information Architecture (IA), refers to the process of evaluating and validating new ideas, concepts, or designs for organizing and presenting information within a digital product or system. It is a crucial step in the IA design process that helps ensure that the proposed information structure meets the needs and expectations of the intended users. During concept testing, designers and researchers present the proposed IA concepts to a representative sample of users, stakeholders, or domain experts, seeking their feedback, opinions, and preferences. The goal is to gather insights and data that can be used to refine and improve the IA design before its full implementation.

Conceptboard

Conceptboard is a collaborative online tool used in the context of Information Architecture (IA). Information Architecture refers to the planning, organizing, and structuring of information within a system or website to support findability and usability. It involves designing the navigation, labeling, and categorization systems that help users easily navigate and understand the information presented to them.

Conceptual Modeling

A conceptual model in the context of Information Architecture (IA) refers to a high-level representation of the structure and organization of information within a system or domain. It is an abstract concept that helps in understanding and communicating the relationships, attributes, and constraints of the information. The purpose of conceptual modeling in IA is to create a shared understanding and a common language among stakeholders about how the information should be organized and accessed. It serves as a blueprint that guides the design and development of the information architecture. Conceptual modeling involves identifying and defining the entities, attributes, and relationships that exist within the information space. Entities represent the different types of objects or concepts that are relevant to the domain. Attributes describe the characteristics or properties of the entities. Relationships represent the associations and connections between entities. During the conceptual modeling process, various techniques can be used, such as entity-relationship diagrams, class diagrams, or semantic networks. These techniques provide visual representations of the conceptual model, making it easier to understand and communicate. The resulting conceptual model serves as a foundation for other aspects of information architecture, such as the development of taxonomies, navigation systems, and search functionality. It helps in organizing the information in a way that is intuitive, efficient, and meaningful for users. Conceptual modeling also helps in identifying potential gaps, inconsistencies, or redundancies in the information structure. It allows for the exploration of different design alternatives and the evaluation of their impacts before implementation. In conclusion, conceptual modeling in the context of Information Architecture is a fundamental process of defining and representing the structure and organization of information. It helps stakeholders to gain a shared understanding of the information space and guides the design and development of effective information architecture.

Conceptual Models

A conceptual model in the context of Information Architecture (IA) refers to the high-level representation of the organization, structure, and relationships of the information within a system, application, or website. It is a conceptual framework that helps designers, developers, and users understand and navigate through the information architecture. The main purpose of a conceptual model in IA is to provide a clear and intuitive mental model of how the information is organized and accessed. It serves as a communication tool between designers and stakeholders, ensuring that everyone has a shared understanding of how the information will be organized and presented to users. Conceptual models in IA can take various forms, such as hierarchical structures, network diagrams, flowcharts, or even narrative descriptions. These models typically depict the main categories, subcategories, and relationships between different chunks of information. One common type of conceptual model in IA is the "site map" or "taxonomy." A site map is a hierarchical representation of the website's pages, often organized into sections or categories. It provides an overview of the entire website's structure, helping users understand the relationship between different sections and how to navigate through the content. Another type of conceptual model is the "user flow" or "task flow" diagram. This diagram illustrates the sequence of steps a user takes to accomplish a specific task or goal within a

13

system or application. It highlights the different screens, actions, and decision points involved in the user journey, helping designers optimize the user experience and identify potential pain points.

Content Accessibility

Content accessibility, in the context of Information Architecture (IA), refers to the practice of designing and structuring digital content in a way that ensures it can be accessed, understood, and used by a wide range of users, including those with disabilities or impairments. It involves applying design principles, techniques, and guidelines to create content that is perceivable, operable, understandable, and robust for all users. Content accessibility aims to remove barriers and provide equal access to information and services for people with various abilities and needs.

Content Architecture

Content architecture, in the context of Information Architecture (IA), refers to the organization, structure, and presentation of content within a digital system or website. It involves the thoughtful arrangement of information to facilitate effective and efficient navigation, search, and comprehension by users. A well-designed content architecture aims to harmonize the needs of both the users and the content creators or administrators. It ensures that the information is logically organized, visually coherent, and easily accessible. The goal is to enable users to find the desired content quickly, understand its context and relevance, and perform their intended actions without confusion or frustration.

Content Audit

A content audit is a systematic process of evaluating and analyzing the content within a website or digital platform in order to gain insights into its effectiveness, relevance, and overall quality. It is an essential practice within Information Architecture (IA), which focuses on organizing and structuring information in a way that is intuitive, helpful, and user-friendly. During a content audit, each piece of content is meticulously examined and categorized based on a set of predefined criteria. These criteria may include factors such as accuracy, relevance, comprehensiveness, and alignment with business goals. The purpose is to gain a comprehensive understanding of the existing content landscape, identify areas for improvement, and inform future content creation and optimization efforts. The process of conducting a content audit typically involves several steps. First, a thorough inventory of all the content within the website or platform is created. This inventory includes not only the main pages and articles, but also any supplementary content such as images, videos, or downloadable files. Each piece of content is then reviewed and evaluated against the predetermined criteria. During the evaluation process, content may be assessed for its accuracy, currency, and accessibility. The quality of the writing style and language used may also be considered, along with the presence of appropriate keywords and metadata. Additionally, the content's structure, organization, and overall user experience are evaluated to ensure that it aligns with IA best practices. The insights gained from a content audit can be used to inform various aspects of the website or platform's development and maintenance. For example, it can help identify content that is outdated, redundant, or in need of revision. It can also reveal content gaps or opportunities for new content creation to address user needs or enhance engagement. In conclusion, a content audit is a valuable IA practice that helps assess the effectiveness and quality of the content within a website or digital platform. By systematically evaluating and categorizing content, it provides insights that can inform content optimization and creation efforts, ultimately enhancing the overall user experience and achieving business goals.

Content Auditing

Content auditing in the context of Information Architecture (IA) refers to the systematic evaluation and analysis of all content within a website or digital platform. It involves assessing the quality, relevance, accuracy, and effectiveness of the content in order to identify any gaps, inconsistencies, or areas for improvement. During the content auditing process, the IA team carefully examines the entire range of content, including text, images, videos, documents, and other media assets. The goal is to gain a comprehensive understanding of the existing content and its alignment with the overall goals and objectives of the website or platform. A content audit typically involves several steps. Firstly, the IA team compiles a complete inventory of all the content elements within the website or platform. This includes not only the main pages and articles but also any supplementary content such as navigation menus, sidebars, footers, and call-to-action buttons. Secondly, the team conducts a thorough analysis of each content element. This involves assessing factors such as the accuracy of the information provided, the clarity and conciseness of the writing, the appropriateness of imagery or visuals used, and the overall user experience provided by the content. Based on this analysis, the team then identifies any content that is outdated, redundant, or no longer relevant to the target audience. They may also flag any content that is poorly structured, hard to navigate, or lacks consistency in terms of style or tone. The ultimate purpose of a content audit is to inform future content strategy decisions. By highlighting the strengths and weaknesses of the existing content, the IA team can make recommendations for content improvements or optimizations. This may involve rewriting or updating outdated content, removing unnecessary or redundant content, or creating new content to fill any identified gaps. In summary, content auditing plays a crucial role in the IA process by providing insights into the effectiveness and relevance of the content within a website or digital platform. It helps ensure that the content aligns with the goals and objectives of the platform while also meeting the needs and expectations of the target audience.

Content Delivery Strategy

A content delivery strategy, in the context of Information Architecture (IA), refers to the plan or approach adopted to efficiently distribute and present content to the intended audience. It encompasses various considerations, such as content organization, delivery channels, content formats, and user preferences, to ensure that the right information reaches the right people at the right time in the most effective manner. The primary goal of a content delivery strategy is to enhance the user experience by facilitating easy access to relevant and meaningful content. This involves organizing the content in a logical and intuitive manner, making it easily discoverable and navigable for users. A well-designed content delivery strategy takes into account the target audience's needs and expectations, and tailors the content presentation accordingly.

Content Governance Framework

A Content Governance Framework in the context of Information Architecture (IA) refers to a set of rules, processes, and guidelines that define how content is planned, created, organized, and maintained within a website or digital platform. The framework is designed to ensure consistent and high-quality content that aligns with the goals, objectives, and user needs of the organization. It provides a structured approach to managing content, promoting collaboration between stakeholders, and enabling effective content management and maintenance.

Content Governance

Content governance refers to the processes, policies, and guidelines that are implemented to ensure the effective management and control of content within an information architecture (IA) framework. It encompasses the rules and procedures that govern the creation, organization, publication, and maintenance of content, allowing for consistency, quality, and accuracy across all digital platforms and channels. Within an IA context, content governance is essential for ensuring that the right content is delivered to the right audience at the right time. It involves establishing a framework that outlines the roles, responsibilities, and decision-making processes for all stakeholders involved in content creation and management.

Content Grouping

Content grouping is a technique used in information architecture (IA) to organize and categorize content into logical groups or categories. It helps to provide a better user experience by making it easier for users to find and access the information they are looking for. In IA, the goal is to create a clear and intuitive structure for the content on a website or application. By grouping similar content together, it becomes easier for users to navigate and understand the information hierarchy. Content grouping can be applied to various types of content, such as articles, products, blog posts, or any other type of information.

Content Hierarchy

Content Hierarchy in the context of Information Architecture refers to the organization and arrangement of content elements in a hierarchical structure. It establishes the relationship between different pieces of information, allowing users to navigate and understand the content more effectively. The content hierarchy defines the order and importance of various content components within a website or digital platform. It helps users easily find and access the information they are looking for, while also aiding in the understanding of the overall structure and purpose of the website.

Content Inventory Analysis

A content inventory analysis is a systematic and comprehensive assessment of all the content within a particular information space, with the goal of understanding its structure, organization, and usefulness. It is an essential component of information architecture (IA), which is concerned with the design and organization of information to support effective navigation and retrieval. The content inventory analysis involves a meticulous examination of each individual piece of content, including web pages, documents, images, videos, and any other resources relevant to the information space. This analysis aims to identify and document various attributes of the content, such as its title, description, URL, format, owner, creation date, and last update date. By conducting a content inventory analysis, IA practitioners can gain insights into the existing information landscape and identify areas for improvement. It helps them understand how content is currently organized and whether it aligns with the needs and expectations of the users. It also highlights any content gaps or redundancies that may exist. During the analysis, IA professionals may use various tools and techniques to gather information about the content, such as automated crawlers, content management systems, or manual human review. They may also interview content owners and subject matter experts to gain a deeper understanding of the context and purpose of the content. Once the content inventory analysis is complete, IA practitioners can use the findings to inform their IA strategy. They can identify opportunities to restructure or reorganize the content to improve its findability, usability, and overall user experience. They may also discover content that needs to be updated, removed, or consolidated. In summary, a content inventory analysis is a comprehensive assessment of all the content within an information space. It enables IA practitioners to understand the structure and organization of content and make informed decisions about its optimization. By conducting this analysis, they can improve the overall information architecture and enhance the usability of the information space for users.

Content Inventory Management

Content Inventory Management in the context of Information Architecture (IA) refers to the systematic organization and documentation of all content assets within a digital ecosystem. It involves the identification, categorization, and evaluation of content to inform strategic decision-making and improve the overall user experience. At its core, content inventory management aims to create a comprehensive overview of the existing content within a website, application, or any other digital platform. It involves analyzing and collecting data about each piece of content, such as its title, format, location, and metadata. The collected information is then organized in a structured manner, enabling content strategists and information architects to gain a holistic understanding of the available resources. The process of content inventory management starts with the discovery phase, where content assets are identified and cataloged. This typically involves conducting a thorough content audit, mapping out the different sections and pages of the digital ecosystem. During this phase, duplicate or outdated content is flagged, and any content gaps are identified, helping the IA team to streamline the overall content structure. Once the content inventory is established, the next step is to categorize and classify the content assets. This process may involve the creation of taxonomies, metadata schemas, or content models to ensure that content is appropriately tagged and labeled. Categorization enables content managers and users to navigate and search for relevant information effectively. Content inventory management also includes the evaluation and analysis of the collected data. This can involve assessing the quality, relevance, and accuracy of content assets, as well as identifying areas for improvement. By analyzing the content inventory, IA professionals can identify content that can be repurposed, consolidated, or retired, helping to optimize the overall user experience and reduce content redundancy. In conclusion, content inventory management within the field of Information Architecture (IA) involves the systematic organization, documentation, and evaluation of content assets within a digital ecosystem. It enables information architects to gain a comprehensive understanding of existing content and make informed decisions to enhance the user experience.

Content Inventory

Content Layout Design

Content layout design in the context of Information Architecture (IA) refers to the organization and arrangement of content elements on a webpage or screen, with the goal of providing clear and intuitive navigation and enhancing the user experience. Effective content layout design involves creating a logical hierarchy and structure that allows users to easily find and understand the information they are looking for. It involves considering factors such as the target audience, the goals of the website or application, and the nature of the content being presented. The content layout design should be visually appealing, balanced, and provide a clear visual hierarchy. This can be achieved through the use of spacing, alignment, typography, and color. Consistent use of these design principles helps to guide and direct the user's attention, highlighting important information and facilitating comprehension. An important aspect of content layout design is the use of grids or columns to organize and structure content. This allows for a cohesive and consistent design across various screen sizes and devices. The use of grids also helps to create balance and harmony on the page, enabling users to easily process and navigate through the content. Furthermore, content layout design should take into consideration the accessibility needs of all users. This includes ensuring that the content is easily readable and navigable for individuals with disabilities, such as those who rely on screen readers. Providing clear headings, labels, and descriptive links can greatly improve the accessibility and usability of the content layout. In summary, content layout design plays a crucial role in the field of Information Architecture, as it determines how information is organized and presented to users. A well-designed content layout enhances usability, information comprehension, and overall user experience.

Content Lifecycle Management

Content Lifecycle Management (CLM) refers to the systematic and structured management of content throughout its entire lifespan, from creation to disposal, within the context of Information Architecture (IA). It encompasses the processes and activities involved in creating, organizing, publishing, maintaining, and retiring content in a way that aligns with the overall goals, strategies, and user needs of an organization. The key objective of content lifecycle management is to ensure that content is effectively managed and utilized throughout its lifespan, enabling organizations to derive maximum value from their content assets. It involves establishing a framework and implementing processes for managing content from its initial creation or acquisition, through various stages of development, to its eventual retirement or archiving. Content creation is the first stage of the content lifecycle, where content authors and creators generate new pieces of information or media based on specific requirements and objectives. This stage often involves the use of various tools and technologies to capture, write, design, or record content in a format suitable for publishing. Once content is created, the next stage in the content lifecycle is organization. This involves classifying, categorizing, and structuring content in a logical and intuitive manner, such as using metadata, tags, or taxonomies. The organization stage aims to ensure that content is easily discoverable, accessible, and understandable for both content creators and end-users. The publishing stage involves making the content available to the intended audience through various channels or platforms, such as websites, intranets, mobile applications, or social media. Publishing may include processes like formatting, localization, or adaptation to different devices or channels to ensure the content is presented in a consistent and compelling manner. Once content is published, it enters the maintenance stage, which involves ongoing updates, revisions, or improvements to ensure its accuracy, relevancy, and quality. This stage may include activities such as content reviews, version control, content governance, or content optimization based on user feedback or analytics. The final stage in the content lifecycle is retirement or disposal. This involves the removal, archiving, or deletion of content that is no longer required or relevant. It may also involve the migration or transfer of content to long-term storage or archival systems, ensuring compliance with legal or regulatory requirements.

Content Management Systems (CMS) IA

17

A Content Management System (CMS) in the context of Information Architecture (IA) refers to a software platform that enables the creation, organization, and management of digital content. It provides a centralized and user-friendly interface for content authors, editors, and administrators to publish and maintain content on a website or application. CMSs facilitate the separation of content from presentation, allowing content creators to focus on the substance of the information without concerning themselves with the technical aspects of design or development. They typically consist of an administrative backend or dashboard and a frontend or public-facing website. The backend provides tools and features for content creation, editing, and organization, while the frontend displays the published content to users. Within the IA framework, a CMS plays a crucial role in managing the information structure and content hierarchy of a digital system. It allows content owners to arrange and categorize content in a logical manner, creating a cohesive and intuitive user experience. Using a CMS, content authors can create and modify content elements such as text, images, videos, and documents. They can also apply metadata, tags, and attributes to enhance searchability and discoverability. A CMS enables collaboration among multiple content contributors, offering features like user roles, permissions, and version control. In addition to content creation and organization, a CMS often includes features for content presentation and delivery. It enables the design and layout of web pages, templates, and themes, providing consistency and a unified visual identity. Content can be dynamically displayed based on user preferences or contextual conditions, enhancing personalization and relevance. CMSs also support content maintenance and governance, facilitating updates, archiving, and content lifecycle management. They may integrate with other systems and technologies, such as analytics, marketing automation, or e-commerce platforms, to enable more advanced functionality and improve the overall digital experience.

Content Management

Content Management in the context of Information Architecture (IA) refers to the process of organizing, categorizing, and managing digital content to ensure its discoverability, accessibility, and usability. It involves creating a system or framework that enables the efficient and effective management of content throughout its lifecycle. The primary goal of Content Management in IA is to create a structure that allows users to easily find and navigate through information. This involves designing a logical and intuitive organization scheme, often in the form of a hierarchical structure or taxonomy. By categorizing content into meaningful and distinguishable groups, users can quickly locate the information they need, leading to improved user experience and satisfaction. Furthermore, Content Management also involves the implementation of metadata, which provides additional context and description to content items. Metadata can include attributes such as title, author, publication date, and keywords, which enable advanced search and filtering capabilities. By utilizing metadata, content can be more easily indexed and retrieved, enhancing the overall findability and accessibility of the information. Another crucial aspect of Content Management in IA is the establishment of a workflow or governance process. This involves defining roles and responsibilities, establishing content creation and approval workflows, and enforcing content management policies. A well-defined workflow ensures that content is consistently updated, reviewed, and maintained, preventing outdated or inaccurate information from being presented to users. Overall, Content Management in the context of Information Architecture plays a vital role in organizing and structuring digital content to provide a seamless and optimal user experience. It involves creating a logical organization scheme, implementing metadata for enhanced searchability, and establishing workflows for efficient content maintenance. By effectively managing content, organizations can ensure that information is easily discoverable, accessible, and usable, leading to improved user satisfaction and successful information retrieval.

Content Mapping

Content mapping is a process in information architecture (IA) that involves organizing and categorizing content to facilitate effective navigation and retrieval of information within a digital product or website. It serves as a blueprint or roadmap for how the content will be structured and presented to users. During the content mapping process, the IA team identifies the different types of content that will be included in the digital product or website and determines how they should be organized and interconnected. This involves analyzing the target audience, their information needs, and how they are likely to search for and consume information. The main goal of content mapping is to create a cohesive and user-friendly information structure that

18

allows users to easily find the content they are looking for and understand the relationships between different pieces of information. It helps to eliminate confusion and reduce cognitive overload by providing clear paths and hierarchies for users to navigate through the content. Content mapping typically involves the creation of a content inventory, which is a comprehensive list of all the content items that will be included in the digital product or website. Each content item is categorized and tagged with metadata to provide additional context and enable more sophisticated search and filtering capabilities. Once the content inventory is complete, the IA team can start organizing the content into a hierarchical structure using techniques such as card sorting or tree testing. This structure is often represented visually in the form of a sitemap or site architecture diagram, which shows the relationships between different content categories and subcategories. The content mapping process also involves considering the user interface and interaction design elements that will be used to present the content to users. This includes deciding on the appropriate navigation menus, labels, and search functionality that will help users navigate and retrieve information effectively. In conclusion, content mapping is a crucial step in IA that involves organizing and categorizing content to create a logical and intuitive information structure. It helps users find and understand content more easily, improves information retrieval, and enhances the overall user experience.

Content Modeling Framework

A content modeling framework is a structured approach to organizing and defining the content within a website or digital application. It serves as a blueprint or guide for information architects to determine the structure, relationships, and attributes of the content elements that will be included within the system. The purpose of a content modeling framework is to ensure consistency, efficiency, and scalability in information architecture. It helps information architects and content strategists define and manage content types, attributes, relationships, and hierarchies in a systematic and standardized manner.

Content Modeling Workshops

A content modeling workshop is a collaborative session that brings together stakeholders to define and map the structure, attributes, and relationships of content within a digital product or platform. This workshop is a critical step in the information architecture (IA) process, which aims to organize and structure content in a way that is intuitive, user-friendly, and aligned with business goals. During the workshop, participants, including content strategists, UX designers, developers, and subject matter experts, collaborate to define content types, their properties, and their relationships. The workshop typically involves a series of activities and exercises designed to elicit insights and facilitate discussions around the content structure. One of the key outputs of a content modeling workshop is a content model. A content model is a representation of the content structure and attributes that will be used as a blueprint for organizing and managing content within a digital platform. It defines the types of content, such as articles, events, or products, and the properties associated with each type, such as title, description, or date. The content model also captures the relationships between different content types. For example, an article may be associated with an author, a category, or related articles. This information is critical to ensure that the content can be easily navigated, discovered, and presented to the users in a coherent and meaningful way. By bringing stakeholders together in a content modeling workshop, the IA process becomes more iterative and inclusive. It allows for a shared understanding of the content structure and its requirements, enabling better decision-making throughout the design and development process. The workshop also serves as a platform for knowledge sharing and cross-functional collaboration, fostering a sense of ownership and alignment among the participants. In conclusion, a content modeling workshop is a collaborative session that plays a crucial role in the IA process. It helps define the content structure, attributes, and relationships through activities and discussions involving various stakeholders. The output of the workshop, a content model, serves as a blueprint for organizing and managing content within a digital platform.

Content Modeling

Content modeling in the context of Information Architecture (IA) refers to the process of organizing and structuring content in a way that reflects its meaning, relationships, and attributes. It involves defining a consistent framework and set of rules for how content should be

19

created, classified, and presented. A content model serves as a blueprint or guide for creating and managing content within a website or digital platform. It helps to ensure that content is organized and structured in a logical and coherent manner, making it easier for users to find and navigate. By establishing a clear structure for content, content modeling also supports the scalability and extensibility of a website or application.

Content Personalization

Content Personalization refers to the process of tailoring information and experiences to individual users based on their preferences, behavior, and needs. In the context of Information Architecture (IA), it involves customizing the content and presentation of a website or application in order to enhance user engagement and satisfaction. By analyzing user data such as demographics, browsing history, search queries, and interactions, IA professionals can create personalized experiences that cater to the specific needs of each individual. This can include customizing the layout, design, and functionality of a website, as well as delivering targeted content and recommendations.

Content Planning

Content Planning in the context of Information Architecture (IA) refers to the strategic process of organizing and structuring content within a digital platform to enhance usability, optimize user experience, and achieve specific business goals. It involves the thoughtful analysis, identification, and categorization of information assets to ensure that they are logically arranged and easily accessible to users. Content Planning takes into consideration the users' needs and expectations, as well as the goals and objectives of the organization.

Content Relationship Mapping

Content Relationship Mapping in the context of Information Architecture (IA) refers to the process of identifying and visualizing the connections and relationships between different pieces of content within a system or website. It helps in understanding the underlying structure and organization of content, allowing for easier navigation, searchability, and accessibility for users. Through content relationship mapping, information architects can determine how various content items relate to one another and how they fit into the broader context of the website or system. This mapping can be represented in the form of diagrams, charts, or other visualizations that illustrate the relationships between different content elements.

Content Relevance

Content relevance in the context of Information Architecture (IA) refers to the degree to which the information presented on a website or other digital platform is pertinent and meaningful to the intended audience and their goals or tasks. It is a critical aspect of IA as it directly influences the effectiveness and usability of the overall user experience. When considering content relevance in IA, it is essential to ensure that the information provided is adequately aligned with the specific needs, interests, and expectations of the target users. This requires a deep understanding of the user base and their context, which can be achieved through user research, personas, and user testing.

Content Strategy Development

Content Strategy Development, in the context of Information Architecture (IA), refers to the systematic planning, creation, management, and delivery of content that aligns with the overall goals, objectives, and user needs of an organization or website. Content Strategy Development is a critical aspect of IA as it ensures that relevant and valuable content is available to users, in a structured and meaningful way, to support their information needs and facilitate their user experience. It involves the development of a clear and comprehensive strategy that outlines the goals, target audience, messaging, and content requirements of an organization or website.

Content Strategy Framework

A content strategy framework in the context of Information Architecture (IA) refers to a comprehensive plan or guide that helps organizations effectively manage and organize their content in order to meet the needs and goals of their users. It encompasses the processes, tools, and methodologies used to create, structure, analyze, and deliver content to users in a way that is meaningful, usable, and relevant. The framework typically includes a set of strategies, best practices, and guidelines that inform the decision-making process related to content creation, organization, and management. It helps organizations define their content goals and objectives, identify their target audience, and determine the most appropriate formats and channels for delivering content. It also takes into account user research and data analytics to ensure that the content is relevant and engaging for the users. One key aspect of a content strategy framework is content modeling, which involves defining the structure and relationships between different content elements. This helps facilitate content reuse, organization, and navigation, ensuring that information is consistent and easily discoverable. Additionally, the framework considers the various stages of the content lifecycle, such as creation, editing, publication, and archival, and provides guidelines for managing content throughout each stage. Another important component of the framework is content governance, which involves establishing clear roles, responsibilities, and workflows for content creation, maintenance, and updates. This helps ensure that content is created and managed in a consistent and efficient manner, and that it aligns with the organization's brand voice, style, and tone. Overall, a content strategy framework in the context of Information Architecture helps organizations address the challenges of creating, organizing, and managing content in an increasingly digital and multichannel environment. It provides a structured approach to content planning and execution, ultimately improving the user experience and achieving the organization's content-related goals.

Content Strategy

A content strategy in the context of Information Architecture (IA) refers to the planning and management of content that is structured, organized, and presented on a website or digital platform. It involves creating a framework and guidelines for the creation, publication, and maintenance of content in order to meet the goals and objectives of the website or digital platform. Content strategy encompasses various elements such as content creation, content organization, content presentation, and content governance. It involves understanding the target audience, their needs and preferences, and aligning the content strategy with the overall objectives of the website or digital platform. The first aspect of content strategy is content creation, which involves defining the purpose and goals of the content, identifying the target audience, and developing a plan for creating relevant and engaging content. This may include conducting research, performing content audits, and developing user personas to guide the creation of content that meets the needs and expectations of the target audience. The second aspect is content organization, which focuses on structuring and organizing content in a logical and meaningful way. This involves developing a taxonomy or classification system to categorize and label content, creating hierarchies and relationships between different pieces of content, and defining metadata to provide additional context and information about the content. The third aspect is content presentation, which involves determining how the content will be presented and displayed to the users. This includes defining the layout and navigation of the website or digital platform, choosing the appropriate visual elements and design elements, and considering the accessibility and usability of the content for different devices and user contexts. The final aspect is content governance, which involves establishing processes and guidelines for the ongoing management and maintenance of content. This includes defining roles and responsibilities, creating workflows and approval processes, and establishing guidelines for content updates, archiving, and version control. In summary, content strategy in the context of Information Architecture encompasses the planning and management of structured and organized content on a website or digital platform. It involves content creation, organization, presentation, and governance to meet the goals and objectives of the website or digital platform.

Content Synchronization

Content synchronization is a process in information architecture that involves the coordination and harmonization of content across different platforms, devices, or channels to ensure consistent and up-to-date information is available to users. In the context of information architecture, content synchronization is essential for maintaining a seamless and unified user experience. It involves the synchronization of content, such as text, images, videos, and other media, across various digital environments, such as websites, mobile apps, social media platforms, and more. The goal is to ensure that users can access and interact with the same content regardless of the platform or device they are using. The process of content synchronization typically involves several steps. First, the content needs to be identified, classified, and organized according to a standardized framework or taxonomy. This helps to establish a consistent structure and categorization for the content, which makes it easier to synchronize across different platforms. Next, a content management system (CMS) or other tools are used to update and manage the content. These tools allow content creators and administrators to make changes, edits, or additions to the content, which are then automatically synchronized across all relevant platforms. This ensures that users are always accessing the most up-to-date information, reducing the risk of outdated or conflicting content. In addition to updating content, synchronization also involves ensuring consistency in presentation and formatting. This includes elements such as layout, typography, color schemes, and branding. By synchronizing these visual aspects, organizations can establish a cohesive and recognizable brand identity across all platforms. Content synchronization is particularly important for organizations that operate in multiple locations or target diverse audiences. It helps to eliminate information silos and ensure that users receive a consistent and unified experience, regardless of their location or demographic. In conclusion, content synchronization is a critical aspect of information architecture that ensures consistency and coherence across different platforms, devices, and channels. By synchronizing content, organizations can provide users with reliable and up-to-date information in a seamless and unified manner.

Content Taxonomy

A content taxonomy, in the context of Information Architecture (IA), refers to the structured classification and organization of content within a website or digital platform. It involves categorizing and organizing information in a hierarchical manner, typically using a tree-like structure of parent and child categories. The purpose of a content taxonomy is to provide a logical and intuitive structure for users to navigate and find content easily. By organizing and classifying content, a taxonomy helps users understand the relationships between different pieces of information and enables efficient information retrieval.

Content Testing

Information Architecture (IA) is a discipline within the field of user experience design that focuses on organizing, structuring, and labeling information in an effective and user-friendly way. It involves creating a hierarchy and navigation system that allows users to easily find and understand the information they are looking for. IA helps to make sense of complex information by categorizing and organizing it in a logical and intuitive manner. It takes into consideration the needs and expectations of the users, ensuring that the information is presented in a way that is easy to navigate and comprehend. IA helps to improve the usability and findability of websites, applications, and other digital products.

Content Wireframing

Content wireframing is a key aspect of Information Architecture (IA) that involves the visual representation and organization of content elements within a digital interface or website. It serves as a blueprint or skeletal structure to illustrate the layout, hierarchy, and placement of various content components on a web page or application. The primary purpose of content wireframing is to map out the structure and flow of information, ensuring that the content and its presentation align with user needs and business goals. It allows designers, developers, and stakeholders to collaboratively discuss and iterate on content-related decisions before moving into the visual design phase.

Contextual Inquiry

Information Architecture (IA) refers to the structural design and organization of information within a system or website. It involves the arrangement and labeling of information components to support effective and efficient navigation, search, and retrieval of information. IA focuses on creating a logical structure that allows users to easily find what they are looking for and understand the relationships between different pieces of information. It aims to enhance clarity, coherence, and usability by defining a clear hierarchy and categorization system.

Contextual Navigation

Contextual navigation in the context of Information Architecture (IA) refers to the technique of providing navigation options that are tailored to the specific context or content of a website or application. It aims to help users easily navigate through the different sections, pages, or components within the system by presenting them with relevant and meaningful choices. Contextual navigation is based on the understanding that users often have different goals and tasks when accessing a website or application. By providing navigation options that are directly related to the current context or content, users can quickly find what they are looking for and navigate to the relevant information or functionality.

Conversational Interface

A conversational interface in the context of Information Architecture (IA) refers to the design and implementation of a user interface that enables natural language conversations between users and a system or application. It is a form of human-computer interaction where users can interact with a system through conversation, typically via text or speech. The conversational interface aims to mimic real-life conversations, allowing users to communicate with the system in a more natural and intuitive way. It utilizes natural language processing (NLP) and machine learning techniques to understand and interpret user input, generating appropriate responses or actions.

Convert

Information Architecture (IA) is the practice of organizing and structuring information to facilitate efficient and effective communication, navigation, and understanding. It involves the design and arrangement of information elements and their relationships to create a coherent and intuitive system. IA encompasses a variety of aspects, including categorization, labeling, hierarchy, and navigation. These elements are carefully planned and executed to ensure that users can easily find and consume the information they need. By organizing information in a logical and meaningful way, IA helps users navigate through complex systems, websites, or applications with ease.

Copper

Crayon

Information architecture (IA) refers to the structural design and organization of information within a system or website. It involves the arrangement and labeling of content, navigation, and functionality to enhance discoverability, usability, and overall user experience. The goal of IA is to facilitate easy and efficient access to information, enabling users to find what they need quickly and intuitively. It involves analyzing user needs and behaviors, identifying key content and features, and creating a coherent and logical structure to present the information. IA ensures that information is organized in a way that makes sense to users, minimizing cognitive load and maximizing usability.

Crazy Egg

Crazy Egg is a web analytics tool that provides insights into user behavior on a website, specifically focused on visualizing user interaction through heatmaps and other visual elements. In the context of Information Architecture (IA), Crazy Egg can be a valuable tool for gathering data and understanding how users navigate and engage with a website. As part of the IA process, it is important to understand how users interact with a website in order to improve its overall usability and user experience. Crazy Egg's heatmaps, scrollmaps, and other visual reports provide a visual representation of where users click, how far they scroll, and what elements they engage with the most. This data helps in identifying patterns and potential issues with the website's information structure. By analyzing the data provided by Crazy Egg, IA professionals can gain insights into how users navigate through the website, which sections they spend the most time on, and which elements attract the most attention. This information can inform IA decisions, such as organizing content in a more logical and intuitive manner, improving the placement and visibility of important elements, or identifying areas where users may be getting confused or frustrated. Crazy Egg also offers A/B testing capabilities, allowing IA professionals to compare different versions of a website or specific elements to determine which version performs better in terms of user engagement. This can help in refining the information structure and making data-driven decisions to optimize the user experience.

Creately

Information Architecture (IA) is a discipline within the field of User Experience (UX) that focuses on organizing, structuring, and classifying information to enhance usability and findability. It involves designing the underlying framework of a digital product or website to ensure that information is logically structured and easily accessible to users. IA plays a crucial role in helping users navigate and understand digital content. By organizing information in a user-centered manner, IA helps users find what they need quickly and easily, improving their overall experience. It involves creating clear pathways and intuitive navigation systems, ensuring that users can easily locate relevant information and perform desired actions.

Cross-Platform IA

Cross-Platform IA refers to the design and organization of information in a way that allows for seamless navigation and access to content across multiple platforms, such as websites, mobile applications, and other digital interfaces. Information Architecture, or IA, is the practice of structuring and organizing information to help users find what they are looking for quickly and easily. It involves creating intuitive navigation systems, clear labeling, and logical categorization of content. Cross-Platform IA takes this a step further by considering the various devices and platforms through which users access information. With the proliferation of smartphones, tablets, and other internet-connected devices, it is important to design IA that accommodates different screen sizes, input methods, and interaction patterns. This is achieved by creating a consistent and cohesive IA framework that can be adapted and customized for each platform. This means that regardless of whether a user is accessing the information on a desktop computer, a mobile device, or a smart TV, they can easily navigate and find what they need. Cross-Platform IA also takes into account the differences in context and user behavior across platforms. For example, users may have different goals and expectations when accessing information on a mobile device compared to a desktop computer. By understanding these differences and designing IA that takes them into consideration, cross-platform experiences can be tailored to meet the needs and preferences of users on each platform. Overall, Cross-Platform IA is about creating a seamless and consistent user experience across different platforms, ensuring that users can easily access and navigate information regardless of the device or platform they are using.

Dark Pattern

A dark pattern in the context of Information Architecture (IA) refers to a deliberate and deceptive design technique used to manipulate or trick users into taking actions that they may not want to or may not fully understand the implications of. It involves the use of psychological and persuasive tactics to exploit user behavior and advance the goals of the designer or organization at the expense of user experience. Dark patterns can take various forms, but they are typically characterized by the following elements: 1. Misdirection: Dark patterns often involve misleading or confusing design elements that redirect user attention or manipulate their perception. This can include tricking users into subscribing to unwanted services, making unintended purchases, or disclosing personal information unknowingly. 2. Hidden Costs: Another common dark pattern is the concealment of additional charges or fees during the checkout process. This can involve adding unexpected fees at the last minute or making it intentionally difficult for users to find information about pricing and billing terms. 3. Forcing Actions: Dark patterns may also involve coercing users into taking certain actions by making alternative options less visible or more complicated to access. This can include making it difficult to unsubscribe from services, intentionally confusing user interfaces, or using manipulative language to guilt-trip users into making specific choices. 4. Privacy Invasion: Some dark patterns exploit user trust and privacy by collecting excessive or unnecessary personal information without clear consent or adequate disclosure. This can be done through misleading consent forms, pre-checked boxes, or excessively detailed and confusing privacy settings. 5. Urgency and Scarcity: Creating a sense of urgency or scarcity is another tactic used in dark patterns. This can include false countdown timers, limited-time offers, or exaggerated claims about product availability, all designed to pressure users into making hasty decisions. In conclusion, dark patterns are deliberate design techniques that exploit user behavior for the benefit of the designer or organization. They deceive and manipulate users through misdirection, hidden costs, coercion, privacy invasion, and urgency tactics. Identifying and avoiding dark patterns is crucial for ethical and user-centered Information Architecture.

Data Schema

A data schema, in the context of Information Architecture (IA), is a formal representation of the structure, organization, and relationships within a database or data repository. It defines a blueprint for how data is stored, organized, and accessed within the system. The main purpose of a data schema is to provide a logical and structural framework for the data to be stored and managed efficiently. It helps in ensuring consistency, integrity, and accuracy of data by defining rules and constraints that need to be followed.

Data Visualization

Data Visualization is a method used in Information Architecture (IA) to present complex data sets or information in a visual format that is easily understandable and accessible to users. It involves the creation of graphical representations, such as charts, diagrams, graphs, and maps, to provide a clear and concise representation of complex information. The primary goal of Data Visualization in the context of IA is to enhance the user experience by making information more engaging, interactive, and easy to comprehend. It helps users quickly grasp patterns, relationships, trends, and insights that may not be apparent from raw data or text-based formats.

Decibel Insight

Decibel Insight is a sophisticated user experience (UX) analytics platform that provides valuable insights into user behavior on websites and mobile applications. Specifically designed for Information Architecture (IA), Decibel Insight helps IA professionals understand how users interact with digital content and make data-driven decisions to enhance the user experience. Decibel Insight allows IA professionals to analyze a wide range of user interactions, including clicks, scrolls, and mouse movements, as well as the time spent on individual pages and the conversion rates of various user journeys. By collecting and analyzing this data, Decibel Insight offers IA professionals a comprehensive view of how users navigate through a website or mobile application and interact with different elements and features.

Design Documentation

Design Documentation in the context of Information Architecture (IA) refers to a collection of documents that articulate the various elements and aspects of the IA design process. These documents provide a comprehensive understanding of the designed information system and serve as a reference for designers, developers, stakeholders, and users.Design Documentation typically includes multiple components, such as: 1. Information Architecture Specification: This document outlines the overall structure and organization of the information system. It includes descriptions of the various information components, such as pages, sections, and navigation menus. The specification also clarifies how these components are interconnected and how users can navigate through them. 2. Wireframes: Wireframes are visual representations of the information system's user interface. They illustrate the placement and layout of different elements, such as text, images, buttons, and interactive features. Wireframes provide a visual blueprint for the design and help stakeholders visualize the proposed user experience. 3. Interaction Design: Interaction design documents describe the behavior and functionality of interactive elements within the system. These documents may include details on user flows, user interactions, and feedback mechanisms. They help ensure that the information system provides a seamless and intuitive user experience. 4. Content Strategy: Content strategy documents outline guidelines for creating and managing content within the information system. They define content types, formats, and guidelines for content creation, organization, and updates. Content strategy documents ensure consistency, relevance, and usability of the system's content. 5. Accessibility Guidelines: Accessibility guidelines outline standards and best practices for designing an information system that is accessible to users with disabilities. These guidelines ensure that the system can be used by individuals with various impairments, such as visual, auditory, or motor impairments. Design Documentation serves as a reference throughout the development process, assisting in the implementation of the information system. It provides clarity and guidance to designers, developers, and stakeholders, helping them make informed decisions and ensuring the successful realization of the designed information system.

Design Guidelines

Design Guidelines in the context of Information Architecture (IA) refer to a set of principles and recommendations that help designers create effective and user-friendly information structures, interfaces, and navigation systems. These guidelines ensure that users can easily find, understand, and interact with information on a website or application. The first design guideline is consistency. Consistency in IA ensures that all elements across different pages or sections of a website have a uniform appearance and behavior. This includes maintaining consistent navigation menus, headings, labels, and icons throughout the site. Consistency reduces cognitive load and allows users to predict what will happen and where to find information. The second design guideline is simplicity. Simplicity in IA emphasizes the importance of keeping the structure and navigation straightforward and intuitive. Complex and convoluted information hierarchies can confuse users and make it difficult for them to find what they are looking for. By simplifying the IA, designers can improve the overall user experience and make it easier for users to navigate and access information. The third design guideline is clarity. Clarity in IA ensures that information is presented in a clear and readable manner. This includes using descriptive and concise labels for navigation elements, headings, and sections. Clear and understandable language helps users quickly grasp the context and purpose of the information they are seeking. The fourth design guideline is accessibility. Accessibility in IA refers to designing information structures and navigation systems that are usable by people with disabilities. This involves providing alternative text for images, using clear and consistent headings, and ensuring that the information can be accessed using assistive technologies. The fifth design guideline is flexibility. Flexibility in IA allows users to personalize their experience based on their preferences and needs. This can include options to customize the layout, choose different display modes, or personalize the navigation menu. Providing flexibility enhances the user experience and increases user satisfaction. In conclusion, design guidelines in the context of Information Architecture are principles and recommendations that aim to create effective, user-friendly, and accessible information structures, interfaces, and navigation systems. By adhering to these guidelines, designers can improve the usability and overall user experience of websites and applications.

Design Patterns

Design Patterns in the context of Information Architecture (IA) refer to reusable solutions to common design problems that occur in the construction and organization of information systems. They provide a structured approach to creating effective IA by offering proven solutions that can be easily applied to various situations. IA Design Patterns are essential tools for designers, developers, and architects to solve common challenges encountered in the design and implementation of information infrastructures. These patterns serve as guidelines and best practices to ensure that IA solutions are consistent, scalable, and user-friendly.

Design Prototyping Tools

Design prototyping tools are software programs or applications that allow designers to create interactive and functional representations of a user interface or experience. These tools enable designers to experiment with different layouts, interactions, and visual elements to test and refine the design before development. In the context of information architecture (IA), design prototyping tools play a vital role in the early stages of the design process. IA is the practice of organizing and structuring information in a way that enables users to find and navigate through content effectively. Prototyping tools help IA designers create and iterate on the structure and layout of information, ensuring a logical and intuitive user experience.

Design Prototyping

Design prototyping is a crucial step in the process of developing an information architecture (IA) for a website or digital product. It involves creating a visual representation or model of the proposed design, allowing stakeholders to evaluate and provide feedback on the overall structure and organization of the information. The purpose of design prototyping is to test and refine the IA before it is implemented, ensuring that it meets the needs and expectations of the users. During the design prototyping phase, the IA is translated into a tangible artifact that can be interacted with and explored. This often involves using specialized software or tools to create wireframes, mockups, or prototypes of the user interface. These prototypes can be low-fidelity, representing the basic layout and structure of the information, or high-fidelity, simulating the final appearance and functionality of the design.

Design Sprint

A Design Sprint, in the context of Information Architecture (IA), refers to a structured approach that enables teams to collectively solve complex IA problems or design challenges. During a Design Sprint, cross-functional teams work together in a time-boxed and highly focused manner to generate, evaluate, and iterate on IA solutions. The primary goal of a Design Sprint is to rapidly prototype and validate ideas before investing significant time and resources into the development of a final IA solution.

Design Thinking

Design Thinking is a systematic approach to problem-solving, rooted in empathy and collaboration, that is used to create innovative and user-centered solutions in the context of Information Architecture (IA). Design Thinking is a framework that helps information architects understand and address complex problems by focusing on the needs and experiences of the users. It involves a series of iterative steps that encourage creativity, experimentation, and continuous learning. The first step in Design Thinking is empathy, where the information architect seeks to understand the users and their needs, goals, and challenges. This involves conducting research, gathering data, and gaining insights from users through interviews, observations, and other methods of data collection. Next, the information architect defines the problem statement, which involves synthesizing the research findings and identifying the key user needs and pain points. This step helps to frame the problem in a way that is specific and actionable. Once the problem is defined, the information architect moves on to ideation, where they generate a wide range of possible solutions. This is a creative and divergent phase where quantity and variety of ideas are encouraged, without judgment or evaluation. The goal is to explore as many different solutions as possible. After ideation, the information architect moves on to prototyping, where they design and build low-fidelity representations of the proposed solutions. This can include sketches, wireframes, or interactive prototypes that allow users to interact with the design and provide feedback. Finally, the information architect tests and iterates on the prototypes based on user feedback and evaluation. This involves gathering feedback from users, analyzing the data, and using the insights to refine and improve the design. This iterative process continues until a viable and user-centered solution is achieved. Overall, Design Thinking is a human-centered approach that puts the users at the center of the design process. It emphasizes collaboration, empathy, and experimentation in order to create innovative and effective solutions in the context of Information Architecture.

Designs.Ai

Information Architecture (IA) refers to the art and science of organizing and structuring information in a way that helps users understand and navigate a digital product or website effectively. It involves the careful planning and design of information hierarchy, labeling, and navigation systems to create a user-friendly and intuitive experience. The primary goal of IA is to ensure that users can find the information they need quickly and easily, without feeling overwhelmed or confused. It focuses on providing both breadth and depth of content, allowing users to explore various topics and go into details when necessary.

Digital Prototyping

Digital prototyping, in the context of Information Architecture (IA), refers to the process of creating interactive and realistic representations of digital products or services. It involves the use of specialized software tools to simulate user interfaces, interactions, and experiences, without the need for physical materials or construction. During the digital prototyping phase, IA professionals work closely with stakeholders, designers, and developers to translate conceptual ideas into tangible prototypes. These prototypes serve as a visual and functional blueprint for the final product, allowing stakeholders to better understand the proposed design and provide feedback for improvements.

Divi

Divi is a powerful and versatile WordPress theme that is widely used in the field of Information

Architecture (IA). It offers a user-friendly interface and a wide range of features that make it ideal for creating and managing complex information structures. As an IA tool, Divi allows designers and developers to visually organize and present information in a way that is intuitive and easy to navigate. It provides a set of pre-designed templates and building blocks that can be customized to create unique and engaging websites.

Dovetail

Dovetail in the context of Information Architecture (IA) refers to the process of aligning and integrating different elements or components within a system to create a smooth and efficient user experience. The term "dovetail" is derived from the woodworking technique where two pieces of wood are joined together with interlocking projections and notches, creating a strong and secure connection. Similarly, in IA, dovetailing involves aligning various aspects of a system to ensure coherence and seamless navigation for the user.

Draw.Io

Draw.io is a web-based diagramming tool that facilitates the creation, editing, and sharing of diagrams. It is commonly used in the field of Information Architecture (IA) to visually represent the structure, organization, and relationships of information within a system or website. With Draw.io, IA professionals can design and refine IA models, such as site maps, wireframes, and flowcharts, to effectively communicate complex information structures to stakeholders, designers, and developers. The tool offers a wide range of pre-built shapes and icons, enabling users to easily create diagrams that accurately reflect the intended IA design.

Dscout

Information Architecture (IA) refers to the practice of organizing and structuring information in a way that enables users to find, navigate, and understand content effectively. It involves the design and arrangement of information within a system or website to support intuitive and efficient user experiences. IA encompasses the organization, labeling, and categorization of information to create a coherent and logical structure. It aims to improve the findability, usability, and overall user satisfaction by considering the user's mental models and information needs. By implementing IA principles, designers can enhance the accessibility and usability of digital products and services.

Easel.Ly

Information Architecture (IA) refers to the organization and structure of information in a digital environment. It involves the design and arrangement of content, navigation, and functionality to ensure usability and findability for users. IA aims to create clear and intuitive pathways for users to navigate and access information. It involves categorizing and labeling information in a way that is logical and meaningful to users, allowing them to easily locate and understand the content they are looking for.

Ecological Interface Design (EID)

Ecological Interface Design (EID) is an approach within Information Architecture (IA) that aims to design user interfaces that support users in performing complex tasks by leveraging their knowledge and skills. EID draws inspiration from ecological psychology, which views the cognitive processes of humans as embedded in their environment. In the context of IA, EID recognizes that users interact with information systems as part of a larger socio-technical system. This approach emphasizes the importance of understanding the user's context, goals, and tasks to design interfaces that align with their mental models and facilitate their decision-making processes.

Edraw MindMaster

Edraw MindMaster is a software tool designed for creating mind maps, flowcharts, and concept maps, specifically in the context of Information Architecture (IA). Mind maps are diagrammatic representations that allow users to visually organize and structure information, ideas, and concepts. The software provides a user-friendly interface with a wide range of predefined templates and shapes, enabling users to effectively capture, organize, and present their thoughts and ideas. In the domain of Information Architecture, Edraw MindMaster offers a variety of features that support the creation of visually appealing and well-organized diagrams. With its drag-and-drop functionality, users can easily add and arrange nodes, branches, and connectors to represent relationships and connections between different elements. The software also allows for the customization of colors, shapes, and styles, enabling users to tailor their diagrams to suit their specific needs and preferences. One of the key advantages of using Edraw MindMaster in the context of Information Architecture is its ability to facilitate the process of designing and structuring complex information systems. The software provides a comprehensive set of tools and features that assist in organizing and categorizing large amounts of information, making it easier to understand and navigate. This can be particularly useful in the development of websites and applications, where the effective organization and presentation of information are essential for optimal user experiences. Moreover, Edraw MindMaster supports collaboration and teamwork by allowing users to share their diagrams with others in various formats, such as image files or interactive presentations. This promotes effective communication and ensures that all stakeholders have a clear and shared understanding of the information architecture. Additionally, the software enables users to export their diagrams to other commonly used formats, such as PDF or Microsoft Office files, for further editing or distribution. In conclusion, Edraw MindMaster is a versatile and user-friendly software tool that supports the creation and visualization of mind maps, flowcharts, and concept maps in the domain of Information Architecture. Its features and functionality facilitate the design, organization, and communication of complex information systems, making it an invaluable tool for IA professionals and designers.

EdrawMax

Information Architecture (IA) in the context of EdrawMax can be defined as the practice of organizing, structuring, and labeling information in a way that enables users to find and navigate through it effectively and efficiently. IA is concerned with the organization and classification of information to enhance usability and ensure that users can easily locate the information they need. It involves the creation of clear and logical structures, the development of intuitive navigation systems, and the establishment of consistent labeling conventions.

Elementor Header Footer Builder

The Elementor Header Footer Builder is a tool designed for Information Architecture (IA) that allows users to create and customize the header and footer sections of their website with ease. It is an essential feature for web designers and developers that helps to enhance the overall user experience and visual appeal of a website. The header and footer sections play a crucial role in the IA of a website as they provide important navigational and branding elements. The header typically contains the logo, main menu, search bar, and other key navigation components, making it accessible and visible to users across all pages. The footer, on the other hand, is located at the bottom of the page and often includes important links, copyright information, contact details, and social media icons.

Elementor

Elementor is a popular drag-and-drop website builder plugin for WordPress that allows users to create and design custom websites without any coding knowledge. It is an essential tool for web designers and developers during the information architecture (IA) phase of website development. Information architecture (IA) refers to the practice of organizing, structuring, and labeling content in an effective and user-friendly manner. It focuses on creating a logical and intuitive structure for a website, making it easier for users to navigate and find the information they need. Elementor plays a crucial role in IA as it allows web designers to visually create and arrange various elements and components on a webpage. With its drag-and-drop interface, users can easily add and position different elements such as text, images, videos, buttons, and more. This flexibility enables designers to experiment with different layouts and structures, ensuring a seamless and well-organized user experience. Furthermore, Elementor provides a wide range of pre-designed templates, blocks, and widgets that can be customized to fit the website's IA requirements. Users can choose from ready-made templates or create their own custom layouts, all within the WordPress environment. This saves time and effort during the IA phase, as designers can quickly prototype and iterate different designs without starting from scratch. By utilizing Elementor's features, web designers can create a coherent and intuitive information architecture for a website. They can define the hierarchy of pages, establish clear navigation menus, and ensure consistent labeling and categorization of content. This enhances the user experience by making it easier for visitors to locate and access information, improving engagement and overall satisfaction. In summary, Elementor is a powerful and user-friendly website builder plugin that is highly useful during the information architecture phase of website development. It enables designers to visually create and arrange various elements on a webpage, facilitating the creation of a logical and intuitive structure for better user experience.

Enterprise Content Management (ECM) IA

Enterprise Content Management (ECM) is a strategic framework that encompasses the policies, processes, and technologies used to effectively capture, manage, store, preserve, deliver, and dispose of an organization's content. It focuses on the systematic organization and retrieval of information, allowing businesses to efficiently manage their digital and physical documents, images, emails, videos, and other forms of content. ECM aims to streamline and automate content-related activities by providing a centralized repository for storing and accessing information, regardless of its format or source. It involves the creation of metadata, which describes the content and enables efficient search and retrieval. Content can be classified, categorized, and tagged to facilitate organization and to ensure the right people have access to the right information at the right time. From an information architecture (IA) perspective, ECM plays a crucial role in structuring and organizing content in a way that enhances findability, usability, and reusability. It involves designing taxonomies, navigation systems, and metadata schemas that align with users' mental models and enable intuitive content discovery and exploration. By employing effective IA principles, ECM improves user experience, promotes content reuse, and optimizes content delivery across various channels and devices. ECM IA encompasses the planning, design, and implementation of a coherent and scalable architecture that accommodates the needs of different user groups and supports the strategic objectives of the organization. It involves considering factors such as information hierarchy, navigation patterns, content relationships, and metadata models. By leveraging IA practices, ECM IA ensures that information is structured, organized, and presented in a way that supports intuitive navigation, efficient searching, and seamless integration with other systems and processes.

Entity-Relationship Diagrams (ERD)

Entity-Relationship Diagrams (ERD) are a visual representation of the relationships between entities or objects within a system or database. In the context of Information Architecture (IA), an ERD helps to organize and understand the structure of information and how different entities relate to one another. An ERD consists of entities, attributes, and relationships. Entities represent the different types of objects or concepts within a system or database. Attributes describe the characteristics or properties of the entities, and relationships indicate how these entities are connected or associated with each other.

Error Message

Information Architecture (IA) refers to the organizational structure and arrangement of information within a system or website. It involves the design and planning of how information is categorized, structured, and presented to users in a way that is intuitive, efficient, and user-friendly. The term "Error Message" in the context of IA refers to a notification or feedback provided to users when the system encounters an error or a problem. It is a crucial element of IA as it helps users understand and recover from errors, improving the overall user experience.

Experience Design

Experience design, in the context of Information Architecture (IA), refers to the intentional and systematic process of creating meaningful and engaging user experiences through the organization and presentation of information. It involves considering the needs, goals, and expectations of the users and aligning them with the information being presented. Experience design aims to provide users with intuitive, efficient, and enjoyable interactions with the information architecture. It encompasses both the visual and functional aspects of the user interface, ensuring that the design is aesthetically pleasing, accessible, and easy to navigate.

Experience Map

An experience map in the context of Information Architecture (IA) is a visual representation or diagram that depicts the user's journey or experience as they interact with a digital product, service, or website. It is a strategic tool used by information architects and UX designers to gain a deep understanding of the user's interaction and emotional responses throughout the entire user experience. An experience map typically consists of different stages or touchpoints that the user goes through, starting from their initial awareness or discovery of the product/service, to their first interaction, ongoing usage, and potential re-engagement. Each stage is represented by a timeline or a horizontal axis, and key user actions, thoughts, and emotions are mapped along the vertical axis. The purpose of an experience map is to visualize and analyze the user's holistic experience, allowing designers to identify pain points, areas of improvement, and opportunities for innovation. By visually connecting different touchpoints and understanding how they impact the user's emotions and perceptions, information architects can create a more cohesive and seamless user experience that aligns with the organization's goals and user needs. The information included in an experience map may vary depending on the specific project and goals. It can incorporate user research findings, such as interviews, surveys, and usability tests, to provide insights into user behaviors, motivations, and expectations. It may also include key performance indicators (KPIs), business goals, and other relevant metrics to evaluate the success of the user experience. Additional information, such as user demographics, personas, and user needs, can also be incorporated to provide a more comprehensive understanding of the target audience. Overall, an experience map is a tool that helps information architects visualize and understand the user's journey, emotions, and interactions with a digital product or service. It serves as a foundation for designing user-centered experiences that are intuitive, delightful, and aligned with the organization's objectives.

ExperienceFellow

ExperienceFellow is an innovative tool that supports the practice of Information Architecture (IA) by providing a platform for capturing and analyzing user experiences. IA is the art and science of organizing and structuring information to support the effective and efficient navigation, retrieval, and understanding of content. In this context, ExperienceFellow serves as a valuable resource for IA professionals, allowing them to gain insights into users' interactions with information systems. ExperienceFellow enables the collection of qualitative data through real-time user feedback. This data can then be used to inform the design and optimization of information architectures. By capturing users' experiences, IA practitioners can identify pain points, discover patterns, and make data-driven decisions to enhance the usability and findability of content. The tool allows IA professionals to create and conduct user studies, utilizing various research methods such as interviews, surveys, and observations. Participants can be engaged in real-world scenarios, accessing information systems in their natural environment. This approach promotes authenticity and ensures that the collected data accurately reflects users' actual experiences. ExperienceFellow provides a user-friendly interface for participants to document their experiences in the form of written narratives, images, and audio or video recordings. These rich insights can uncover both explicit and implicit user behaviors, preferences, and needs, providing valuable context for IA decision-making. The tool's analytical capabilities enable IA professionals to analyze and visualize the collected data, identifying key themes, trends, and challenges. This information aids in the development of effective information structures, navigation systems, and labeling strategies that align with users' mental models and expectations. Overall, ExperienceFellow empowers IA practitioners to create user-centered information architectures by capturing and leveraging the authentic experiences of users. By integrating user feedback into the design process, IA professionals can optimize the organization and presentation of information, resulting in enhanced user experiences.

Expert Review

Information Architecture (IA) refers to the art and science of organizing and structuring information to facilitate efficient and effective navigation, retrieval, and understanding of information within a digital environment. The goal of IA is to create a user-centric information structure that enables users to find and use information easily, quickly, and intuitively. This is achieved through the careful organization and categorization of information, the creation of logical and meaningful relationships between pieces of information, and the establishment of clear and coherent navigation systems.

Eye Tracking

Eye tracking is a research method utilized in the field of Information Architecture (IA) that involves monitoring and recording the eye movements and gaze patterns of individuals to understand how they interact with digital interfaces and visual information. It relies on specialized hardware and software, such as eye trackers, to accurately measure and analyze the precise location and duration of eye fixations, saccades, and other eye movements. By examining eye tracking data, IA professionals can gain valuable insights into user behavior, attention, and cognitive processes, which can inform the design and optimization of websites, applications, and other digital experiences. Eye tracking studies can provide IA practitioners with valuable information about the visual attention and engagement of users when navigating through digital content. This includes identifying which areas of a webpage or screen receive the most attention, how individuals scan and process information, and the order in which they explore different elements and features. Eye tracking data can reveal patterns and trends in user behavior, allowing IA professionals to optimize the layout, organization, and prioritization of content to improve usability, user experience, and information comprehension.

Faceted Navigation

Faceted Search

Faceted search, in the context of Information Architecture (IA), is a search technique that allows users to refine and narrow down their search results by selecting multiple filters or categories known as facets. These facets are predefined attributes or metadata associated with the information being searched, such as price, location, date, or content type. With faceted search, the user is presented with a dynamic interface that displays a variety of available facets and their respective values. By selecting one or more facets, the search results are instantly updated to only show the information that matches the chosen criteria. This iterative process enables users to explore and refine their search queries, making it easier to find the most relevant and specific content.

Feedback Loop

A feedback loop in the context of Information Architecture (IA) refers to an ongoing process of collecting and incorporating feedback from users and stakeholders to improve the design and usability of a website or application. It is a crucial component of the IA design process as it allows for iterative improvements and ensures that the final product meets the needs and expectations of its users. The feedback loop typically involves the following steps: 1. Soliciting Feedback: Designers and developers actively seek feedback from users and stakeholders through various channels such as user testing, surveys, interviews, and user feedback forms. This enables them to gather insights into the strengths and weaknesses of the current IA design and identify areas for improvement. 2. Analyzing Feedback: Once feedback is collected, it needs to be carefully analyzed and categorized. Designers review the feedback to identify recurring themes, patterns, and common pain points or areas of confusion. This analysis helps in understanding the user's perspective and prioritizing the changes needed in the IA design. 3. Implementing Changes: Based on the analysis of feedback, designers start implementing changes and improvements to the IA design. This could involve restructuring navigation, reorganizing content, improving search functionality, or making other modifications to enhance usability and user experience. 4. Testing and Evaluation: After implementing changes, the revised IA design is tested to validate the improvements and ensure that they effectively address the identified issues. Usability testing, A/B testing, and other evaluation methods are employed to gather further feedback and assess whether the changes have positively impacted the user experience. 5. Repeating the Feedback Loop: The process of soliciting feedback, analyzing it, implementing changes, and testing the revised IA design is an iterative one. The feedback loop is repeated multiple times throughout the design and development process, allowing for continuous learning, refinement, and optimization of the IA design. The feedback loop in IA is crucial for creating user-centered designs that successfully meet the needs and expectations of the target audience. It ensures that the IA design is continuously improving and evolving based on user feedback, resulting in a valuable and usable digital product or service.

Figma

Figma is a cloud-based design and prototyping tool that helps Information Architects (IAs) create and collaborate on visual designs, wireframes, and interactive prototypes. As a crucial tool for IA, Figma allows IAs to create and organize the structure and layout of information within a digital product or website. With its intuitive interface and robust features, Figma empowers IAs to effectively plan and communicate the arrangement of content, navigation, and functionality to stakeholders and other design team members.

Findability

The term "findability" in the context of Information Architecture (IA) refers to the ease with which users can locate and access desired information within a system or website. It is a key aspect of user experience and plays a crucial role in ensuring that information is readily available and discoverable. Findability encompasses various factors that contribute to the overall searchability and accessibility of information. These factors include the organization and labeling of content, the effectiveness of search functionality, and the overall structure and navigation of the system.

Fitts's Law

Fitts's Law is a fundamental principle in Information Architecture that describes the relationship between the size of a target, the distance to the target, and the time it takes to move to and select the target. It provides a mathematical model for predicting the time it takes for a user to point to and click on a specific element within a graphical user interface (GUI). In simple terms, Fitts's Law states that the time required to launch a target (e.g., clicking on a button) is determined by the distance to the target and its size. The law is based on the observation that it takes longer to move and click on smaller or farther away targets compared to larger or closer targets. The equation used to calculate the time required to select a target based on Fitts's Law is: $T = a + b * log2(D/W + 1)$ Where: - T represents the time required to select the target, - a and b are empirically derived regression parameters, - D represents the distance to the target, and - W represents the width or size of the target. From an Information Architecture perspective, Fitts's Law helps in designing user interfaces that optimize the efficiency and ease of use by placing frequently accessed or important elements (e.g., navigation menus, call-to-action buttons) closer to the user and making them larger in size. By understanding how Fitts's Law affects user interaction, IA professionals can enhance the usability of their designs by reducing the cognitive and physical effort required to navigate and interact with the interface. Fitts's Law also has implications for the placement of interactive elements within a website or application. By considering the target size and distance, IA professionals can ensure that users can easily and accurately select the desired targets, improving overall user experience and reducing the likelihood of errors or frustration. Additionally, Fitts's Law can help inform the decision-making process when designing touch-based interfaces, as finger size and range of motion are important factors to consider when determining target size and placement.

Flairbuilder

Flairbuilder is a software tool used in the context of Information Architecture (IA) to create interactive wireframes and prototypes for websites and web applications. It allows designers and IA professionals to visually represent the structure and organization of information, as well as the navigation flow and user interactions within a digital product. With Flairbuilder, users can easily drag and drop various UI components, such as buttons, forms, menus, and panels, onto a canvas to build wireframes. These wireframes can then be linked together to create clickable prototypes, simulating the actual user experience of navigating through different screens or pages of a website or application.

Flare

Flare refers to a concept within the field of Information Architecture (IA). In IA, flare is used to describe the visual emphasis or importance given to certain elements or sections of a website or application interface. When designing the information hierarchy of a website or application, IA professionals determine which elements should grab the user's attention and how much emphasis should be placed on each. This is achieved through the use of flare, which can include various design techniques such as size, color, contrast, typography, and placement.

Flinto For Mac

Flinto for Mac is a powerful prototyping tool specifically designed for creating interactive and animated prototypes for user interface (UI) design. It plays a significant role in the field of Information Architecture (IA) by allowing designers to conceptualize, visualize, and present their ideas in a more interactive and engaging manner. With Flinto for Mac, designers can create interactive prototypes that mimic the behavior of various user interfaces, helping stakeholders better understand the flow and functionality of a digital product or website. The tool provides a wide range of features and tools that enable designers to easily create and customize transitions, animations, and gestures to simulate real user interactions. Flinto for Mac allows designers to organize their prototypes using screens, which can be linked together to create a coherent user experience. Additionally, designers can design and customize various UI elements within Flinto, including buttons, forms, menus, and more, to accurately represent the intended design and functionality. This enables stakeholders to clearly visualize the layout and structure of the final product, helping them make informed decisions and provide feedback during the design process. The tool also offers collaboration features, allowing designers to share their prototypes with team members, clients, and stakeholders for feedback and review. This collaborative approach facilitates effective communication and ensures that all parties involved are aligned and have a shared understanding of the design and its intended functionality. In conclusion, Flinto for Mac is a valuable prototyping tool within the realm of Information Architecture. It empowers designers to create interactive and animated prototypes that accurately represent the intended user experience. By providing a visual and interactive representation of the design, Flinto allows stakeholders to engage with the design and make informed decisions during the design process. Through collaboration features, the tool facilitates effective communication and ensures a shared understanding among all parties involved.

Flinto

Flinto is a software tool that facilitates the creation of interactive prototypes for digital products within the field of Information Architecture (IA). It enables IA professionals to design and develop prototypes that closely resemble the final product, allowing stakeholders to visualize and experience its functionality and user interface before implementation. By emulating realistic user interactions, Flinto allows designers to test and refine their IA solutions in a simulated environment.

Flow State

Flow state, in the context of Information Architecture (IA), refers to a mental state in which a user becomes immersed and fully focused on a particular task or activity while interacting with a digital interface. It is a state of deep concentration and engagement that typically leads to enhanced user experience and optimal performance. During the flow state, users experience a sense of effortless control, complete absorption, and a loss of self-awareness. They become fully engrossed in the information and tasks at hand, experiencing a seamless and intuitive interaction with the interface. In this state, users are able to navigate through the IA with ease, effortlessly finding and processing the information they need and accomplishing their goals.

Flowcharts

Flowcharts in the context of Information Architecture (IA) serve as visual representations or diagrams that depict the structure, organization, and flow of information within a system or website. These charts are designed to illustrate the relationships between different components, pages, or elements within the IA, facilitating a better understanding of the content, user interactions, and overall navigation of a digital platform. IA flowcharts typically consist of various shapes, lines, and symbols to represent different elements and their connections. These shapes commonly include rectangles to represent pages or content sections, diamonds to indicate decision points or conditional branches, and arrows to show the direction of the flow between components. By visually mapping out the information flow, flowcharts enable designers, developers, and stakeholders to identify potential gaps, redundancies, or inefficiencies in the IA design. One essential aspect of IA flowcharts is the identification of user pathways or navigation routes. By illustrating the possible paths users can take through the website or system, designers can better understand how users may interact with the content and ensure that the IA supports intuitive navigation and seamless user experiences. Furthermore, IA flowcharts also assist in documenting and communicating the IA structure to various stakeholders involved in the development process. They provide a clear visualization of the website's information hierarchy, content relationships, and user interactions, making it easier for designers, developers, and content creators to align their efforts and work towards a cohesive and well-organized IA design. In summary, IA flowcharts are visual representations that depict the structure, organization, and flow of information within a system or website. They help communicate the IA structure, identify user pathways, and facilitate a better understanding of the content relationships and user interactions. This enables designers and stakeholders to optimize the IA design for improved usability and user experiences.

Fluid UI

Fluid UI is a design tool used in the field of Information Architecture (IA) that allows designers to create interactive prototypes of user interfaces for websites or applications. With Fluid UI, designers can easily simulate the flow and behavior of a user interface by linking different screens and components together. The tool provides a drag-and-drop interface, making it intuitive for designers to create and modify their prototypes. Fluid UI offers a wide range of pre-built UI components, such as buttons, menus, forms, and navigation bars, which can be easily customized to match the desired visual style and functionality of the interface being designed. These components can be positioned and resized on the canvas, allowing designers to create a layout that accurately represents the structure and organization of content within the interface. When designing with Fluid UI, designers can define interactions and transitions between screens, enabling them to showcase the flow of navigation and demonstrate how different elements of the interface respond to user actions. This helps designers to effectively communicate their design concepts and ideas to stakeholders, developers, and other members of the design team. Fluid UI also supports collaboration among team members by allowing multiple designers to work on a prototype simultaneously. Designers can share their prototypes with others, gather feedback, and make iterative improvements based on the input received. In addition, Fluid UI provides features for testing and validating the usability of the designed interface. Designers can simulate user interactions, such as tapping or swiping, to test how the interface responds to different scenarios. This allows for early identification and resolution of any usability issues, leading to a more user-friendly and intuitive interface. In conclusion, Fluid UI is a powerful design tool in the realm of Information Architecture that aids designers in creating interactive prototypes of user interfaces. Its intuitive interface, pre-built components, collaborative capabilities, and usability testing features make it an invaluable tool for designing, iterating, and validating user interfaces in a digital context.

Folksonomy

A folksonomy is a user-generated classification system that organizes information and resources based on user tags or keywords. It is a bottom-up approach to information organization, where individuals assign their own labels to content rather than relying on predefined categories. In the context of Information Architecture (IA), folksonomies can be used to enhance the findability and discoverability of content within a website or online platform. By allowing users to tag and label content, folksonomies provide an alternative way of organizing information that reflects the users' own mental models and interests.

Form Follows Function

Form Follows Function is a fundamental principle in Information Architecture (IA), which states that the design of a digital system should be primarily based on its intended purpose and functionality rather than aesthetic considerations. This principle emphasizes the importance of understanding the user's needs and ensuring that the structure and organization of information align with those needs. In the context of IA, Form Follows Function means that the layout, navigation, and overall design of a website or application should be derived directly from its intended purpose and the tasks it is meant to enable users to perform. The goal is to create an

35

intuitive and efficient user experience by designing the system around the information and tasks that are most important to the users.

Framer Classic

Framer Classic is an interactive design and prototyping tool that allows designers to create and test interactive user interfaces. In the context of Information Architecture (IA), Framer Classic can be used to improve and optimize the navigation and organization of a website or application. Information Architecture (IA) refers to the structural design and organization of information within a system, such as a website or application. It involves categorizing, labeling, and organizing information to facilitate efficient navigation and retrieval. Framer Classic can help designers create and test different IA solutions, allowing them to see how users interact with the information and make adjustments based on their feedback and behavior.

Framer Motion

The Framer Motion is a powerful and flexible animation library that is commonly used in the field of Information Architecture (IA). It provides an extensive set of tools and components to create smooth and responsive animations for web applications, enhancing the user experience and improving the overall visual appeal. With Framer Motion, IA professionals can easily define and control the motion of various elements on a website or application. The library offers a wide range of animation options, including transitions, keyframes, and physics-based animations, allowing designers to create dynamic and interactive interfaces.

Framer Web

Framer Web is an interactive design tool that allows users to create and prototype responsive web designs. In the context of Information Architecture (IA), Framer Web can be used to visualize and organize the structure, content, and functionality of a website or web application. Information Architecture is the practice of organizing and structuring information in a way that makes it easy to find, understand, and navigate. It involves designing the organization, labeling, and navigation of a website or web application to ensure that users can easily locate and access the information or functionality they need.

Framer X

Framer X is a powerful tool for designing and prototyping interactive user interfaces. In the context of Information Architecture (IA), Framer X helps to define the structure, organization, and navigation of the information within a digital product or website. With Framer X, designers can create and visualize the hierarchy and relationships between different elements of the user interface, such as pages, screens, sections, and components. This allows them to effectively map out the flow of information and ensure a seamless user experience.

Framer

Information Architecture (IA) in the context of web design refers to the structural design and organization of information within a website or application. It involves the creation of a coherent and intuitive navigation system and categorization scheme that allows users to easily find and understand the content or functionality they are seeking. IA encompasses several key elements including site maps, navigation menus, hierarchical categorization, and labeling systems. These elements work together to establish a logical and user-friendly structure that facilitates efficient information retrieval and enhances the overall user experience.

Freshmarketer

Information Architecture (IA) refers to the organization, structure, and labeling of information in a digital environment. It involves creating a clear and efficient navigational system that allows users to easily find and access the information they need. IA helps to ensure that a website or application is user-friendly, with intuitive and logical pathways for users to follow. It aims to improve the overall user experience by making information readily available and easily understandable.

Froont

Information Architecture (IA) is the systematic organization, structuring, and labeling of information to enhance its usability and findability within a digital product or website. IA focuses on designing a clear and intuitive structure for information, ensuring that users can easily navigate and comprehend the content. It involves creating a blueprint for organizing information, which includes determining the content hierarchy, defining navigation pathways, and labeling categories and elements.

FullStory

FullStory is an information architecture (IA) tool that provides detailed insights into user interactions and behavior on a website or application. It allows IA professionals to understand how users navigate through the website, what actions they take, and any obstacles they encounter during their journey. With FullStory, IA professionals can visualize user journeys, track clicks and scrolls, and analyze user interactions in real-time. The tool captures and records every user session, allowing IA professionals to replay these sessions and gain a comprehensive understanding of user behavior. This helps them uncover pain points and identify areas for improvement in the IA design.

Functional Prototype

A functional prototype, in the context of Information Architecture (IA), refers to a preliminary version of a digital system or website that demonstrates its intended functionality and user experience. It serves as a tangible representation of the proposed design, allowing stakeholders and users to test and evaluate its features before the full development stage. The primary purpose of a functional prototype is to validate the IA design and ensure that it meets the requirements and expectations of both the business and the end users. It provides a means to identify and address usability issues, navigation problems, and content organization challenges early in the process, thus reducing the risk of costly revisions and misunderstandings later on. HTML is a crucial tool for creating functional prototypes. With HTML, designers can build interactive web pages that mimic the behavior of the final product. By utilizing HTML, they can showcase the proposed website's layout, navigation structure, and basic functionality. This is achieved by incorporating HTML elements such as hyperlinks, text fields, buttons, and menus to allow users to navigate through the prototype and interact with its key features. The structure of the prototype should align with the planned IA elements, such as the main navigation menu, search functionality, and content organization. Elements should be labeled appropriately, ensuring that users can easily understand their purpose and functionality. Visual cues, such as contrasting colors or underlined text for hyperlinks, can be incorporated to indicate interactive elements and enhance the user experience. Functional prototypes built with HTML provide a powerful medium for designers and stakeholders to gather valuable feedback and make informed decisions during the IA design process. They offer a hands-on experience that enables users to test navigation paths, interact with content, and better understand the overall information flow. This iterative approach allows for refinements and improvements based on user insights, ensuring that the final product effectively supports users' needs and objectives. In conclusion, a functional prototype in the context of Information Architecture is a preliminary digital representation of a system or website that demonstrates its intended functionality. By utilizing HTML, designers can create interactive prototypes that closely resemble the final product, enabling stakeholders and users to provide feedback and validate the IA design before full development.

Game Interface Design

The game interface design refers to the visual and structural organization of elements within a game, aimed at enhancing the user experience and facilitating interactions between the player and the game. It is an integral part of the Information Architecture (IA) discipline, which focuses on the organization and structure of information within a system. The game interface design involves the arrangement of various elements such as menus, buttons, icons, and graphical representations of game objects, in a way that allows players to easily navigate, understand, and interact with the game. This includes the layout of screens, the use of color, typography, and visual hierarchy to guide players' attention, and the placement of controls for game mechanics. In the context of IA, the game interface design contributes to the overall usability and findability of game-related information. An effective game interface design employs principles of clarity, consistency, and simplicity to provide players with an intuitive and enjoyable gaming experience. It ensures that important information is readily accessible, actions are easily executable, and feedback is timely and informative. Furthermore, the game interface design takes into consideration the target audience and the specific goals of the game. For example, a game designed for casual mobile gamers may prioritize simplicity and ease of use, while a complex strategy game may require a more intricate interface to accommodate a wide range of actions and interactions. To summarize, the game interface design is a crucial aspect of IA in the gaming context. It involves the arrangement and organization of various elements within a game to create an intuitive and visually appealing interface that enhances the overall user experience.

Genially

Information Architecture (IA) is a discipline that focuses on how information is organized, structured, and presented within a system. It encompasses the design and organization of information to improve usability and accessibility, making it easier for users to navigate, understand, and find the information they need. IA plays a vital role in the design and development of websites, applications, and other digital platforms. It involves defining and arranging the various components of information, such as content, labels, menus, and navigational elements, to create a clear and logical structure. The goal is to ensure that information is organized in a way that is intuitive and meaningful for users. One of the key principles of IA is the concept of findability, which refers to the ease with which users can locate specific information within a system. IA helps achieve findability by organizing information into categories, creating labels and metadata, and implementing effective search functionality. By structuring information in a logical manner, IA enables users to quickly find what they are looking for, enhancing their overall experience. Another important aspect of IA is the consideration of user tasks and goals. By understanding the tasks that users want to accomplish and the goals they want to achieve, IA can guide the design of a system to support those activities. This involves determining the most efficient and effective ways to present information, ensuring that it is accessible and actionable for users. IA also considers the context in which information is presented. This includes understanding the needs and preferences of the target audience, as well as the device or platform on which the system will be used. IA takes into account factors such as screen size, input capabilities, and user behavior to optimize the organization and presentation of information. In summary, Information Architecture is the discipline that focuses on organizing and structuring information within a system to improve usability, accessibility, and findability. By creating a clear and intuitive structure, IA enhances the user experience and enables users to quickly find and interact with the information they need.

Gestalt Principles

Gestalt Principles are a set of principles in Information Architecture (IA) that explain how human beings perceive and interpret visual information. These principles are derived from the field of psychology and provide guidance on how to structure and organize information in a way that is meaningful and intuitive for users. One of the key Gestalt Principles is the principle of proximity, which states that elements that are close to each other are perceived as belonging together. In the context of IA, this principle suggests that related pieces of information should be grouped together. By placing related elements in close proximity, users are able to easily identify and understand the relationships between them. This principle helps to create a sense of organization and helps users navigate and comprehend the information more effectively. Another important Gestalt Principle is the principle of similarity, which states that elements that share similar visual attributes, such as color, size, or shape, are perceived as belonging together. In IA, this principle suggests that similar elements should be visually consistent and distinguishable from other elements. By using consistent visual cues, such as color coding or icons, users can quickly identify and differentiate between different categories or types of information. This principle helps to create a sense of structure and makes the information more visually digestible for users. The principle of closure is another essential Gestalt Principle in IA. This principle states that humans have a tendency to perceive incomplete or fragmented information as complete and meaningful. In IA, this principle suggests that designers can use visual cues, such as borders or shapes, to create the perception of closure and completeness.

By visually connecting related elements, designers can help users understand the relationships between different pieces of information and make sense of the overall structure. Other Gestalt Principles that are relevant to IA include the principles of continuity, figure-ground, and common fate. The principle of continuity states that humans tend to perceive continuous lines or patterns as connected and flowing. The principle of figure-ground suggests that humans will naturally perceive elements that stand out as the figure, while the surrounding elements become the background. The principle of common fate states that elements that move or change together are perceived as being related. These principles can be applied in IA to create a sense of flow, emphasize important information, and indicate relationships between elements.

GetResponse

GetResponse is an email marketing platform that provides tools and features for managing and executing email marketing campaigns. In the context of Information Architecture (IA), GetResponse can be seen as a component of a larger system that helps in organizing and structuring information related to email marketing. In IA, the focus is on creating a clear and logical structure for information so that users can easily find and access the content they need. GetResponse contributes to this goal by offering features that allow users to create, manage, and send emails to their target audience. The platform provides a user-friendly interface that assists users in organizing and categorizing their email lists, designing email templates, and scheduling email campaigns.

Glass Morphism

Glass Morphism is a design trend used in Information Architecture (IA) that aims to create a sense of transparency and depth through a combination of blurred backgrounds, frosted glass, and soft lighting effects. It involves the use of elements with a frosted glass-like appearance, typically achieved by applying a semi-transparent background color along with a blurred background image. This gives the impression that the elements are floating or suspended in space, creating a visually pleasing and modern user interface.

Gliffy

Gliffy is a web-based diagramming tool that is commonly used in the field of Information Architecture (IA). It allows users to create and collaborate on various types of diagrams, such as flowcharts, wireframes, and sitemaps, which are integral components of IA. As an IA tool, Gliffy enables designers and architects to visually represent information structures and interactions in a clear and organized manner. It provides a wide range of pre-built shapes and symbols that can be easily dragged and dropped onto the canvas, allowing users to create diagrams efficiently and accurately.

Global Navigation

Global Navigation in the context of Information Architecture (IA) refers to the consistent and uniform navigation system that allows users to navigate through a website or application from anywhere within its structure. It provides users with a sense of orientation, allowing them to understand the hierarchy and structure of the content and easily move between different sections or pages. Global Navigation typically includes elements such as menus, links, and search functionality that are present on every page of a website or application. It is designed to be accessible and visible to users at all times, usually positioned in a prominent location, such as the top or side of the page. By providing a consistent navigation experience, global navigation enables users to efficiently explore and access different sections and features without getting lost or confused.

GlooMaps

GlooMaps is an online tool designed to help information architects create visual representations of information architecture (IA) for websites or other digital projects. It allows IA professionals to easily develop hierarchical site maps and understand how different sections of a website or application are organized and connected. The primary purpose of GlooMaps is to provide a simple and intuitive interface for creating and editing site maps. It offers a drag-and-drop functionality that enables users to effortlessly rearrange and connect different pages or sections within the IA structure. This visual representation is crucial for effectively communicating the hierarchy and flow of information within a website or application. One of the key features of GlooMaps is its ability to handle complex IA structures. It allows the creation of multiple levels and sub-levels, making it suitable for even the most intricate websites or applications. Users can easily expand or collapse sections to simplify the view or focus on specific areas of the IA architecture. GlooMaps also facilitates collaboration between team members by allowing them to share and edit site maps in real-time. This feature enables information architects to work together and make necessary revisions or improvements to the IA structure. Additionally, GlooMaps provides the option to export the site maps in various file formats, such as PDF or PNG, for offline use or further documentation purposes. In conclusion, GlooMaps is a valuable tool for information architects to visually represent and communicate the structure and hierarchy of information within a website or application. Its intuitive interface, flexibility for complex IA structures, and collaborative features make it an essential asset in the IA design process.

Golden Ratio

The Golden Ratio, in the context of Information Architecture (IA), refers to a mathematical concept that is often used to guide the layout and proportions of visual elements in a design. It is based on the ratio of approximately 1.618 and is believed to result in aesthetically pleasing and harmonious designs. In IA, the Golden Ratio can be applied to determine the size and placement of various elements within a website or application. By following this ratio, designers can create balanced and visually appealing interfaces that are pleasing to users.

Gravit Designer

Gravit Designer is a versatile vector graphics editor that allows users to create and manipulate visual elements for various digital platforms. In the context of Information Architecture (IA), it serves as a valuable tool for designing and organizing the structure, navigation, and overall user experience of a website or application. With its intuitive interface and powerful features, Gravit Designer supports the creation of wireframes, sitemaps, and prototypes that help IA professionals visualize and communicate their ideas effectively. Its vector-based approach enables the creation of scalable and high-quality designs that can be easily shared and refined.

Gutenberg

Gutenberg is an information architecture framework developed by WordPress as the default content editor. It aims to streamline the creation and management of web content by providing a flexible and intuitive user interface. Gutenberg is designed to replace the traditional WordPress editor, which had a more basic and limited set of formatting options. With Gutenberg, users can create dynamic and visually appealing pages by using blocks to organize and structure their content.

Happy Addons For Elementor

Happy Addons for Elementor is a plugin that enhances the functionality of the Elementor page builder by providing additional elements and features. It allows users to create more dynamic and interactive designs for their websites. Information Architecture (IA) refers to the organization and structure of information within a website or application. It involves categorizing and labeling content in a way that is logical and intuitive for the user. IA helps users navigate and find information easily, improving their overall experience.

Heap

A heap in the context of Information Architecture (IA) refers to a hierarchical structure or arrangement of information, where elements are organized based on their relationships and are stored in a way that allows for efficient retrieval and manipulation of the data. Heaps are commonly used in IA to organize and manage information in a manner that facilitates easy browsing, searching, and navigation for users. The hierarchical structure of a heap is typically represented by a tree-like arrangement, with each element (or node) having a parent and zero or more children.

Heuristic Analysis

The heuristic analysis is a method used in Information Architecture (IA) to evaluate the usability and effectiveness of a website or digital product. It involves the systematic assessment of a website's interface and user experience based on a set of predefined usability principles or heuristics. During a heuristic analysis, an expert evaluator reviews the website or product and identifies any potential usability issues or violations of the established heuristics. These heuristics are general guidelines or best practices that have been developed based on research and industry standards. The evaluation process typically involves examining various aspects of the interface including navigation, layout, content organization, labeling, and interaction design. The evaluator assesses how well the website or product adheres to the heuristics and identifies areas where improvements can be made to enhance the overall user experience. The goal of a heuristic analysis is to identify and prioritize usability problems so that they can be addressed and resolved before the website or product is launched. The analysis helps in identifying issues that may not be apparent through other usability testing methods such as user testing or surveys. Some commonly used heuristics in IA include clarity and simplicity of interface, consistency in design and navigation, visibility of system status, match between system and the real world, user control and freedom, error prevention, and help and documentation. By conducting a heuristic analysis, IA professionals can gain insights into the strengths and weaknesses of a website or product from a usability perspective. This analysis can guide the design process and inform decisions about interface improvements, content organization, and interaction design to create a more user-friendly and effective digital experience.

Heuristic Evaluation

A heuristic evaluation is a method used in the field of Information Architecture (IA) to evaluate the usability of a digital interface or system. It involves using a set of predefined guidelines or heuristics to assess the overall user experience and identify any potential design flaws or usability issues. The evaluation is typically conducted by a group of experts or evaluators who have a deep understanding of IA principles and best practices. They examine the interface or system and apply the heuristics to determine how well it meets the needs of its users.

Hierarchical Navigation

Hierarchical navigation in the context of Information Architecture (IA) refers to a method used to organize and present content in a structured and hierarchical manner, allowing users to easily navigate through different levels of information within a website or application. In hierarchical navigation, content is grouped into categories or topics, with each category being further divided into subcategories. This creates a hierarchical structure, where the main categories are at the top level, and subcategories are nested beneath them. Users can then navigate through the different levels by clicking on the respective category or subcategory links, drilling down into more specific information. This type of navigation is commonly represented using menus or navigation bars, where each level is visually indicated through indentation or spacing. The top-level categories are typically displayed prominently, while the subcategories are indented or located beneath their parent category. Hierarchical navigation offers several benefits in terms of organizing and accessing information. It provides a clear and intuitive structure that helps users understand the relationships between different pieces of content. By organizing information hierarchically, it becomes easier for users to locate specific information and navigate through a website or application. Furthermore, hierarchical navigation allows for scalability and flexibility, as new categories or subcategories can be easily added to accommodate expanding content. It also enables content authors and administrators to efficiently manage and update the structure of the website or application. Overall, hierarchical navigation is a fundamental approach in Information Architecture that aids in organizing and presenting content in a structured manner. By providing a clear hierarchy and logical structure, it enhances the usability and navigability of websites and applications, resulting in a better user experience. Simple Example: Hierarchical navigation facilitates the structured and intuitive organization of content, allowing users to easily navigate through various levels. It involves grouping content into categories and subcategories, enabling users to drill down into specific information. This type of navigation is commonly represented using menus or navigation bars, where each category or subcategory is visually indicated through indentation or spacing. Hierarchical navigation offers several benefits such as clear structure, scalability, and enhanced usability, ultimately resulting in a better user experience.

Hierarchical Taxonomy

A hierarchical taxonomy is a classification system that organizes information in a tree-like structure, where each category is subcategorized under a broader category. In the context of Information Architecture (IA), a hierarchical taxonomy is an effective method to organize and navigate information, facilitating easy exploration and understanding for users. In a hierarchical taxonomy, categories are organized in a hierarchical manner with a parent-child relationship. The top-level category represents the broadest classification and is often referred to as the root category. Subcategories are then created under the parent category, forming a branching structure. Each subcategory can have its own set of subcategories, further dividing and refining the information. The hierarchical taxonomy helps users locate information by navigating through levels of categories. It allows for a simple and intuitive browsing experience, as users can easily drill down through the categories to find the desired information. This hierarchical structure provides a clear overview of the information architecture and allows for easy comprehension and organization of large amounts of data. One of the key advantages of a hierarchical taxonomy is its scalability. As new information is added, it can easily be integrated into the existing taxonomy by creating new categories or subcategories. This flexibility allows for the taxonomy to grow and evolve over time, accommodating changes and expansions in the information system. The hierarchical taxonomy also helps in content discovery and information retrieval. Users can navigate through the categories, starting from a broad topic and gradually narrowing down to a specific subtopic. This hierarchical browsing experience aids in serendipitous discovery, as users may come across related information or topics of interest during their exploration. In conclusion, a hierarchical taxonomy is a classification system that organizes information in a hierarchical structure, allowing for easy navigation, scalability, and content discovery. It plays a crucial role in Information Architecture by providing a clear overview of the information system and facilitating intuitive exploration and understanding for users.

High-Fidelity Wireframes

High-Fidelity Wireframes are detailed, highly polished visual representations of the final user interface design, typically created during the later stages of the Information Architecture (IA) process. They provide a realistic view of how the website or application will look and function, incorporating specific elements such as colors, typography, and interactive components. These wireframes aim to accurately simulate the final product, enabling stakeholders and developers to understand and evaluate the user experience, interactions, and overall usability. They serve as a bridge between the conceptual ideas and the final design, helping to refine and validate the Information Architecture before moving on to the development phase.

HotGloo

HotGloo is a web-based prototyping and collaboration tool specifically designed for Information Architecture (IA) professionals. It allows designers, developers, and stakeholders to create and iterate on wireframes, mockups, and interactive prototypes, facilitating the communication and understanding of complex website structures. With HotGloo, IA professionals can easily organize and structure their website content, ensuring that users can find information quickly and efficiently. The tool offers a variety of features and functionalities that support the creation and management of information hierarchies, navigation systems, and interaction flows. One of the key features of HotGloo is its drag-and-drop interface, which enables users to easily build and arrange website elements. IA professionals can quickly create and modify wireframes, allowing them to visualize and refine the layout and structure of web pages. Additionally, the tool provides a wide range of pre-designed UI components and icons, helping to speed up the prototyping process. Collaboration is another essential aspect of HotGloo. Multiple users can simultaneously work on the same project, allowing for real-time collaboration and feedback. IA professionals can invite clients, stakeholders, or team members to review and comment on the prototype, streamlining the feedback process and ensuring all parties are aligned. HotGloo also offers features for usability testing, providing IA professionals with the ability to gather user feedback and validate their design decisions. The tool allows them to add interactive elements such as clickable areas and navigation links, enabling users to navigate through the prototype and provide feedback on the user experience. In summary, HotGloo is a powerful and intuitive prototyping and collaboration tool designed for Information Architecture professionals. It enables the creation, visualization, and refinement of website structures and layouts, promoting effective communication and understanding within project teams.

Hotjar

Hotjar is a web analytics tool that helps information architects analyze and understand user behavior on websites. It provides valuable insights into how users interact with a website, allowing IA professionals to make informed decisions about organizing and designing web content. Hotjar offers a range of features that assist in gathering and interpreting user data. One of its key functionalities is heatmaps, which visually represent user activity on a webpage. By showing which areas of the page receive the most attention, heatmaps aid in identifying popular content and areas that may need improvement. This information helps information architects optimize the layout of a website to enhance user experience.

Human-Centered Design (HCD)

Human-Centered Design (HCD) is an approach to designing systems, processes, and artifacts that prioritize the needs, behaviors, and preferences of the end-users. In the context of Information Architecture (IA), HCD focuses on creating intuitive and user-friendly information structures that facilitate efficient and effective navigation, retrieval, and understanding of information. IA, as a discipline within the broader field of user experience (UX) design, is concerned with organizing content and designing navigational systems that assist users in finding and interacting with information. HCD complements IA by placing the user at the center of the design process, ensuring that the information structures align with their mental models, language, and contextual understanding.

Human-Computer Interaction (HCI)

Human-Computer Interaction (HCI) refers to the study of how humans interact with computers and the design of user interfaces that facilitate this interaction. It focuses on understanding the needs, behaviors, and capabilities of users and incorporating this knowledge into the design process to create effective and user-friendly interfaces. In the context of Information Architecture (IA), HCI plays a crucial role in ensuring that the structure and organization of information are optimized for user interaction. IA involves designing the navigation, organization, and labeling of information within a system or website, with the goal of making it easy for users to find and understand the information they need. When designing information architecture, HCI principles help to ensure that the organization and presentation of information meet the users' needs and expectations. This involves understanding the users' mental models, preferences, and cognitive abilities, as well as considering the context and goals of their interactions. An effective IA should provide clear, concise, and meaningful labels for navigation and content, making it easy for users to locate and understand the information. The structure of the IA should be intuitive and logical, following familiar patterns and conventions that users are accustomed to. Additionally, the IA should support various methods of information retrieval and exploration, such as browsing, searching, and filtering, to accommodate different user preferences. By applying HCI principles in IA design, designers can create interfaces that are user-centered, efficient, and enjoyable to use. This results in improved user satisfaction, increased productivity, and reduced errors and confusion. Overall, HCI provides the foundation for creating information architectures that meet the needs of users and support their goals in interacting with digital systems.

IA Best Practices

Information Architecture (IA) refers to the practice of organizing, structuring, and labeling information in a way that facilitates efficient navigation, retrieval, and understanding. It involves developing a clear and intuitive structure for websites, applications, or other digital platforms, ensuring that users can easily find and access the information they need. IA involves several key components, including organization systems, navigation systems, and labeling systems. An organization system defines how information is grouped and categorized, helping users locate content based on their needs or interests. This can be achieved through hierarchical structures, such as menus or categories, or through more dynamic systems, such as tags or filters. A navigation system provides a means for users to move through the information and navigate the interface. It should be designed in a way that is easy to understand and use, with clear and consistent navigation elements. This can include menus, breadcrumbs, search functions, or other interactive elements that guide users through the content. Labeling systems are used to describe and tag different pieces of information, making them easier to identify and locate. Labels should be concise, clear, and consistent, using familiar and meaningful language to avoid confusion or ambiguity. Effective labeling can improve the findability and usability of information. IA also considers the user experience and the overall goals of the platform. It should prioritize the needs and expectations of the users, making it easy for them to accomplish their tasks or find the information they are looking for. By organizing information in a logical and intuitive way, IA enhances usability, reduces cognitive load, and improves the overall user experience.

IA Documentation

Information Architecture (IA) in the context of web design refers to the organization, structure, and labeling of content on a website or digital platform. It involves strategically arranging and categorizing information to help users navigate and find what they need efficiently. IA focuses on creating a logical and intuitive information hierarchy that supports users' mental models and goals. This includes determining the main navigation elements, organizing subcategories, and establishing relationships between different pieces of information.

IA Evaluation

Information Architecture (IA) can be defined as the structural design and organization of information to facilitate effective navigation and user experience. It involves organizing, labeling, and categorizing information in a way that allows users to easily find what they are looking for and understand the relationships between different pieces of information. In the context of websites and digital platforms, IA focuses on creating a logical and intuitive information structure that enhances usability and findability. This involves determining the hierarchy of information, designing navigation systems, and creating clear and concise labels for different sections and categories.

IA Governance

IA Governance refers to the set of policies, processes, and guidelines that guide the development and management of Information Architecture (IA) in an organization or project. The aim of IA Governance is to establish a framework that ensures consistency, usability, and effectiveness of IA throughout the organization. It provides a structured approach to managing information resources and ensures that they are aligned with the business goals and user needs. IA Governance encompasses various aspects, including the roles and responsibilities of IA stakeholders, the decision-making processes, and the documentation of IA standards and best practices. One of the key components of IA Governance is the establishment of an IA Steering Committee or a similar governing body. This committee is responsible for setting the strategic direction of IA, making decisions on IA-related matters, and ensuring the implementation of IA standards and guidelines. IA Governance also involves defining and documenting IA principles and guidelines. These principles outline the fundamental concepts and approaches that guide the development of IA. Guidelines, on the other hand, provide more specific instructions and techniques for implementing IA within projects. Another important aspect of IA Governance is the establishment of IA review and approval processes. These processes ensure that IA artifacts, such as site maps, navigation structures, and metadata schemes, are reviewed and approved by appropriate stakeholders before implementation. This helps to ensure that IA remains consistent, coherent, and aligned with the organization's goals. Furthermore, IA Governance includes the establishment of IA training and awareness programs. These programs aim to educate stakeholders about the importance of IA and provide them with the knowledge and skills necessary to effectively contribute to IA-related activities. In summary, IA Governance provides a framework for the development, management, and governance of IA within an organization or project. It ensures consistency, usability, and effectiveness of IA by establishing policies, processes, and guidelines that guide IA-related activities.

IA Patterns

IA Patterns, in the context of Information Architecture (IA), refer to recurring solutions or approaches used to solve common design problems in organizing and structuring information. These patterns are established guidelines that help designers create consistent and user-friendly experiences by providing a framework for organizing and presenting information in a logical and intuitive manner. IA Patterns serve as a set of best practices that enable designers to effectively structure information, facilitate navigation, and support user tasks. They offer a systematic approach to organizing contents, ensuring that users can easily find what they are looking for and understand the relationships between different pieces of information. By following these patterns, designers can enhance the overall user experience and improve the usability of a website or application.

IA Prototyping

IA Prototyping is a method used in Information Architecture (IA) to visually represent and simulate the structure and organization of information within a digital product or system. It involves the creation of low-fidelity, interactive prototypes that allow designers to test and refine their IA concepts before the actual development phase. The primary goal of IA prototyping is to explore and iterate on different ways of organizing and presenting information to ensure a seamless user experience. By creating prototypes, designers can gather valuable feedback from users and stakeholders, identify potential issues or areas of improvement, and make informed decisions about the final IA design. IA prototypes are typically built using wireframing or prototyping tools, which allow designers to quickly and easily create interactive simulations of the proposed information structure. These prototypes often include basic navigational elements, such as menus and links, to replicate the user's interaction with the system. However, the level of fidelity can vary depending on the specific project requirements and stage of the IA design process. During the IA prototyping phase, designers may employ various techniques to explore different IA concepts and interactions. This can involve creating multiple prototypes with alternative organizational structures, testing different navigation systems, or experimenting with different labeling and categorization approaches. The prototypes created during IA prototyping may be presented to users or stakeholders for feedback through usability testing or other evaluation methods. These feedback sessions allow designers to observe how users interact with the prototype, understand their mental models and expectations, and identify areas that may require improvement. By leveraging IA prototyping, designers are able to gain valuable insights into the usability and effectiveness of their information structures. This iterative process helps refine the IA design, ensuring that the final product or system is intuitive, easy to navigate, and meets the needs of its users. In summary, IA prototyping is a fundamental method in the field of Information Architecture that involves the creation of interactive prototypes to visually represent and refine the organization and structure of digital information. Through these prototypes, designers can gather feedback, identify opportunities for improvement, and ultimately create a seamless user experience.

IA Software Tools

IA Software Tools refer to a set of computer programs or applications that are specifically designed and developed to assist information architects in performing their tasks more effectively and efficiently. Information Architecture (IA), in the context of web development or digital design, focuses on organizing, structuring, and labeling information to enhance usability and findability for users. IA Software Tools support information architects in various stages of the IA process, including analysis, planning, design, and implementation. These tools provide functionalities that aid in the creation of information structures, navigation systems, content categorization, and metadata management.

IA Wireframes

IA Wireframes are visual representations that outline the structure, layout, and functionality of a website or application. They are an essential tool in the field of Information Architecture (IA) as they help designers, developers, and stakeholders understand the organization and hierarchy of content, features, and user interactions. Wireframes provide a skeletal framework for the user interface, focusing on the placement of key elements such as navigation, content blocks, forms, and interactive components. They are created in the early stages of the design process and serve as a blueprint, guiding the development of the final product.

IA Workflow

Information Architecture (IA) Workflow is a systematic approach that outlines the process of designing and organizing information within a digital product or website to enhance its usability and findability. It involves several steps that ensure the structure, navigation, and labeling of content are intuitive and user-friendly. The first step in the IA workflow is to define the project objectives and gather requirements. This includes understanding the target audience, their needs, and the goals of the digital product. Once these are clear, the next step is to perform a thorough content audit. This involves analyzing existing content, identifying gaps, and determining what content is necessary to achieve the project objectives. After the content audit, the IA designer moves on to creating a sitemap. A sitemap is a hierarchical representation of the website's structure, showing the relationship between different pages and content elements. It provides a high-level view of the entire website and helps in planning the overall navigation. The next step is creating wireframes, which are low-fidelity visual representations of the website's layout and functionalities. Wireframes help in defining the placement of elements, such as headers, footers, navigation menus, and content sections, without getting into the specific visual details. They help ensure that the information is properly organized and accessible to users. Once the wireframes are approved, the IA designer proceeds to define the labeling and categorization of content. This step involves creating a controlled vocabulary, such as a taxonomy or classification scheme, to classify and categorize different types of content. This ensures that users can easily find and navigate through the information they are looking for. The final step in the IA workflow is to conduct usability testing and gather feedback from users. This helps in identifying any usability issues or areas for improvement in the information architecture. The feedback collected is used to iterate and refine the IA design before the final implementation. In conclusion, the IA workflow is a structured process that involves defining project objectives, performing content audits, creating sitemaps and wireframes, defining labeling and categorization, and conducting usability testing. It ensures that the information within a digital product is organized in a way that enhances user experience and helps users find the information they are looking for efficiently.

IA For Chatbots

Information Architecture (IA) for chatbots refers to the process of organizing, structuring, and labeling the information within a chatbot system to optimize user experience and facilitate efficient communication between the user and the chatbot. IA for chatbots involves designing the conversation flow, content organization, and navigational structure to ensure that users can easily find and access the information they need. It focuses on creating a seamless and intuitive user interface that enables effective interaction and understanding between the user and the chatbot.

IA For E-Learning Systems

E-Learning Systems is an umbrella term that encompasses various digital platforms and tools designed to facilitate online education and training. In the context of Information Architecture (IA), E-Learning Systems refer to the organization and structuring of information within these online learning environments to optimize user experience and knowledge retention. IA for E-Learning Systems involves the development and implementation of a coherent and intuitive navigation system that allows learners to easily locate and access the information they need. This includes the arrangement of content, resources, and interactive features in a logical and user-friendly manner. An effective IA for E-Learning Systems should prioritize the needs and preferences of both learners and instructors. It should consider factors such as the targeted educational objectives, the diversity of learners' backgrounds and learning styles, and the availability and format of the content being delivered. To achieve optimal IA, careful consideration should be given to the organization of content within different categories, such as courses, modules, lessons, and assessments. A hierarchical structure can be implemented to allow learners to navigate through these levels and access relevant materials at each stage of their learning journey. Additionally, clear labeling and consistent terminology should be employed to reduce cognitive load and enhance comprehension. Well-designed menus, search functionalities, and learning pathways can further assist users in finding specific information and progressing through the course effectively. IA for E-Learning Systems also encompasses the design of user interfaces and interactions. Visual cues, such as icons, colors, and typography, can be utilized to aid navigation and provide feedback. Furthermore, interactive elements, such as quizzes, discussions, and multimedia components, should be seamlessly integrated into the system to enhance engagement and knowledge application. Regular assessment and refinement of IA for E-Learning Systems is essential to ensure its continued effectiveness. User feedback, analytics, and usability testing can provide valuable insights into areas that may require improvement or adjustment. In summary, IA for E-Learning Systems focuses on the organization and structuring of information within online learning environments to optimize user experience and knowledge retention. It involves the development of intuitive navigation systems, clear labeling, consistent terminology, and interactive interfaces. Regular assessment and refinement are crucial to maintain the effectiveness of IA in supporting learners' educational goals.

IA For Internet Of Things (IoT)

The Internet of Things (IoT) refers to the network of physical devices, vehicles, appliances, and other objects embedded with sensors, software, and network connectivity that enables these objects to collect and exchange data. Information Architecture (IA) in the context of IoT focuses on structuring, organizing, and categorizing the vast amount of data generated by these interconnected devices to ensure effective storage, retrieval, and analysis of information.

IA For Smart Environments

Information Architecture (IA) for Smart Environments can be defined as the practice of organizing, structuring, and labeling information in a way that enables users to easily navigate and find what they need within smart environments. IA involves creating a clear and intuitive information structure that supports efficient information retrieval and use. In the context of smart environments, IA plays a critical role in facilitating seamless interactions between users and the vast amount of connected devices, sensors, and services present in these environments. It aims to optimize the user experience by ensuring that the right information is presented to the right user at the right time and in the right context.

IA For Virtual Assistants

Information Architecture (IA) for Virtual Assistants is a design discipline that focuses on organizing and structuring information in a way that makes it easily accessible and understandable for users of virtual assistants. IA helps in the development of efficient and user-friendly virtual assistants by defining the way information is categorized, labeled, and presented within the system. The main goal of IA for Virtual Assistants is to create a coherent and intuitive information structure that facilitates the interaction between users and the virtual assistant. This involves determining the most effective ways to organize and present information, ensuring that it is logically organized and easy to navigate. IA professionals for virtual assistants also strive to ensure that the information provided is consistent, up-to-date, and relevant to the user's needs. The IA process for virtual assistants typically includes several key activities. These include information analysis, where the IA professional assesses the content and determines its relevance and importance to users. They also define the information structure, which involves creating a hierarchical organization of topics and subtopics. This structure helps users navigate the virtual assistant and find the information they need efficiently. Another important activity in IA for virtual assistants is labeling and categorization. This involves assigning appropriate names and descriptions to different topics and categories, making it easier for users to understand and find the information they are looking for. IA professionals also collaborate with stakeholders and content creators to ensure that the information is accurately represented and presented in a user-friendly manner. Overall, IA for Virtual Assistants plays a crucial role in improving the user experience and ensuring that virtual assistants are effective and helpful tools. By organizing and structuring information in a logical and intuitive way, IA professionals contribute to the usability and functionality of virtual assistant systems, making them valuable tools for users in various domains and industries.

IA For Wearable Devices

Information Architecture (IA) for Wearable Devices encompasses the organization, structure, and navigation of information within these devices. It focuses on providing a seamless and intuitive user experience by effectively organizing and presenting information. The primary goal of IA for Wearable Devices is to ensure that users can easily access and navigate through the information they need, while minimizing cognitive load and maximizing efficiency. This is achieved through careful consideration of the following aspects: 1. Content Organization: IA for Wearable Devices involves grouping and categorizing information in a logical manner. This facilitates easy retrieval and assists users in quickly finding the relevant information. Content organization should be driven by user needs and tasks, considering the context and limitations of wearable devices. Information may be organized hierarchically, through menus or cards, or using other appropriate structures. 2. Navigation: Effortless navigation is crucial in wearable devices due to their small screens and limited input methods. IA for Wearable Devices employs strategies such as clear and concise navigation labels, breadcrumb trails, or gesture-based navigation to ensure users can easily move between different sections and retrieve information intuitively. Navigation should be intuitive and provide a clear mental model for users. 3. Search: As wearable devices often have smaller screens, typing can be challenging. Therefore, IA for Wearable Devices integrates effective search interfaces to allow users to quickly find information through voice search or other simplified input methods. This includes presenting search results in a meaningful and organized manner. 4. Contextual Information: Wearable devices often leverage various sensors to gather contextual information. IA for Wearable Devices takes advantage of this data to personalize and tailor information to the user's current context. This could involve presenting relevant information based on location, time, or user preferences. In summary, Information Architecture for Wearable Devices revolves around effectively organizing and presenting information in a manner that ensures seamless navigation, easy information retrieval, and personalized experiences based on context. By focusing on content organization, navigation, search, and contextual information, IA for Wearable Devices enhances the overall usability and user experience of these devices.

In-Context Navigation

In-Context Navigation, in the context of Information Architecture (IA), refers to the navigation system that allows users to easily move between different sections or pages of a website or application without losing context or getting disoriented. It is a crucial aspect of IA as it helps users smoothly navigate through the content, ensuring a positive user experience. In-Context Navigation is designed to guide users within the information space, providing clear pathways and relevant links based on their context.

InVision Studio

InVision Studio is a powerful design tool that is used in the field of Information Architecture (IA) to create interactive prototypes and design user interfaces for digital products. It allows designers to visually organize and structure information in a way that enhances user experience and usability. With InVision Studio, IA professionals can easily create wireframes, flowcharts, and navigation models to represent the structure of a website or application. These visual representations help stakeholders and team members understand the overall layout and organization of content, allowing for effective collaboration and decision-making.

InVision

InVision is a web-based prototyping tool that plays a crucial role in the field of Information Architecture (IA). In the context of IA, InVision is a powerful platform that enables designers and stakeholders to collaborate in the creation and validation of interactive prototypes. With InVision, designers can easily upload their design files and transform them into interactive prototypes. The platform offers a range of tools and features that allow designers to link different screens and create interactive hotspots. This allows stakeholders to experience the prototype as if it were a real website or application, enabling them to provide feedback and make informed decisions about the IA.

Inclusive Design

Inclusive Design, in the context of Information Architecture (IA), refers to the practice of designing digital products and services that are accessible and usable by a wide range of users, including individuals with disabilities or age-related impairments. It involves considering the diverse needs, preferences, and abilities of users during the design process to ensure that the final product is inclusive and provides equal access to information and functionality for all users.

This approach to design recognizes that accessibility is not just a legal requirement or a nice-to-have feature, but an essential aspect of creating an inclusive and user-centered experience. Inclusive Design acknowledges that individuals have different physical, cognitive, and sensory abilities, and that these differences should be accommodated to provide equal opportunities and experiences. When implementing Inclusive Design in the context of IA, designers need to consider various aspects: - Structure and organization: The IA should be designed in a way that is easy to navigate, understand, and interact with for all users. Clear and consistent labeling, logical grouping of content, and intuitive navigation pathways contribute to an inclusive IA. - Content presentation: Inclusive design considers different users' preferences and needs by providing flexible options for presenting content. This could include offering multiple formats, such as text alternatives for non-text content, resizable text, or the ability to change color contrasts and fonts to improve legibility. - Interaction and functionality: Designers should ensure that interactive elements and functionalities are accessible and usable by users with different abilities. This may involve providing keyboard navigation options, allowing sufficient time for users to complete tasks, and ensuring that form fields are properly labeled and easy to understand. Inclusive Design in the context of IA aims to create digital environments that are welcoming and inclusive for everyone, regardless of their abilities or disabilities. By considering the diverse needs of users from the early stages of the design process, designers can create information architectures that meet the needs of a wider range of users and provide a more equal and inclusive digital experience.

InfoMapper

InfoMapper refers to a tool or framework used within the context of Information Architecture (IA) to help visualize and organize information. It serves as a guide or blueprint for designing the structure and navigation of a website or digital system. With InfoMapper, the information architect can map out the relationships and connections between different pieces of information. It provides a visual representation of how information should be organized and presented to the user, ensuring a seamless and intuitive user experience.

Information Design Principles

Information Design Principles in the context of Information Architecture (IA) refer to a set of guidelines and principles that help in organizing, structuring, and presenting information in a clear, intuitive, and meaningful way. These principles are essential for creating effective and user-friendly IA systems where users can easily navigate, find, and understand the desired information. The first principle is Clarity, which emphasizes the importance of ensuring that the information presented is clear, concise, and easily understood. This involves using plain language, avoiding jargon and complex terminology, and using consistent and standardized terminology across the IA system. Clarity also involves choosing appropriate visual elements, such as fonts, colors, and icons, that aid in clear communication and understanding. The second principle is Organization, which focuses on arranging and grouping information logically and intuitively. This involves creating categories, hierarchies, and taxonomies that reflect the users' mental models and expectations. Organizing information facilitates efficient navigation and retrieval, reducing cognitive load and enhancing the overall user experience. The third principle is Consistency, which emphasizes the importance of establishing and maintaining consistent patterns, structures, and interfaces throughout the IA system. Consistency enhances user familiarity and reduces learning curve, allowing users to quickly understand and navigate the system. This includes consistent labeling, layout, and navigation conventions, ensuring that similar actions and information are displayed in a consistent manner. The fourth principle is Discoverability, which focuses on enabling users to easily find and access relevant information within the IA system. This involves providing clear and visible navigation menus, search functionalities, and breadcrumb trails. Discoverability also entails effective use of information scent, where visual cues and indicators help users understand where they are and where they can go within the system. The fifth principle is User-Centricity, which puts the users' needs, goals, and tasks at the center of the IA design process. User-centric IA systems are designed with empathy and understanding of the users' context, preferences, and information seeking behavior. User research and testing inform the design decisions, ensuring that the IA system meets the users' expectations and supports their information needs effectively. By adhering to these Information Design Principles, an IA system can be designed and implemented in a way that optimizes the accessibility, usability, and overall user experience. These principles guide the architect in making informed decisions regarding information organization, presentation, and interaction, resulting in an IA system that is intuitive, efficient, and effective.

Information Design

Information design in the context of Information Architecture (IA) refers to the process of organizing and presenting information in a clear, intuitive, and visually appealing way. It involves the strategic arrangement of content, navigation systems, and interactive elements to enhance the user experience and enable efficient access to information.Information design aims to convey complex information in a simple and concise manner, ensuring that users can easily find and understand the information they are seeking. This involves considering the needs and goals of the users and designing the structure, layout, and presentation of information accordingly.

Information Ecosystem

The Information Ecosystem in the context of Information Architecture (IA) refers to the interconnected network of information sources, platforms, and processes that collectively contribute to the creation, dissemination, and consumption of information. In an increasingly digital world, the Information Ecosystem encompasses a wide range of elements, including websites, databases, content management systems, social media platforms, search engines, and various other information sources and tools. These components work together to support the discovery, organization, and delivery of information to users.

Information Filtering

Information filtering, in the context of Information Architecture (IA), refers to the process of selecting and delivering relevant and valuable information to users based on their specific needs, preferences, or characteristics. It involves the systematic organization and categorization of information to facilitate efficient retrieval and presentation. The goal of information filtering is to reduce information overload and enhance user experience by presenting only the most relevant and useful content. It helps in streamlining the access to information by identifying and eliminating irrelevant or redundant information, allowing users to focus on the information that matters to them.

Information Flow Analysis

Information Flow Analysis in the context of Information Architecture (IA) refers to the process of mapping and analyzing the movement of information within a system or network. It aims to understand the path, direction, and interactions of information within an information architecture framework. At its core, Information Flow Analysis helps in identifying how information is created, stored, retrieved, shared, and utilized by different users or stakeholders. It examines the flow of information across various components of an information system, including databases, applications, websites, and other digital platforms.

Information Foraging

Information foraging is a concept in the field of Information Architecture (IA) that refers to the process by which users search, browse, and navigate through information in an online environment, with the aim of maximizing their information gain while minimizing their effort. The term "foraging" is derived from the analogy of animals searching for food in their natural habitats, where they constantly assess the cost and benefit of each potential food source. Similarly, information foragers evaluate the available options and make strategic decisions in order to obtain the most relevant and valuable information.

Information Governance

Information Governance refers to the strategic management of an organization's information, ensuring that it is effectively utilized, protected, and compliant with relevant regulations and policies. In the context of Information Architecture (IA), it refers to the processes and practices involved in organizing and structuring information assets to support effective information management and decision-making. IA plays a crucial role in Information Governance by providing the framework for organizing and categorizing information assets in a way that facilitates easy retrieval, navigation, and understanding. It involves defining the taxonomy, metadata, and structure of information, as well as the relationships between different information elements. Effective Information Governance through IA requires careful consideration of various factors. This includes understanding the information needs and requirements of different stakeholders within the organization, such as employees, customers, and regulatory bodies. By aligning the organization's information assets with these needs, IA helps ensure that the right information is available to the right people at the right time. Furthermore, IA also enables organizations to implement and enforce data security and privacy measures. By structuring information assets in a way that reflects their sensitivity and criticality, IA helps identify and protect sensitive data from unauthorized access, while also facilitating data sharing and collaboration where appropriate. Another important aspect of Information Governance in IA is compliance with relevant regulations and policies. This includes ensuring that the organization's information assets adhere to legal, industry, and organizational requirements, such as data retention policies, data protection regulations, and intellectual property rights. In summary, Information Governance in the context of IA involves the strategic organization and management of an organization's information assets to ensure their effective utilization, protection, and compliance. It requires robust IA practices to define the taxonomy, metadata, and structure of information, as well as considerations for stakeholders' information needs, data security, and regulatory compliance.

Information Mapping

Information Mapping is a method of organizing and presenting information in a structured and intuitive manner, optimized for efficient retrieval and comprehension. It is a fundamental component of Information Architecture (IA), which focuses on the design and organization of digital information systems. The main goal of Information Mapping is to break down complex information into smaller, more manageable units, known as information chunks. These chunks are then organized and classified based on their content and context, allowing users to easily navigate and locate the information they need. This method utilizes a hierarchical structure, where information is grouped into categories, subcategories, and further subcategories, forming a tree-like structure. Each level of the hierarchy represents a different level of detail, allowing users to drill down into specific topics or zoom out to see the bigger picture. Information Mapping also emphasizes the use of consistent and standardized templates for presenting information. These templates include headings, subheadings, and sections, which help users quickly scan and understand the content. This consistent formatting not only enhances readability but also enables users to compare and contrast information across different sections. Additionally, Information Mapping advocates for the use of visual elements, such as diagrams, charts, and icons, to supplement textual information. These visuals provide users with alternative ways of understanding and processing information, catering to different learning styles and preferences. In summary, Information Mapping is a systematic approach to organizing and presenting information, aiming to improve findability, comprehension, and usability. By breaking down complex information into smaller chunks, utilizing hierarchical structures, employing consistent templates, and incorporating visual elements, Information Mapping enables users to navigate and make sense of digital information more efficiently and effectively.

Information Presentation

Information Architecture (IA) is the practice of organizing and structuring information in a logical and meaningful way to facilitate efficient and effective access, retrieval, and communication of information within a system. IA involves designing the structure, organization, labeling, and navigation systems of digital products, websites, and other information systems to enhance the user experience and help users find the information they need quickly and easily.

Information Retrieval

Information Retrieval is a discipline within Information Architecture that focuses on the effective and efficient retrieval of information from a collection or database. It involves the development and implementation of methods, algorithms, and systems to search, retrieve, and organize information to meet the needs and requirements of users. Information Retrieval encompasses various techniques and processes to facilitate the searching and retrieval of information. These techniques include indexing, retrieval models, query processing, and relevance ranking. The goal is to provide users with accurate and relevant information that satisfies their information needs.

Information Scent

Information Scent is a concept in Information Architecture (IA) that refers to the degree of relevancy and clarity of information presented to users when they are navigating a website or digital interface. It is a crucial component of user experience design, as it impacts how easily users can find and access the desired information. When users interact with a website or application, they follow various cues or paths to locate the information they need. These cues can include visual cues (such as headings, links, and buttons), textual cues (such as labels and descriptions), and interactive cues (such as search fields and navigation menus). The strength and effectiveness of these cues determine the information scent. Effective information scent is achieved when users can effortlessly follow the cues provided and find relevant information. It helps users make informed decisions about where to go next and encourages exploration and engagement. On the other hand, poor information scent can lead to frustration and confusion, increasing the likelihood of users abandoning the site or interface. One way to enhance information scent is through the use of clear and descriptive labels and headings. Labels should accurately represent the content or functionality they correspond to, helping users predict what they will find when they click or interact. Similarly, headings should provide a clear hierarchy and structure to guide users through the information architecture. Another important aspect of information scent is the use of consistent and recognizable visual and interactive cues. Users rely on familiar patterns and conventions when navigating digital interfaces. Therefore, maintaining consistent design elements, such as color schemes, button styles, and menu placements, helps users quickly understand and interact with the interface. In conclusion, information scent plays a vital role in the usability and effectiveness of digital interfaces. By providing clear and relevant cues, designers can guide users to the information they seek, improving their experience and increasing engagement.

Information Seeking Behavior

Information seeking behavior refers to the process individuals go through to find, evaluate, and use information to meet their specific needs. In the context of Information Architecture (IA), information seeking behavior is an important concept as it helps designers understand how users search for and interact with information in digital environments. When designing an effective IA, it is crucial to consider the different types of information seeking behaviors users might exhibit. These behaviors can be categorized into three main types: known-item searching, exploratory searching, and undirected monitoring. Known-item searching occurs when users have a specific piece of information in mind and conduct a focused search to find it. In this behavior, users often rely on search engines or specific databases to locate the exact information they are looking for. Designers should ensure that the IA includes clear and intuitive search functionality, allowing users to easily enter their search terms and retrieve relevant results. Exploratory searching, on the other hand, happens when users have a broader information need and are open to exploring different sources and options. These users may navigate through a website or system, following links and browsing categories to find relevant information. In IA design, it is important to provide clear navigation paths and categorization systems that allow users to easily browse and discover information in an intuitive manner. Undirected monitoring refers to the passive information seeking behavior where users keep themselves updated on specific topics or areas of interest. This behavior often occurs through subscription services, RSS feeds, or social media platforms that deliver relevant information to the users. IA designers should ensure that the system provides options for users to subscribe, follow, or receive notifications for updates in order to support this type of information seeking behavior.

Information Structure

The information structure in the context of Information Architecture (IA) refers to the way information is organized, classified, and presented on a website or any other digital platform. It plays a crucial role in ensuring that users can easily find and understand the information they are looking for. The information structure is designed to provide a logical and intuitive framework that facilitates navigation and supports effective information retrieval. Essentially, the information structure encompasses the organization and arrangement of content elements such as pages, sections, categories, and tags. It establishes the relationships and hierarchy between these elements, defining how they are interconnected and how users can navigate between them. The main goal is to create a hierarchical structure that is both meaningful and user-friendly. A key aspect of information structure is the use of navigation systems. These systems consist of menus, links, and other navigation elements that guide users through the digital platform. They allow users to move seamlessly between different sections and levels of information, ensuring that they can easily navigate to the content they are interested in. Another important element is the use of metadata and labeling. Metadata provides additional information about the content, such as the date of creation, author, or related topics. This metadata is used to categorize and classify the content, making it easier for users to find relevant information. Labels, on the other hand, are used to provide clear and concise descriptions of the content, making it easier for users to understand what they will find on a particular page or section. The information structure also takes into consideration the principle of findability. It aims to make information easily discoverable by using clear and descriptive labels, providing search and filtering functionalities, and using consistent navigation and labeling conventions throughout the digital platform. In summary, the information structure in Information Architecture refers to the organization, arrangement, and presentation of information on a digital platform. It encompasses the hierarchical relationships between content elements, the use of navigation systems, the application of metadata and labeling, and the principle of findability. A well-designed information structure is essential for providing a seamless user experience, ensuring that users can easily find and understand the information they need.

Information Visualization

Information Visualization is a discipline within Information Architecture that focuses on presenting complex data or information in a visual format. It involves transforming raw data into visual representations, such as charts, graphs, maps, or diagrams, to facilitate understanding and analysis of the information. The purpose of Information Visualization is to enhance cognition and decision-making by making information more accessible, organized, and meaningful. It leverages the human visual system's ability to process and interpret visual stimuli more efficiently than textual or numerical data alone.

Informational Content

Informational Content refers to the textual, visual, or audiovisual information presented within a website or application. It is an integral part of Information Architecture (IA) and plays a critical role in guiding users to find and understand the content they are seeking. Informational Content encompasses various types of data, including articles, blog posts, product descriptions, tutorials, videos, images, and audio files. Its purpose is to provide users with useful, relevant, and reliable information that meets their needs and supports their goals. One of the key goals of Information Architecture is to organize and structure informational content in a way that facilitates easy navigation and discovery. This involves categorizing content into logical, meaningful sections, and creating clear hierarchies and paths for users to follow. Effective Information Architecture ensures that informational content is presented in a readable and understandable format. It emphasizes the use of clear headings, concise and engaging text, relevant visuals, and easy-to-follow navigation menus. Informational Content should be created with a focus on the target audience. User research and analysis help identify users' information needs, preferences, and behaviors, allowing designers to tailor the content to their specific requirements. Considering the diverse range of devices and platforms users may access content from, Information Architecture also needs to account for responsive design principles. This ensures that the informational content adapts and displays correctly on different screen sizes and resolutions. In conclusion, Informational Content in the context of Information Architecture is the textual, visual, or audiovisual information presented within a website or application. It aims to provide users with relevant and reliable information in a readable and understandable format. Effective Information Architecture structures and organizes this content to facilitate easy navigation and discovery, while considering the specific needs of the target audience and the requirements of various devices and platforms.

Informational Scent

Informational scent in the context of Information Architecture (IA) refers to the cues or indicators provided by a website or digital interface that help users determine the relevance and potential usefulness of a particular piece of information or content before they click on it. It is a design principle used to guide users through a website or application, providing clear pathways to information and helping users make informed decisions about which links or buttons to click. Informational scent is crucial in IA as it helps users quickly and efficiently navigate through complex information ecosystems. Well-designed informational scent can enhance the user experience by reducing cognitive load and increasing the findability of relevant content. It provides users with a sense of confidence and control, allowing them to make informed choices and find the information they are looking for without getting lost or overwhelmed.

Input Modalities

Input Modalities in the context of Information Architecture (IA) refer to the various ways through which users can interact with a system or application to input information or provide commands. These modalities serve as the channels or methods users employ to communicate their intentions or requests to the system. Input modalities can be classified into different categories based on the nature of the interaction they enable. Some common input modalities include: 1. Visual Modalities: Visual modalities involve using visual cues or stimuli to input information or commands. This could include clicking buttons or links on a graphical user interface (GUI), selecting options from a dropdown menu, or dragging and dropping elements. Visual modalities rely on the user's ability to perceive and interpret visual information. 2. Auditory Modalities: Auditory modalities involve using sound or speech to input information or commands. This could include voice recognition technology, where users speak commands or dictate text to be transcribed by the system. Auditory modalities are particularly useful for individuals with visual impairments or when hands-free interaction is desired. 3. Tactile Modalities: Tactile modalities involve using touch or physical feedback to input information or commands. This could include touchscreens, touchpads, or physical buttons. Tactile modalities rely on the sense of touch and provide haptic feedback to the user, enhancing the overall user experience. 4. Gestural Modalities: Gestural modalities involve using gestures or body movements to input information or commands. This could include swiping, pinching, or tapping on touchscreens, or using motion-sensing devices like accelerometers or cameras to detect and interpret specific gestures. Gestural modalities provide a more natural and intuitive way of interacting with a system. By considering and incorporating multiple input modalities in IA, designers can cater to a broader range of user preferences and abilities. This can enhance usability and accessibility, ensuring that users can effectively and efficiently interact with the system, regardless of their individual needs or constraints.

Inspectlet

Inspectlet is a web analytics tool that focuses on providing insights into user behavior on websites. It is often used in the context of Information Architecture (IA) to study how users interact with a website and optimize its design and structure. Inspectlet offers a range of features that help IA professionals understand user behavior. One of its key features is session recording, which captures and replays user sessions on a website. This allows IA professionals to observe how users navigate through the site, what actions they take, and any issues they encounter. The session recordings can be filtered and searched based on various criteria, such as location, device type, and page views. This helps IA professionals identify patterns and trends in user behavior. Another important feature of Inspectlet is heatmaps. Heatmaps visually represent user interactions by highlighting areas of a webpage that are most frequently clicked, scrolled, or focused on. This provides valuable insights into what content or features are most engaging or important to users. Heatmaps can be generated for individual pages or across the entire website, helping IA professionals identify areas of improvement or potential issues. Inspectlet also offers form analytics, which tracks and analyzes user interactions with forms on a website. It provides metrics such as form completion rate, field abandonment rate, and time taken to complete each field. These insights can help IA professionals optimize form layouts and reduce friction in the user experience. Furthermore, Inspectlet provides a real-time dashboard that displays key performance metrics, such as the number of active visitors, average visit duration, and conversion rates. This allows IA professionals to monitor website performance and make data-driven decisions to improve user experience. Overall, Inspectlet is a powerful tool that aids IA professionals in analyzing user behavior and optimizing website design and structure. By leveraging its session recording, heatmaps, form analytics, and real-time dashboard, IA professionals can make informed decisions to enhance user engagement and satisfaction.

Instapage

Information Architecture (IA) is the structural and organizational design of information within a website or application. It involves the arrangement and categorization of content, navigation systems, and overall user experience. IA focuses on how information is organized, labeled, and presented to users. It aims to create a clear and intuitive structure that helps users find and understand information easily. The goal is to improve usability, enhance user satisfaction, and support efficient interaction between users and the system.

Interaction Design (IxD)

Interaction Design (IxD) in the context of Information Architecture (IA) refers to the practice of designing how users interact and engage with digital products, systems, and services in order to optimize their experience and achieve their goals. It encompasses the elements, behaviors, and interactions that shape the overall user experience. IxD involves the strategic planning and meticulous execution of the design process to ensure that users can easily navigate and interact with information and functionality within a digital product or system. It focuses on creating intuitive, efficient, and enjoyable interactions that support users in accomplishing their tasks and achieving their objectives.

Interaction Flow

The interaction flow in the context of Information Architecture (IA) refers to the sequence of steps or actions that a user takes while navigating through a digital product or system. It outlines the paths, transitions, and interactions that users go through to achieve their desired goals within the system. The interaction flow is guided by the structure and organization of the information within the IA, including the placement of content, navigation menus, buttons, and links. It ensures that users can easily find, understand, and interact with the information they need.

Interaction Patterns

Interaction patterns, within the context of information architecture (IA), refer to the recurring structures or frameworks that guide the way users engage and interact with a digital product or system. These patterns are designed to facilitate efficient, intuitive, and user-friendly interactions, ensuring that users can easily navigate, access information, and complete tasks within a digital environment. The goal of interaction patterns is to establish consistent and predictable behaviors across different interfaces, platforms, or applications. By following established patterns, designers can leverage users' existing mental models and prior experiences, which can enhance usability and reduce cognitive load. In IA, there are several commonly used interaction patterns, including: 1. Navigation patterns: These patterns define how users move through information and content within a system. Examples include hierarchical menus, breadcrumb trails, and tabbed interfaces. Navigation patterns play a crucial role in helping users orient themselves, locate desired information, and traverse between different sections or pages. 2. Search patterns: Search patterns provide users with a way to find specific information or items within a system. This may include search bars, filters, or advanced search options. Effective search patterns allow users to formulate queries, submit requests, and receive relevant results efficiently. 3. Input patterns: Input patterns define how users enter data, interact with forms, or provide feedback within a system. This may include input fields, checkboxes, radio buttons, dropdown menus, or buttons. Well-designed input patterns ensure that users can easily input or select information, minimizing errors and streamlining the interaction process. 4. Feedback patterns: Feedback patterns provide users with information about their actions or system status. This may include error messages, success notifications, loading indicators, or progress bars. Effective feedback patterns help users understand whether their actions were successful or not, reducing frustration and providing a sense of control. 5. Content patterns: Content patterns refer to the way information is structured and presented within a system. This may include article layouts, card-based designs, image carousels, or grid-based displays. Content patterns play a vital role in organizing information, highlighting key details, and facilitating effective information consumption. By incorporating these established interaction patterns into their IA designs, designers can create user-friendly systems that promote a seamless and intuitive user experience. Consistency and predictability in interactions not only enhance usability but also contribute to users' overall satisfaction and engagement with the digital product or system.

Interactive Prototype

An interactive prototype, in the context of Information Architecture (IA), is a representation of a digital product or system that allows users to interact with its functionalities and features in a simulated environment. It serves as a visual demonstration of the proposed design, layout, and navigation of the product, helping stakeholders and designers to evaluate and refine the user experience. The interactive prototype is typically created during the early stages of the design process, before the development of the actual product or system begins. It allows designers to test and validate their design concepts and user flows, gather feedback and input from stakeholders and potential users, and identify potential issues or improvements in the user experience. The HTML format is one of the commonly used formats for creating interactive prototypes. By using HTML, designers can create multiple static web pages that are interconnected through hyperlinks, enabling users to navigate from one page to another and mimic the flow and structure of the final product. The interactive prototype should be designed in a way that reflects the intended functionality and user interface of the final product. This includes incorporating elements such as buttons, menus, forms, and interactive elements that allow users to interact with the prototype and simulate actions they would perform in the actual product. The goal of an interactive prototype is to provide a realistic and immersive representation of the final product, enabling stakeholders and designers to evaluate and refine the user experience, identify design flaws, and make informed decisions about the product's functionality and features. In summary, an interactive prototype in the context of Information Architecture is a visual representation of a digital product or system, created using HTML or other interactive tools, that allows stakeholders and designers to evaluate and refine the user experience. It serves as a simulated environment for users to interact with the proposed design and functionality, gather feedback, and make informed decisions about the final product.

IxD (Interaction Design)

Interaction Design (IxD) is a field within Information Architecture (IA) that focuses on creating meaningful and effective interactions between users and digital products or services.IxD is concerned with how users interact with the user interface (UI) and how information is presented and organized to facilitate a smooth and engaging user experience (UX).

Justinmind

Information Architecture (IA) refers to the organization and structure of digital information in a way that allows users to easily navigate and understand content. It involves creating a clear and intuitive interface that helps users find and interact with the information they need. The main goal of IA is to provide users with a seamless and efficient experience when accessing information. It aims to organize and classify content in a logical and consistent manner, ensuring that users can easily locate and retrieve the information they are looking for.

Kameleoon

Kameleoon is a software platform designed to optimize and personalize the user experience on websites. It is used to implement and manage A/B testing, personalization, and behavioral targeting strategies. Kameleoon integrates seamlessly with websites, allowing marketers and webmasters to create and modify website elements without requiring any coding skills. As a tool for Information Architecture (IA), Kameleoon plays a crucial role in organizing and structuring the content and navigation of a website. It enables IA professionals to design and implement effective information hierarchies, ensuring that users can easily find the information they are looking for.

Kinetic Scrolling

Kinetic scrolling is a user interface (UI) interaction technique that allows users to smoothly scroll through content by using touch or mouse gestures, providing a more natural and fluid browsing experience. In the context of Information Architecture (IA), kinetic scrolling plays a crucial role in enhancing the usability and accessibility of websites, applications, and other digital platforms. By implementing kinetic scrolling, IA designers aim to improve the overall user experience (UX) by enabling users to easily navigate and consume large amounts of content.

Kite Compositor

Kite Compositor is a powerful tool used in Information Architecture (IA) to design and create interfaces for digital products. It allows IA professionals to visually organize and structure information in a way that enhances the user experience and usability of a website, application, or system. With Kite Compositor, IA professionals can easily create wireframes, prototypes, and interactive designs that help stakeholders and development teams understand the flow and functionality of a digital product. It provides a comprehensive set of features and functionalities that enable the creation of user-friendly and intuitive interfaces.

Knowledge Organization

Knowledge organization in the context of Information Architecture (IA) refers to the systematic arrangement and structuring of information to facilitate easy access, retrieval, and understanding. It involves organizing information in a way that takes into account the needs and expectations of users, as well as the relationships between different pieces of information. Knowledge organization involves various processes and techniques, including classification, categorization, metadata creation, and indexing. These processes help to identify the main themes, concepts, and relationships within a particular information space, allowing for efficient navigation and searching.

Landingi

Landingi is a software platform that specializes in creating and managing landing pages for online marketing campaigns. As an integral part of Information Architecture (IA), Landingi helps with the organization and structure of content, ensuring that these pages are designed to effectively capture leads and drive conversions. With Landingi, marketers can easily create custom landing pages without any coding knowledge. The platform offers a drag-and-drop editor that allows users to customize the look and feel of their pages, including the layout, fonts, colors, and images. This flexibility ensures that the landing pages align with the overall branding and messaging of the campaign. Information Architecture plays a crucial role in helping users navigate through a website or digital product. It focuses on organizing and structuring content in a way that is intuitive and user-friendly. Landingi contributes to IA by providing templates and design elements that are optimized for conversion. By integrating user-generated content such as testimonials and reviews, Landingi helps build trust and credibility, further enhancing the user experience. Additionally, Landingi offers various features to optimize landing pages for search engines (SEO) and improve conversion rates. The platform allows for A/B testing, enabling marketers to compare different versions of a landing page to determine which one performs better. This data-driven approach helps refine the IA of these pages and maximize their effectiveness. In conclusion, Landingi is a powerful tool that assists marketers in creating and managing landing pages as part of their overall Information Architecture strategy. By offering an easy-to-use platform with customization options and optimization features, Landingi helps drive conversions and improve the user experience, ultimately leading to the success of online marketing campaigns.

Law Of Prägnanz

The Law of Prägnanz, also known as the Law of Good Form or the Law of Simplicity, is a fundamental principle in Information Architecture (IA). It states that humans tend to perceive and interpret complex shapes or patterns in the simplest and most organized way possible. According to this principle, people will instinctively seek out and prefer designs that are clear, organized, and easy to understand. In the context of IA, the Law of Prägnanz plays a crucial role in designing and structuring information to ensure optimal user experience. IA aims to organize and present information in a way that facilitates efficient navigation, comprehension, and retrieval of content. By applying the Law of Prägnanz, IA professionals can create intuitive interfaces and seamless user journeys. To adhere to the Law of Prägnanz in IA, several guidelines and best practices can be followed: 1. Simplicity: Minimize complexity by keeping designs and structures clean, straightforward, and free from unnecessary elements. Avoid clutter and prioritize the most important information. 2. Consistency: Use consistent and familiar patterns, icons, and labels throughout the information structure. This helps users build mental models and navigate more smoothly. 3. Grouping: Group related content together to create meaningful associations. Use visual cues such as proximity, color, size, or typography to indicate logical groupings and relationships. 4. Hierarchy: Establish a clear hierarchical structure to guide users through the information. Organize content in a way that highlights the most important elements and provides a clear path to deeper levels of detail. 5. Visual cues: Utilize visual cues such as icons, graphics, and typography to assist users in understanding the content and its context. Employ appropriate contrast, spacing, and alignment to aid legibility and scanability. By applying the Law of Prägnanz to IA, designers can create information spaces that are visually appealing, efficient, and easy to navigate. This ultimately enhances the overall user experience, improves findability, and increases user satisfaction. In conclusion, the Law of Prägnanz emphasizes the importance of simplicity, clarity, and organization in information design. It serves as a guiding principle for IA professionals to create intuitive and user-friendly structures that optimize the presentation and comprehension of information.

Leadpages

Leadpages is a web-based software tool that helps users quickly and easily create high-converting landing pages, websites, and pop-ups. It offers a streamlined way to design and publish web pages without the need for coding or technical skills. With Leadpages, users can choose from a wide range of customizable templates and elements to build their web pages. The software provides a drag-and-drop interface that allows users to add and rearrange various components, such as text, images, forms, buttons, and more. Leadpages also includes features like A/B testing, analytics, and integrations with popular email marketing and CRM platforms. These features enable users to test and optimize their pages for better conversion rates, track performance metrics, and seamlessly connect with their existing tools and workflows. The main goal of Leadpages is to help businesses and marketers generate more leads and sales through effective landing page design and optimization. By providing a user-friendly interface and a range of powerful features, Leadpages empowers users to create visually appealing and high-performing web pages that drive conversions. In terms of information architecture (IA), Leadpages organizes and structures the content and functionality of web pages in a way that enhances usability and user experience. The software enables users to categorize and arrange their content, ensuring that it is easily accessible and digestible for visitors. Leadpages also facilitates the navigation of web pages by implementing intuitive menus and links. This helps users and visitors find the information they need quickly and effortlessly. The software's IA ensures that the overall layout and organization of web pages are logical and coherent, enhancing the overall usability and user satisfaction. Overall, Leadpages is a powerful tool for creating and optimizing web pages, delivering a seamless user experience, and driving conversions. Its IA-focused approach allows users to effectively structure and present their content, resulting in enhanced usability and improved user engagement.

Lickert Scale

The Lickert Scale is a psychometric scaling technique used in Information Architecture (IA) to measure attitudes or opinions of individuals towards a given set of statements or concepts. It allows IA professionals to gather qualitative data and assess user preferences, satisfaction, or experiences. The scale consists of a series of statements or concepts presented to participants, who are then asked to rate their level of agreement or disagreement. The scale typically includes five or seven response options, ranging from strongly agree to strongly disagree or from very satisfied to very dissatisfied. The options are evenly spaced to provide a balanced scoring range. The Lickert Scale helps IA professionals in understanding users' perceptions and preferences, enabling them to make informed decisions regarding the design and organization of information resources. It provides quantitative data that can be used to identify trends, patterns, and correlations, aiding the development of user-centered IA solutions. By analyzing the responses on the scale, IA professionals can evaluate different aspects of information resources, such as the clarity of labels, the effectiveness of navigational structures, or the relevance of content. They can identify areas for improvement and make data-driven decisions to enhance the usability and user experience of systems, websites, or applications. The Lickert Scale also allows for the comparison of different IA options or alternative designs. By administering the scale to different user groups or conducting A/B testing, IA professionals can gather feedback on the viability and preference of different IA solutions. This enables them to choose the most effective design based on user feedback and align IA with user expectations.

Live Composer

Live Composer is an effective solution that pertains to Information Architecture (IA). It is an innovative tool used in web development that enables users to create and customize websites effortlessly. The focus of Live Composer lies in providing users with the ability to modify and design the structure, layout, and appearance of their websites without requiring advanced technical knowledge or coding skills. This powerful tool allows users to visually build and arrange website elements, such as headers, footers, sidebars, and content sections. It offers a convenient drag-and-drop interface, allowing users to select and position various components on their webpages with ease. Additionally, Live Composer provides an extensive library of pre-designed elements and templates, facilitating the quick creation of visually appealing and functional websites. With Live Composer, users have the flexibility to make real-time adjustments and modifications, eliminating the need for constant reloading or previewing. It empowers users to experiment with different layouts, color schemes, and content arrangements until they achieve the desired result. This dynamic approach enhances the efficiency of website development and design, as it enables quick prototyping and iteration. Furthermore, Live Composer promotes collaboration within the web development process. It allows multiple users or teams to work simultaneously on different sections of a website, enhancing productivity and facilitating efficient project management. This feature is particularly beneficial for large-scale projects that involve multiple stakeholders working remotely. Importantly, Live Composer supports the principles of Information Architecture by providing a user-friendly platform that optimizes the organization and presentation of content. By offering visual design capabilities, it fosters the creation of clear and intuitive navigation structures, promoting an enhanced user experience and enabling easy access to information. Overall, Live Composer serves as an essential tool in the field of Information Architecture, providing users with the means to construct visually attractive and functional websites. Through its intuitive interface and collaborative features, it empowers users to create and modify website layouts efficiently, while adhering to the principles of effective information organization and presentation.

Local Navigation

Local navigation, in the context of Information Architecture (IA), refers to the menu or set of links that provide direct access to specific sections or pages within a website or application. It serves as a means for users to navigate within a particular section or subset of content, aiding in the overall information organization and ease of access. Local navigation is typically located within a specific section or page of a website, such as a submenu within a main navigation menu or a sidebar menu within a content area. It provides users with the ability to quickly jump between related content or different subsections within the same context.

Lookback

Information Architecture (IA) is a discipline within the field of User Experience (UX) design that focuses on the organization, structure, and labeling of information to enhance its usability and findability. It involves the strategic design and planning of how information is structured, categorized, and presented within a system or website. The goal of IA is to create intuitive and meaningful connections between information and users, allowing them to easily navigate and understand the content. It involves analyzing user needs and behaviors, as well as the organization's goals, to determine the most effective way to organize and present information.

Loop11

Loop11 is a web-based usability testing software that helps in evaluating the usability of websites, applications, and digital products. In the context of Information Architecture (IA), Loop11 plays a crucial role in improving the overall user experience by gathering valuable insights and data about user interactions and behaviors. Loop11 enables designers, researchers, and stakeholders to conduct remote usability testing, which means that users can access and interact with a website or application from their own devices and environments. This allows for more natural and authentic user feedback. The software provides a wide range of features and tools to facilitate the testing process, such as task scenarios, user surveys, heatmaps, and clickstream analysis.

Low-Fidelity Wireframes

Low-fidelity wireframes refer to simplified visual representations of a website or application that focus primarily on the basic skeletal structure, content hierarchy, and overall layout. They serve as a blueprint for website or application development and are commonly used in the field of Information Architecture (IA) to communicate and document the initial design concepts and layout ideas. Unlike high-fidelity wireframes that are more detailed and polished, low-fidelity wireframes are intentionally rough and sketch-like in appearance. They are typically created quickly and with minimal effort, using simple shapes, basic lines, and placeholder text. Their primary purpose is to convey the broad concepts and flow of information, rather than the finer design details such as color, typography, or precise positioning.

Lucidchart

Lucidchart is an online platform designed to facilitate the creation, collaboration, and communication of visual diagrams and flowcharts, particularly in the realm of Information Architecture (IA). It provides users with a range of pre-built templates and shapes to represent different components and relationships within an information structure. Lucidchart is specifically tailored to support IA practitioners in organizing and mapping complex information systems, such as website navigation, content taxonomy, and user flows. It enables users to visually depict the hierarchical structure of information, the interconnections between different elements, and the overall flow of content across various pages or sections.

Lucidspark

Lucidspark is an innovative digital tool designed to facilitate the practice of Information Architecture (IA) for professionals in various fields. IA involves the organization and structuring of information to enhance its accessibility and usability, making it easier for users to find and navigate through content. With Lucidspark, IA practitioners can visually map out the relationships between different elements of information, such as content, users, processes, and technology. By creating and manipulating diagrams, flowcharts, and other visual representations, IA professionals can gain a clearer understanding of how information should be organized to meet user needs and achieve specific business goals.

Lumzy

Information Architecture (IA) is a discipline within the field of user experience (UX) design that focuses on organizing and structuring information in a way that allows users to easily find and navigate through it. It involves the process of determining how information should be organized, labeled, and presented in order to make it intuitive, efficient, and user-friendly. IA aims to create logical and coherent structures for information, both in physical and digital environments. It involves analyzing the content and understanding the needs and mental models of the target audience to develop a clear and effective information hierarchy. This hierarchy helps users understand the relationships between different pieces of information and enables them to navigate through the system with ease.

Mappio

Mappio is an information architecture tool that helps in organizing and displaying complex data structures in a user-friendly and intuitive manner. It enables users to create visual representations of the relationships between different pieces of information, allowing for easy navigation and understanding of the overall structure.

Marvel

Information Architecture (IA) in the context of Marvel refers to the organization, structure, and labeling of content within the Marvel universe. It involves the systematic arrangement of information to enhance its accessibility, usability, and overall user experience. IA in Marvel encompasses various elements such as characters, storylines, events, locations, and other related content. The goal of IA is to facilitate efficient and intuitive navigation, making it easier for users to explore and comprehend the vast Marvel universe.

Matrix Navigation

Matrix navigation in the context of Information Architecture (IA) is a method used to organize and navigate through complex information structures by representing the relationships between different categories or topics in a matrix-like format. This approach helps users easily understand the connections and hierarchies within the information system, allowing them to navigate between different sections in an intuitive and efficient manner. The matrix navigation technique typically involves the use of a two-dimensional grid, where the rows and columns represent different categories or topics. This grid can be visualized as a table or a matrix, with each cell containing links or references to specific content related to the intersection of categories or topics. This method offers several advantages in terms of information organization and navigation. Firstly, it allows for flexible and dynamic relationships between categories or topics. By placing them in a matrix, different connections and associations can be established, enabling users to explore related content in a non-linear fashion. Secondly, matrix navigation facilitates multi-dimensional exploration. Users can navigate not only horizontally and vertically within the matrix, but also diagonally, following cross-references or related topics. This adds depth and richness to the exploration process, enabling users to discover diverse content they may not have encountered through traditional linear navigation methods. Thirdly, matrix navigation provides a visual representation of the overall information structure, helping users understand the relationships and hierarchies between different categories or topics at a glance. This can reduce cognitive load and enhance the user experience by providing a clear and meaningful overview of the information space. In conclusion, matrix navigation is a valuable technique in the field of Information Architecture, offering an effective and dynamic way to organize and navigate complex information structures. By representing categories or topics in a matrix-like format, users can easily explore and discover relevant content, while gaining a holistic understanding of the information system.

Maze

A maze, in the context of Information Architecture (IA), refers to a complex structure or arrangement of interconnected pathways or choices that users encounter while navigating a website or application. In IA, a maze is designed to guide users through a series of interconnected pages or screens, presenting them with choices and options along the way. The purpose of a maze is to help users find relevant information or complete specific tasks by providing a clear and logical path.

Metadata Schema

Metadata Schema is a standardized framework that defines the structure, content, and encoding of metadata for a specific domain or purpose. It provides a set of rules and guidelines for organizing and describing information in a consistent and uniform manner. Within the context of Information Architecture (IA), metadata schema serves as a crucial tool for organizing and categorizing information in a meaningful way. It helps in enhancing findability, discoverability, and usability of information by providing a structured framework for describing and identifying the various attributes and characteristics of data.

Microinteractions

Microinteractions refer to the small, subtle interactions that occur within a digital interface, providing feedback to users, guiding them through tasks, and enhancing their overall experience. These interactions are often overlooked or taken for granted, but they play a vital role in creating a seamless and intuitive user interface. In the context of Information Architecture (IA), microinteractions are crucial in helping users navigate and interact with the information presented to them. They serve as a means of communication between the users and the system, allowing users to understand the consequences of their actions, providing feedback on their progress, and giving them a sense of control over the system.

Mind Mapping

Mind Mapping is a visual tool used in Information Architecture (IA) to organize and represent complex information. It is a graphical representation technique that allows users to gather, structure, and visualize thoughts, ideas, and concepts in a non-linear manner. With mind mapping, information architects can create a hierarchical structure of key concepts and relationships, fostering a better understanding of the overall information landscape. It helps identify the main topics or themes and their interconnections, facilitating the design and arrangement of content within a website or application.

Mind Maps

Mind Maps are a visual tool used in the field of Information Architecture (IA) to represent and organize complex information. They are a graphical representation of connections between ideas and concepts, allowing users to visually explore and understand relationships between different pieces of information. A Mind Map consists of a central idea or topic, represented by a main node, surrounded by related subtopics or key points, connected by lines or branches. These branches can then be further expanded into sub-branches or sub-subtopics, creating a hierarchical structure. Mind Maps in IA help to simplify and clarify complex information by breaking down concepts into smaller, more manageable pieces. They provide a visual overview of the information landscape, making it easier to identify patterns, connections, and gaps in knowledge. In IA, Mind Maps are often used as a brainstorming tool to generate ideas and organize thoughts. They provide a flexible and non-linear approach to information organization, allowing for easy addition, removal, and rearrangement of nodes and branches as needed. Mind Maps can also be used to aid in the navigation and exploration of information systems. By visually representing the structure and relationships within a system, users can quickly locate and access relevant information. In addition to their use in IA, Mind Maps can be applied to various other fields, such as education, project management, and problem-solving. They encourage creativity, critical thinking, and information synthesis. In conclusion, Mind Maps are a valuable tool in the field of Information Architecture. They facilitate the organization and understanding of complex information by visually representing connections, hierarchies, and relationships. By using Mind Maps, IA professionals can better analyze, communicate, and navigate information systems.

Mind42

Information Architecture (IA) is a discipline that focuses on organizing and structuring information to enhance the usability and findability of a website or application. It involves the design and arrangement of content, navigation systems, and labeling schemes to create intuitive and efficient user experiences. IA aims to create clear pathways for users to access and understand information within a complex digital environment. It involves analyzing user needs, business goals, and content requirements to develop a logical and user-centric information structure.

MindManager

MindManager is a versatile information architecture (IA) tool that allows users to visually organize, manage, and communicate ideas, concepts, and data in a structured way. By providing a digital canvas for capturing and mapping information, MindManager assists in creating clear, coherent, and easily navigable frameworks. With MindManager, users can easily create and manipulate various elements such as topics, subtopics, and branches. These elements serve as containers for storing and linking relevant data, enabling users to establish meaningful connections and hierarchies. The intuitive drag-and-drop interface allows for effortless rearrangement and reorganization of information, facilitating flexible and dynamic IA development. One of the key features of MindManager is its ability to visualize complex structures and relationships. Users can employ different visual elements, such as colors, icons, and shapes, to distinguish and categorize various components of their IA. This visual representation aids in grasping and understanding the underlying structure and logic, making it easier to comprehend and analyze complex information. MindManager also supports collaboration and information sharing. Multiple users can work on the same IA simultaneously, making real-time updates and contributions. This collaborative aspect enhances team productivity, fosters creativity, and allows for a collective perspective on IA development. Furthermore, MindManager enables users to integrate various types of media and data into their IA maps. This includes attaching files, embedding websites, inserting hyperlinks, and linking to external resources. By incorporating multimedia content, users can enrich their IA with additional context, references, and supporting materials, thus enhancing the overall user experience. Overall, MindManager is a powerful IA tool that empowers users to create structured and visual representations of information. By enabling the organization, management, and communication of ideas and data, MindManager facilitates efficient decision-making, improved knowledge sharing, and enhanced collaboration.

MindMeister

MindMeister is a web-based visual mapping tool that facilitates the creation and organization of ideas and information for effective Information Architecture (IA). Through its intuitive interface and collaborative features, MindMeister enables users to visually represent and connect concepts, brainstorm ideas, and structure content in an interactive way. This allows for efficient planning and designing of an information system, ensuring a cohesive and user-friendly experience for the audience.

MindMup

Information Architecture (IA) refers to the practice of organizing and structuring information to facilitate effective navigation and findability. It involves the design and arrangement of information within a system to ensure that users can easily locate and comprehend the content they require. IA encompasses various principles and techniques, including organization schemes, labeling systems, and navigation structures. Proper IA implementation enhances user experience and usability by reducing cognitive load and allowing users to quickly and intuitively access information.

MindNode

MindNode is a visual brainstorming and organization tool that utilizes information architecture principles. It helps individuals or teams to create and manage complex ideas, concepts, and information by visually representing them in a hierarchical format. At its core, MindNode incorporates the principles of information architecture (IA), which is the practice of organizing and structuring information to enhance usability and accessibility. IA is particularly important in digital spaces, such as websites and applications, where a well-organized structure can greatly improve the user experience. MindNode allows users to create a central idea or topic and then branch out into related subtopics or ideas. This hierarchical tree-like structure enables individuals to see the relationships and connections between different concepts or pieces of information. Users can add text, images, or icons to each node, enhancing the visual representation and making it easier to understand the content at a glance. The visual nature of MindNode makes it an effective tool for brainstorming, planning, organizing, and managing information. It allows users to capture and explore ideas in a non-linear manner, helping to stimulate creativity and facilitate problem-solving. By visually connecting related ideas and concepts, MindNode aids in comprehending complex topics and encourages critical thinking and analysis. Overall, MindNode is a valuable tool in the field of information architecture as it leverages visual representation and hierarchical structure to help individuals or teams organize and interpret complex information effectively. By utilizing IA principles, MindNode enhances usability and accessibility, making it a powerful tool for brainstorming, planning, and managing information in various contexts.

Mindomo

Mindomo is a web-based application that is used in the field of Information Architecture (IA) to create and organize visual representations of complex information structures. It is a powerful tool that allows IA professionals to plan, design, and manage the organization and navigation of information within a digital system. With Mindomo, IA practitioners can create mind maps, concept maps, and other visual diagrams that help to illustrate the relationships between

63

different elements of an information system. These diagrams can be used to communicate complex ideas, identify patterns and connections, and facilitate collaborative problem-solving.

Miro

Information architecture (IA) is the practice of organizing and structuring information to enhance the usability and findability of a system or website. It involves designing how information is labeled, categorized, and prioritized to optimize user navigation and retrieval of information. IA aims to create intuitive and logical information structures that support users in easily and efficiently finding the information they need. It is concerned with the arrangement of content elements, such as headings, links, and navigation menus, to create a coherent and meaningful user experience.

Mixpanel

Mixpanel is an advanced web analytics tool that provides detailed insights and analysis on user behavior, allowing businesses to make data-driven decisions and optimize their websites or applications. It offers powerful tracking and reporting capabilities, enabling organizations to understand user interactions, measure the success of specific actions or events, and segment users based on a variety of criteria. With its powerful analytics engine, Mixpanel allows businesses to track and analyze events or actions performed by users, such as clicking on buttons, submitting forms, or navigating through specific pages. This deep understanding of user behavior helps organizations identify patterns, trends, and bottlenecks, allowing them to optimize their websites or applications for improved user experience and conversion rates.

Mobile App Design Patterns

Mobile App Design Patterns refer to commonly used solutions or approaches for designing the user interface and interaction of a mobile application. These patterns help create consistency, improve user experience, and make the app more intuitive for users. In the context of Information Architecture (IA), design patterns play a crucial role in organizing and structuring the information within the app. One commonly used mobile app design pattern in IA is the Drawer Navigation pattern. This pattern involves using a navigation drawer, which is a hidden panel that can be swiped from the edge of the screen to reveal a menu of navigation options. The drawer navigation pattern is often used in apps where there are multiple sections or screens that need to be accessed easily. By organizing the navigation options in a drawer, users can quickly access different sections of the app without cluttering the main interface. Another important IA design pattern is the Tab Bar pattern. This pattern is frequently used in apps where there are multiple categories or sections that users can switch between. It involves placing a horizontal bar at the bottom or top of the screen, with each tab representing a different section of the app. When a user taps on a tab, the corresponding section is displayed. The tab bar pattern helps users navigate through different sections of the app effortlessly and provides them with a clear visual hierarchy of the available options.

Mobile Gestures

Mobile Gestures refer to the actions performed by users on a mobile device's touchscreen interface to manipulate or interact with the content and features of an application or website. These gestures often replace traditional input methods, such as keystrokes or mouse clicks, and are designed to be intuitive and convenient for mobile users. Mobile gestures can be categorized into two main types: touch gestures and motion gestures. Touch gestures involve direct physical contact with the touchscreen, while motion gestures detect and respond to the movement of the device itself.

Mobile IA

Mobile IA, also known as Mobile Information Architecture, refers to the organization and structure of information within a mobile application or website. It involves the design and planning of how information is presented, accessed, and navigated on smaller screens, such as smartphones and tablets. The goal of Mobile IA is to create a seamless and intuitive user experience, allowing users to easily find and interact with the content they are looking for. It involves understanding the needs and behaviors of mobile users, and designing the information architecture accordingly.

Mobile Navigation Patterns

Mobile navigation patterns refer to the various design and layout strategies used in mobile information architecture (IA) to enable users to navigate smoothly and efficiently through the content and features of a mobile application or website. These patterns play a crucial role in enhancing the user experience by providing intuitive and accessible navigation options. The complexity and limitations of mobile devices, such as smaller screen sizes and touch-based interactions, require careful consideration of IA in mobile design. The choice of navigation patterns depends on factors like the content structure and user goals. It involves creating a logical flow of information and designing navigation elements that are easy to understand and interact with on mobile devices. Some commonly used mobile navigation patterns include: 1. Hamburger Menu: This pattern is characterized by a three-horizontal-line icon (resembling a hamburger) that expands into a vertical menu when tapped. It conserves screen space by hiding the menu options until needed. 2. Tab Navigation: Tabs are used to organize content into categories or sections, allowing users to switch between them by tapping on the corresponding tab. It provides a straightforward and visible navigation option. 3. Bottom Navigation Bar: Placed at the bottom of the screen, this pattern offers quick access to essential features or main sections of the app. It is easily reachable by users, especially on larger mobile devices. 4. Swipeable Tabs: This pattern combines tabs with horizontal swipe gestures, allowing users to swipe between different sections of an app. It provides a fluid and engaging navigation experience. 5. Floating Action Button (FAB): The FAB is a circular button positioned above the content, usually used for a primary call to action. It provides quick access to frequently used functions. Overall, mobile navigation patterns serve as the backbone of an effective IA, ensuring that users can easily understand the content structure and navigate through the mobile app or website. By strategically selecting and implementing these patterns, designers can create seamless and intuitive navigation experiences that enhance user satisfaction.

MockFlow

MockFlow is an online platform that serves as a collaborative tool for creating and visualizing information architecture (IA) designs. It allows designers, developers, and stakeholders to efficiently plan, prototype, and communicate the structure and layout of websites, applications, and other digital products. With MockFlow, users can easily create wireframes, sitemaps, flowcharts, and other IA artifacts that help map out the user experience and navigation flow of a digital product. The platform provides a range of pre-built UI components and icons, as well as the ability to customize and create reusable components to speed up the design process and ensure consistency across designs. One of the key features of MockFlow is its collaborative functionality, which enables multiple team members to work together on IA designs in real-time. This allows for efficient feedback gathering, brainstorming, and decision-making, improving the overall design process and reducing the need for lengthy email chains or in-person meetings. The platform also supports version control, allowing users to track changes, compare different versions, and revert to previous iterations if needed. This ensures that the design remains consistent and easily manageable, especially when dealing with complex IA structures and frequent updates. MockFlow offers integration with popular design tools such as Sketch and Adobe Creative Cloud, allowing users to import and export design assets seamlessly. It also provides the ability to share designs with stakeholders and gather feedback through comments and annotations, ensuring clear communication and alignment throughout the design process. In summary, MockFlow is an online collaborative platform that facilitates the creation and visualization of information architecture designs. Its range of tools and features, along with its collaborative functionality, enable efficient planning, prototyping, and communication of IA structures, helping designers and teams streamline their design processes and create user-centered and well-structured digital products.

Mockingbird

Mockingbird in the context of Information Architecture (IA) refers to a technique or process of creating a visual representation or blueprint of a website's structure, layout, and navigation hierarchy. It involves creating wireframes, which are simplified and skeletal designs that outline the different pages, content, and functionality of a website. Mockingbird plays a crucial role in IA as it helps designers and stakeholders to visualize and understand the overall structure and organization of a website before it is fully developed. By creating wireframes, designers can identify and address any potential usability and navigation issues, ensuring a user-friendly experience. Mockingbird also allows for collaborative discussions and decision-making about the architecture and design elements of a website.

Mockplus

Mockplus is a software tool used in the field of Information Architecture (IA). With a focus on user experience (UX) design, Mockplus helps designers and developers create interactive prototypes and wireframes for websites and mobile applications.Through its drag-and-drop interface, Mockplus enables users to quickly and easily build and visualize their IA concepts and ideas. It offers a library of pre-designed components, such as buttons, forms, and menus, that can be customized and rearranged to fit the specific IA requirements of a project.

Mockup Builder

A Mockup Builder is a tool used in the field of Information Architecture (IA) to create visual representations of a website or application's layout and user interface. It allows designers and developers to quickly and easily generate mockups, which are rough drafts of a website or app that can be used for testing and feedback before moving on to the development phase. Mockup Builders typically provide a range of pre-designed components, such as buttons, forms, and navigation menus, that can be easily dragged and dropped onto a canvas to build a mockup. These components can be customized in terms of size, color, typography, and other visual properties to match the desired design aesthetic.

Mockup.lo

Mockup.io is a web-based tool designed to assist in the development of information architecture (IA). IA is a discipline that focuses on the organization, structure, and labeling of digital information to ensure effective and intuitive user experiences. Mockup.io helps IA professionals visually represent and communicate their information architecture by creating interactive digital mockups. These mockups are representations of the information structure, hierarchy, and flow that users will encounter when navigating a website, application, or system.

Mood Board

A mood board, in the context of Information Architecture (IA), is a visual representation of the overall look and feel, style, and atmosphere that a designer or team wants to create for a particular project or website. It is a curated collection of images, colors, patterns, textures, and typography samples that help communicate the desired mood and aesthetic of the design. The purpose of a mood board is to establish a shared vision and understanding among team members and stakeholders about the design direction. It serves as a starting point for discussions and decision-making during the design process, as it helps align everyone's expectations and ensure that the design concept matches the project goals and objectives.

Moqups

Moqups is an online tool used for creating wireframes and mockups in the field of Information Architecture (IA). It allows designers to visually represent the structure and layout of a website or application, facilitating the planning and communication of its overall design. With Moqups, designers can easily create and manipulate various elements such as pages, containers, widgets, and text boxes, which can be resized, rearranged, and customized according to their specific needs. These elements provide a basis for organizing and arranging content, functionality, and navigation within a digital product, helping to define its information structure.

Motion Design

Motion design refers to the art and technique of incorporating movement into visual elements to enhance user experience and convey information effectively. In the context of Information Architecture (IA), motion design plays a crucial role in creating interactive and engaging digital experiences for users. Motion design can be utilized to guide users through a website or application by using carefully designed animations and transitions. By animating certain elements, such as buttons, menus, or images, motion design helps provide visual feedback and affordances, making it easier for users to navigate and interact with the interface. In the realm of IA, motion design can also be utilized to convey complex information or data in a more digestible and visually appealing manner. By animating graphs, charts, or infographics, motion design helps bring data to life, making it easier for users to understand and interpret. Additionally, motion design can be used to create microinteractions, which are small animations triggered by user actions or system events. These microinteractions can provide valuable feedback, such as highlighting a selected item or confirming a successful action, thereby enhancing the overall user experience. Overall, motion design in the context of IA focuses on using animation and motion to improve the usability and user experience of digital interfaces. By incorporating well-designed animations and transitions, motion design helps guide users, provide feedback, and convey information in a dynamic and engaging manner. Motion design is an essential consideration for information architects as it can greatly impact how users perceive and interact with digital experiences. Through carefully crafted animations and transitions, motion design enhances the usability of interfaces and helps convey complex information effectively.

Mouseflow

Mouseflow is a web analytics tool that provides valuable insights into user behavior and interactions on a website. It helps information architects in understanding how users navigate through a website, enabling them to optimize the IA for improved user experience. Mouseflow captures and analyzes user interactions, such as mouse movements, clicks, scrolling, and form filling. By recording and aggregating this data, information architects can gain a comprehensive understanding of how users engage with different elements and pages on the site. With Mouseflow, information architects can visualize user sessions and heatmaps to identify patterns and trends in user behavior. Heatmaps provide a visual representation of where users are clicking or scrolling the most, helping architects identify popular areas of the site or potential usability issues. Furthermore, Mouseflow offers session replay features that allow information architects to watch recorded user sessions in real-time. This feature provides a detailed view of the user's journey, enabling architects to pinpoint any bottlenecks or frustrations in the IA. Mouseflow also offers form analytics to evaluate the performance of online forms. Information architects can analyze form abandonment rates and identify fields that may cause confusion or frustration for users. This data helps architects make informed decisions about form design and layout. Overall, Mouseflow is a powerful tool for information architects to gather quantitative and qualitative data about user interactions on a website. By leveraging these insights, architects can make data-driven decisions to improve the IA, enhance user experience, and achieve their website's goals.

Muffin Builder

Muffin Builder is a concept in Information Architecture (IA) that refers to a systematic approach for creating and organizing website content and structure. It aims to enhance the user experience by providing a clear and logical framework for users to navigate through the website. When using the Muffin Builder methodology, the website is divided into smaller components called muffins, which represent individual sections or pages of the website. Each muffin can contain different types of content, such as text, images, videos, or interactive elements. This method allows designers and developers to build websites in a more modular way, making it easier to manage and update the content. By breaking down the website into smaller components, changes or updates can be made to specific muffins without affecting the entire website. Furthermore, Muffin Builder emphasizes the importance of consistent and intuitive navigation. The IA of a website using this approach is structured to guide users through a logical flow, ensuring that they can easily find the information they are looking for. Another key aspect of Muffin Builder is the use of metadata. Each muffin is associated with relevant metadata, such as tags or categories, which help with searchability and information retrieval. This allows users to filter or search for specific content based on their preferences or needs. In conclusion, Muffin Builder is a methodology in IA that focuses on creating and organizing website content in a modular and structured manner. It enhances the user experience by providing clear navigation and searchability through smaller components called muffins, while also allowing for easy content updates and management.

Multi-Channel Navigation

Multi-channel navigation in the context of Information Architecture (IA) refers to the design and implementation of navigation systems that allow users to seamlessly navigate across multiple channels or platforms. These channels can include websites, mobile applications, social media platforms, and any other digital interfaces that provide access to information or services. The goal of multi-channel navigation is to create a consistent and user-friendly experience for users, regardless of the channel they are using. This is important because users often interact with the same organization or brand through different channels, and they expect a cohesive experience throughout their journey. By providing a unified navigation system, users can easily find what they are looking for and navigate between different channels without confusion or frustration.

Multi-Touch

Multi-Touch refers to a user interface technology that allows multiple points of contact or input on a touch-enabled device, facilitating simultaneous interaction with the content and functions on the screen. In the context of Information Architecture (IA), Multi-Touch plays a crucial role in enhancing user experience, enabling more intuitive and efficient navigation and interactions. With the advent of touch-enabled devices such as smartphones, tablets, and interactive kiosks, Multi-Touch has become an integral part of modern IA design. It enables users to manipulate and navigate through digital content by using various gestures such as tapping, pinching, swiping, and rotating. Multiple fingers or touch points can be utilized simultaneously to perform different actions or access different functionality.

Multilingual IA

Information Architecture (IA) is the practice of organizing and structuring information in a clear and intuitive manner to enhance the usability and findability of digital products and systems. It involves the design and organization of content, functionality, and navigation systems to provide users with a seamless and efficient experience. IA is a multidisciplinary field that draws upon principles from information science, cognitive psychology, and user-centered design to create coherent and meaningful information structures. It aims to ensure that users can easily locate, understand, and interact with the information they need.

Mural

A mural in the context of Information Architecture (IA) refers to a visual representation or graphic element that is used to communicate information or enhance the user experience within a digital or physical interface. Murals are often employed in IA to convey complex ideas, concepts, or relationships between different elements in a visually appealing and intuitive manner. They serve as a means of simplifying and organizing large amounts of information, making it more easily digestible for users. By using visual elements such as images, icons, colors, and typography, murals can help users quickly understand and navigate through the content or functionality of a system or website.

Narrative Interface

The narrative interface is a form of user interface design that focuses on presenting information and guiding users through a sequence of events or a story. It is particularly relevant in the context of Information Architecture (IA) as it offers a way to structure and organize content to create a coherent and engaging user experience. With a narrative interface, information is presented in a linear or non-linear fashion, following a specific narrative structure. This can be achieved through various design elements such as storytelling techniques, visual cues, and interactive features. The goal is to create a sense of flow and progression, allowing users to easily navigate and understand the content.

Navigation Cards

Navigation Cards are a user interface design element used in Information Architecture (IA) to visually present and organize a set of navigation options or links. They help users navigate through different sections or categories of a website or an application. The primary purpose of Navigation Cards is to provide a clear and intuitive navigation structure that allows users to easily locate and access the content or features they are looking for. They serve as visual cues to help users understand the overall organization and hierarchy of the information within the system.

Navigation Design Principles

Navigation design principles in the context of Information Architecture (IA) refer to the fundamental guidelines and best practices followed to create effective and user-friendly navigation systems within digital interfaces. These principles aim to enhance the user experience by providing clear, intuitive, and efficient navigation methods, allowing users to easily find and access the desired content or functionality. The first principle is clarity, which emphasizes the importance of presenting navigation options in a clear and understandable manner. This involves using concise and straightforward wording for navigation labels, avoiding technical jargon or ambiguous terms. Additionally, visual cues such as icons or graphical elements can be used to aid in comprehension and recognition. Another principle is consistency, which ensures that the navigation design remains uniform across different sections or areas of the interface. Consistency allows users to quickly understand and adapt to the navigation system. This includes consistent placement of navigation elements, maintaining consistent terminology, and adhering to standard interaction patterns. Efficiency is an essential principle in navigation design, aiming to minimize the cognitive effort required by users to navigate through the interface. This involves organizing the navigation options logically, grouping related items together, and providing clear pathways to common or frequently accessed information. Additionally, the use of hierarchical structures, such as menus or submenus, can help users navigate through complex content hierarchies. Navigation design principles also emphasize the importance of responsiveness, ensuring that the navigation system adapts seamlessly across different devices and screen sizes. Responsive design techniques, such as collapsible menus or adaptive navigation bars, can be employed to provide optimal user experiences on both desktop and mobile devices. Overall, navigation design principles in the context of IA serve as a foundation for creating user-centered and intuitive navigation systems. By following these principles, designers can help users easily navigate through digital interfaces, improving findability, usability, and overall satisfaction.

Navigation Design

The navigation design in the context of Information Architecture (IA) refers to the process of creating an intuitive and efficient system for users to navigate through a website or application. It involves organizing and structuring the information in a way that allows users to easily find and access the content they are looking for. In IA, navigation design aims to provide users with a clear and logical path that helps them understand the overall structure of the website or application. It involves deciding on the placement, labeling, and functionality of navigation elements such as menus, links, buttons, and search options.

Navigation Diagram

A navigation diagram, in the context of Information Architecture (IA), is a visual representation of the structure and organization of a website's navigation system. It portrays the hierarchy and relationships between different pages or sections of a website, allowing users to easily navigate and find the desired content. The main purpose of a navigation diagram is to provide a clear and intuitive roadmap for users to navigate through a website. It helps users understand the navigational paths available to them and how different sections or pages are interconnected. By presenting a high-level overview of the website's structure, a navigation diagram enables users to quickly locate the information they need and efficiently move between different sections. Typically, a navigation diagram consists of nodes or boxes representing different pages or sections, connected by lines or arrows to indicate the flow and relationships between them. The nodes are labeled with the page or section names, providing an at-a-glance understanding of the website's organization. Navigation diagrams are an essential tool in the design and development of websites. They serve as a foundation for creating a logical and coherent navigation system that aligns with the goals and objectives of the website. By visualizing the website's structure, designers can identify potential navigation issues, such as overly complex hierarchies or confusing paths, and make informed decisions to improve the user experience. Additionally, navigation diagrams facilitate communication and collaboration among designers, developers, and stakeholders. They provide a common reference point for discussions and ensure everyone involved has a shared understanding of the website's structure and navigation. In conclusion, a navigation diagram is a visual representation of a website's navigation system, depicting the hierarchy and relationships between different pages or sections. It serves as a visual roadmap for users, helping them easily navigate through the website and find the desired content. Navigation diagrams are crucial for designing a logical and intuitive navigation system and facilitating collaboration among stakeholders in the website development process.

Navigation Flowchart

A navigation flowchart is an organized visual representation of the hierarchical structure and the sequence of navigational paths within a website or application. It outlines the various pages, sections, categories, and subcategories, along with the relationships and connections between them. The primary purpose of a navigation flowchart in the context of Information Architecture (IA) is to create a clear and intuitive navigation system that allows users to easily find and access the desired content. It serves as a blueprint for designing the website's navigation menus, links, and overall user interface. The flowchart typically starts with a homepage or main landing page at the top, representing the starting point of the navigation. From there, it branches into different sections or categories, each leading to specific pages or subcategories. The flowchart visually illustrates the hierarchy, showing how different pages are grouped together and how users can navigate from one section to another. In addition to the hierarchical structure, the navigation flowchart also captures the sequence of navigational paths. It shows the possible user journeys within the website, allowing designers to identify the most common and important paths. This helps in organizing the content and optimizing the navigation system to prioritize these paths, ensuring a seamless user experience. Navigation flowcharts can be created using a variety of visual tools such as diagrams, wireframes, or mind mapping software. Designers often use standardized symbols or conventions to represent different types of pages, links, and navigational elements. These symbols help to communicate the flow and relationships effectively, aiding collaborative discussions and decision-making during the IA design process. By visualizing the navigation structure and user paths, a navigation flowchart serves as a valuable reference for both designers and stakeholders. It helps designers in planning and organizing the website's content and navigation system, facilitating efficient information retrieval and enhancing overall usability. Stakeholders can evaluate and provide feedback on the proposed navigation system, ensuring that it aligns with the website's goals and meets the users' expectations. In conclusion, a navigation flowchart is a visual representation of the hierarchical structure and sequence of navigational paths within a website or application. It serves as a blueprint for designing an intuitive and user-friendly navigation system, facilitating efficient information access and seamless user experiences.

Navigation Labels

Navigation Labels in the context of Information Architecture (IA) refer to the textual or visual elements used to denote the different links or sections within a website or application that help users navigate through its content. These labels serve as a means of presenting the available options or pathways to users, enabling them to easily find and access the desired information or functionality. The main purpose of navigation labels is to provide clear and intuitive cues to users, allowing them to understand the structure and hierarchy of the information presented. By utilizing descriptive and concise labels, designers can enhance the user experience by minimizing confusion and facilitating efficient navigation.

Navigation Pathways

Navigation Pathways in the context of Information Architecture (IA) refer to the organized routes or sequences that users can follow to navigate through a website or application. These pathways help users locate and access the desired information or perform specific tasks within the digital system. Navigation pathways are designed to enhance user experience by providing clear and intuitive directions, ensuring that users can move seamlessly through the website or application without getting lost or confused. They enable users to understand the structure and hierarchy of the information presented, facilitating efficient exploration and retrieval of content.

Navigation Structure

Navigation structure, in the context of Information Architecture (IA), refers to the hierarchical organization and arrangement of navigation elements within a website or application. It determines how users can browse, locate, and access different sections, pages, or features of the digital environment. A well-designed navigation structure is crucial for creating a user-friendly and intuitive experience, as it enables users to easily understand the content and functionalities available within the system. It serves as a roadmap that guides users through the digital space, allowing them to find the information they are looking for efficiently and effectively.

Navigation Taxonomy

Navigation Taxonomy is a classification system used in Information Architecture (IA) to organize and categorize the navigation components of a website or application. It refers to the hierarchical structure and arrangement of navigation elements, such as menus, links, buttons, and tabs, with the aim of improving the usability and findability of information. The purpose of Navigation Taxonomy is to provide users with a clear and intuitive way to navigate through the website or application, making it easier for them to find the content or functionality they are looking for. By organizing navigation elements into logical groups and hierarchies, users can quickly understand the structure of the information and the relationships between different pages or sections. Navigation Taxonomy typically involves the creation of a navigation menu or toolbar that acts as the primary means of navigating within the website or application. This menu is often placed in a consistent location, such as the top or side of the interface, to provide a familiar and predictable navigation experience for users. To create an effective Navigation Taxonomy, it is important to consider the target audience and their specific needs and mental models. The taxonomy should be designed in a way that aligns with users' expectations and enables them to easily understand and predict where they can find certain types of information. Furthermore, Navigation Taxonomy should be flexible and adaptable, allowing for future growth and changes to the website or application. As new content or functionality is added, the taxonomy should be able to accommodate these updates without disrupting the overall navigation structure. In conclusion, Navigation Taxonomy is a crucial aspect of Information Architecture that focuses on organizing and categorizing navigation elements in a hierarchical structure. By creating a clear and intuitive navigation system, users can easily navigate through a website or application, improving their overall user experience and satisfaction.

Navigation Usability

Navigation usability is a crucial component of Information Architecture (IA) that refers to the ease and efficiency with which users can navigate and explore a website or application to find the information or functionality they seek. It encompasses the design and organization of navigation elements, such as menus, links, breadcrumbs, search bars, and filters, to guide users through the content and facilitate their interactions. Effective navigation usability ensures that users can easily understand the structure and hierarchy of a website or application, allowing them to locate desired information or complete tasks efficiently, without confusion or frustration. It involves principles of clarity, simplicity, and consistency, aligning with user expectations and mental models to enable intuitive exploration.

Negative Space

Negative space, in the context of Information Architecture (IA), refers to the empty or blank areas in a design or layout that surround and separate content elements. These areas play a crucial role in creating a well-organized and easily navigable user interface. The effective use of negative space helps in reducing visual clutter and improving the user's ability to comprehend and interact with the information presented. By providing breathing room between different elements, negative space aids in establishing visual hierarchy and enhancing the overall clarity and legibility of the interface.

OmniGraffle

OmniGraffle is a specialized software used in the domain of Information Architecture (IA) to create visual representations of complex systems and information. It is a powerful tool that allows IA professionals to design, analyze, and communicate the structure, organization, and relationships within a digital or physical information space. With OmniGraffle, IA practitioners can create diagrams and flowcharts that help in mapping out the various components, interactions, and hierarchies of a system. These diagrams, also known as IA models, provide a clear and visual representation of how information is organized and accessed within a website, application, or any other information system.

Onboarding

Onboarding in the context of Information Architecture (IA) refers to the process of introducing new users or team members to the IA framework and guiding them on how to navigate and understand the organization's information structure. During onboarding, individuals are familiarized with the key components and principles of IA, including the organization's taxonomy, metadata, navigation systems, and content hierarchy. They are provided with the necessary knowledge and tools to effectively contribute to the development and maintenance of the IA within their respective roles and responsibilities.

Ontology

Ontology is a foundational concept in Information Architecture (IA) that refers to the organization and classification of information resources within a specific domain. It involves the identification and definition of the various entities, relationships, and properties that exist within the domain, as well as the hierarchical structure that governs their organization.Ontology provides a means to represent knowledge and information in a systematic and structured manner, allowing for better understanding, retrieval, and management of information. It serves as a framework for organizing and categorizing content, facilitating efficient navigation and search experiences for users.

Open Card Sorting

Open card sorting is a method used in the field of information architecture (IA) to organize and categorize content or information. It involves presenting participants with a set of cards, each representing a piece of content or information, and asking them to sort and group these cards in a way that makes sense to them. The participants are free to create their own categories and arrange the cards as they see fit. This method is called "open" card sorting because there are no predefined categories given to the participants. Instead, they have the freedom to define their own categories based on their understanding and mental models. This allows for a more user-centered approach, as users can express their own perspectives and organizational patterns. Open card sorting is typically conducted in a facilitated session, either in person or remotely. The facilitator explains the purpose of the exercise and provides instructions on how to perform the sorting task. Participants are encouraged to think out loud and share their thought processes as they sort the cards. Once participants have completed the card sorting task, the facilitator collects the sorted cards and analyzes the results. The collected data from multiple participants can be combined to identify common patterns and themes. These patterns can then be used to inform the development of an information architecture that better aligns with users' mental models and expectations. Open card sorting can help with several aspects of information architecture, such as: 1. Content organization: It can provide insights into how users naturally group and categorize information, which can inform the structure and navigation of a website or application. 2. Labeling and naming: Participants often provide labels for their categories, which can help in determining appropriate wording and terminology for navigation menus and links. 3. User feedback: Through open card sorting, participants have the opportunity to express their preferences, expectations, and frustrations with the content or information provided. This feedback can be valuable in refining the overall user experience. In conclusion, open card sorting is a user-centered method used in information architecture to involve users in the organization and categorization of content. By allowing participants to define their own categories, this method provides insights into how users mentally group information, helping to create more intuitive and user-friendly information architectures.

Optimal Workshop

Optimal Workshop is an online research platform that specializes in providing tools and resources for conducting user research and usability testing in the field of Information Architecture (IA). Information Architecture (IA) is the practice of organizing and structuring information in a way that allows users to easily find and navigate through content. It involves the design and implementation of systems that facilitate the organization, storage, retrieval, and dissemination of information, ensuring that it is accessible and understandable to users. The goal of IA is to create a user-friendly and intuitive information environment that enhances the user experience.

OptimalSort

The term OptimalSort refers to a web-based card sorting tool that is commonly used in the field of Information Architecture (IA). It is a user research method used to determine the most effective and intuitive ways of organizing information on a website or application. OptimalSort allows researchers to conduct card sorting studies with participants, enabling them to categorize and group information in a way that makes sense to them. This tool provides a platform for both remote and in-person card sorting studies, making it a convenient option for researchers.

OptimizePress

OptimizePress is a software tool designed to optimize website performance and enhance user experience through a range of customizable features. It falls under the category of Information Architecture (IA) as it focuses on organizing and structuring website content to improve usability and navigation. IA encompasses the way information is organized, categorized, and presented to users. It involves creating a clear and intuitive structure that allows users to easily find the information they are looking for. OptimizePress plays a crucial role in IA by providing tools and resources to help website owners enhance the overall architectural design of their sites.

Optimizely

Optimizely is a platform and tool that is used in the field of Information Architecture (IA) to improve and optimize the design and performance of websites and digital products. It allows IA professionals to conduct experiments and gather data to make data-driven decisions that enhance the user experience and achieve business goals. Through its user-friendly interface and powerful features, Optimizely provides IA specialists with the ability to easily test different variations of a website or application and determine which design elements, navigation structures, or content implementations are the most effective in achieving specific objectives. This process is commonly known as A/B testing.

Origami Studio

Origami Studio is an interactive design and prototyping tool developed by Facebook specifically for creating and testing user interfaces. In the context of Information Architecture (IA), Origami Studio can be utilized to visually represent and explore the structure and organization of information within a digital product or system. Origami Studio provides designers and information architects with a canvas to create and manipulate user interface elements, such as buttons, sliders, and text fields, allowing them to simulate and refine their proposed IA solutions. By using Origami Studio, designers can rapidly prototype and iterate upon different information structures, enabling them to evaluate the effectiveness and usability of their designs before implementation.

Overflow

Overflow is a term used in the context of Information Architecture (IA) to describe the behavior of content that exceeds the allocated space within a container or element. This phenomenon occurs when the content within a designated area, such as a text box, image container, or a web page layout, is too large to fit within its given dimensions. When this happens, the excess content is not visible, and the container undergoes an overflow. The overflow behavior can be described in different ways, depending on the CSS (Cascading Style Sheets) property applied to the container.

Page Builder Sandwich

Page Builder Sandwich is an Information Architecture (IA) tool that allows users to design and build web pages using a visual interface, without the need for coding or technical knowledge.

With Page Builder Sandwich, users can create, edit, and customize web pages by dragging and dropping elements onto the canvas, rearranging them, and modifying their properties. The tool provides a wide range of pre-designed templates, widgets, and modules that users can choose from, making it easy to create professional-looking websites.

Page Builder By SiteOrigin

Page Builder by SiteOrigin is a drag-and-drop content editor plugin for WordPress websites that allows users to build web pages without the need for coding or technical knowledge. In the context of Information Architecture (IA), Page Builder provides a visual interface for organizing and structuring website content, enhancing the user experience and improving the efficiency of content creation. With Page Builder, website administrators can easily create and arrange different types of content elements, such as text, images, videos, and widgets, using a simple and intuitive interface. This tool enables the creation of complex page layouts by allowing users to customize the arrangement, size, and appearance of elements within a grid-based system. By eliminating the need for manual coding, Page Builder enables website owners to structure and organize their content effectively, aligning with the principles of IA. This empowers them to create well-structured and navigable websites that allow users to easily find and access the desired information. Page Builder also offers features such as row and column customization, pre-designed templates, responsive design options, and live front-end editing. These features allow users to optimize their website's layout for different screen sizes and device types, ensuring a consistent and seamless user experience across various platforms. Moreover, Page Builder integrates seamlessly with other WordPress plugins and themes, providing compatibility and extensibility. This enables users to enhance their websites with additional functionalities, such as contact forms, social media integration, and e-commerce capabilities, further improving the overall user experience and supporting the goals of IA.

Paper Prototype

A paper prototype is a low-fidelity representation of a digital product or system, typically made using paper or cardboard. It is used in the field of Information Architecture (IA) to conduct user testing and gather feedback on the design and functionality of a website or application before it is fully developed. Creating a paper prototype involves sketching out the user interface and designing the layout, navigation, and content organization of the digital product. This can be done using pens, markers, or even printing and cutting out screens from a design software. The prototype should mimic the intended interactions and functionalities of the final product, allowing users to interact with it as if it were a real application.

Paper Prototyping

Paper prototyping is a method used in the field of Information Architecture (IA) to design and test user interfaces prior to development. It involves creating hand-drawn or printed representations of screens or web pages, which are then used to simulate the user experience. During the paper prototyping process, IA professionals use paper, pens, and other physical materials to create a low-fidelity version of the intended digital interface. This allows them to quickly iterate and make changes based on user feedback, without investing time and resources into coding and development.

Paradigm Shift

Paradigm Shift in the context of Information Architecture (IA) refers to a fundamental change in the way that IA is understood, conceptualized, and practiced. It signifies a departure from traditional approaches and frameworks and the adoption of new methodologies, ideas, and technologies. In IA, a paradigm shift occurs when there is a significant transformation in the underlying principles, assumptions, and models that guide the design and organization of information. This shift is often driven by advancements in technology, changes in user needs and behaviors, and new insights gained from research and practice.

Participatory Design

Participatory Design is a process used in Information Architecture (IA) that involves involving end-users and stakeholders in the design process, ensuring their active participation and contribution. It aims to create user-centered systems through collaboration, co-creation, and shared decision-making. In Participatory Design, the focus is on designing information systems that meet the needs and expectations of the users. It recognizes the importance of involving end-users in the design process as they possess valuable domain knowledge and insights. Their active participation helps improve the efficiency, effectiveness, and usability of the information system.

Pattern Languages

A pattern language in the context of Information Architecture (IA) is a set of recurring solutions to common design problems in the organization and structure of information. It provides a way for designers and architects to communicate and share their knowledge and experience, as well as a framework for approaching complex design challenges. The concept of a pattern language originated from the field of architecture, where architect Christopher Alexander popularized the idea in his book "A Pattern Language" in the 1970s. It has since been adapted and applied to various disciplines, including IA.

Pattern Libraries

Pattern Libraries are a set of reusable design elements and components that are organized and documented to provide consistency and efficiency in the design and development process. In the context of Information Architecture (IA), Pattern Libraries serve as a central repository of standardized UI patterns and layouts that can be used across different digital products or platforms. The main goal of Pattern Libraries in IA is to establish a shared understanding and language amongst designers, developers, and stakeholders. By defining and documenting common patterns, designers can create a consistent user experience, while developers can efficiently implement these patterns in code without reinventing the wheel. This leads to time and cost savings, as well as improved user satisfaction and comprehension.

Pattern Recognition

Pattern Recognition in the context of Information Architecture (IA) refers to the process of identifying and categorizing patterns or trends within a set of data or information, with the goal of organizing and structuring that information in a meaningful and intuitive way. Pattern recognition involves analyzing and understanding the inherent relationships and similarities that exist between different pieces of information. This can include recognizing similarities in content, layout, navigation, or user behaviors. By identifying patterns, IA professionals can create a logical framework that allows users to easily find and navigate through the information. In the field of IA, pattern recognition is crucial for creating effective and user-friendly information structures. It enables designers to group related information together, making it easier for users to understand and navigate the content. By recognizing patterns, designers can also anticipate and meet user expectations, providing a more intuitive and efficient information system. Pattern recognition in IA can be applied at various levels. At a high level, it involves recognizing patterns in the overall structure and organization of information, such as identifying common themes or topics. At a more granular level, pattern recognition can involve identifying patterns in the arrangement of content elements within a page or screen, such as the consistent placement of navigation menus or the repetition of certain design elements. To effectively recognize and apply patterns in IA, designers must have a deep understanding of user needs and behaviors. By studying user interactions and feedback, IA professionals can identify patterns in how users search for and consume information, allowing them to design IA solutions that align with those patterns. In conclusion, pattern recognition is a fundamental concept in IA that involves identifying and categorizing patterns or trends within a set of information. By applying pattern recognition techniques, IA professionals can create information architectures that are intuitive, efficient, and aligned with user expectations.

Pencil Project

Information Architecture (IA) is a discipline that focuses on organizing and structuring digital information in a clear and intuitive way. It involves designing the layout, navigation, and labeling systems of websites and other digital products to enhance user experience and help users find and understand information more easily. IA aims to create logical and meaningful structures for information by considering the needs, goals, and behaviors of users. This involves analyzing user research, conducting usability tests, and studying user interactions to inform the organization of information. IA also takes into account content strategy, ensuring that the right content is available in the right place, at the right time.

Pencil And Paper

Information Architecture (IA) is a discipline within the field of User Experience (UX) Design that focuses on organizing, structuring, and labeling content in websites, applications, and other digital products to enhance usability and findability. It involves creating an intuitive navigation system and categorizing information in a way that supports the user's mental model and helps them locate and retrieve information efficiently. IA aims to simplify complex information and make it more accessible and understandable to users. It involves careful planning and consideration of the needs, goals, and behaviors of the target audience. A well-designed IA enhances the overall user experience, facilitating seamless information retrieval and interaction with the digital product.

PencilBlue

PencilBlue is an open-source content management system (CMS) that is designed to facilitate the creation and management of websites and web applications. It provides a platform for developers to build and customize websites using a modular and flexible approach. With a focus on Information Architecture (IA), PencilBlue offers tools and features that help organize, structure, and present content in a logical and intuitive manner. It allows developers to create and define content types, attributes, and relationships between different data elements. This enables the implementation of a consistent and coherent information structure across the website.

Pendo

Pendo is a Customer Success platform that provides product analytics and user guidance to help businesses optimize their software products and enhance the user experience. It offers a suite of tools and features that allow companies to gain insights into how customers are using their applications and make data-driven decisions to improve their products. Within the context of Information Architecture (IA), Pendo can be utilized to support the organization and structuring of information within a digital product or website. It helps architects and designers understand how users interact with the content and identify opportunities for improvement.

Persona Development

A persona in the context of Information Architecture (IA) refers to a fictional representation of a target user group that expresses their goals, needs, and behaviors when interacting with a digital product or service. Personas are created by gathering information from user research, interviews, surveys, and other data sources to develop a deep understanding of the target audience. This understanding is used to create a concise but detailed persona profile that can be used as a reference throughout the design and development process.

Persona Profiling

Persona profiling in the context of Information Architecture (IA) refers to the process of creating fictional representations or archetypes of target users. These personas are based on research and data collected about real users and are used to better understand their needs, behaviors, and motivations. Persona profiling helps IA practitioners to design more user-centric and effective information architectures. The process of persona profiling involves collecting and analyzing user data from various sources, such as user interviews, surveys, analytics, and market research. This data is used to identify patterns, common characteristics, and goals among different user groups. Based on this analysis, personas are created that represent the different user groups and their goals, needs, motivations, and preferences. Personas in IA are often depicted as fictional characters with names, backgrounds, and personal details that help make them more relatable. These fictional characters are not meant to represent individual users, but rather represent groups of users who share similar characteristics and goals. Personas are typically given descriptive labels or titles, such as "technology enthusiast" or "busy professional," to easily identify the target user group they represent. The purpose of persona profiling in IA is to ensure that the information architecture is designed to meet the needs and expectations of the target users. Personas help IA practitioners to make informed decisions about the organization, labeling, and structure of information on a website or other digital platform. By understanding the goals and behaviors of different user groups, IA practitioners can create intuitive navigation, prioritize content, and design meaningful user experiences. In conclusion, persona profiling is a vital component of Information Architecture. It enables IA practitioners to gain a deeper understanding of user needs and behaviors, which in turn allows them to design user-centric information architectures that meet the requirements of the target audience.

Persuasive Design

Persuasive design refers to the practice of using information architecture (IA) techniques to influence or change user behavior, attitudes, or beliefs. It involves the strategic placement and presentation of content, functionality, and design elements to encourage specific actions or outcomes. In the context of IA, persuasive design focuses on optimizing the structure and organization of information to guide users towards desired goals. This can include designing intuitive navigation menus, creating clear and concise labels, and arranging content in a logical and meaningful way.

Pidoco

Pidoco is a web-based prototyping software tool that is used in the field of Information Architecture (IA). It allows designers to create and simulate interactive wireframes, mockups, and prototypes of websites or other digital products. Information Architecture is the practice of organizing and structuring information in a way that is intuitive and user-friendly. It involves creating a clear and logical structure for content, navigation, and interactions within a digital product. This is crucial for guiding users through the information effectively and ensuring a positive user experience.

PlaybookUX

PlaybookUX is an information architecture (IA) tool that helps UX designers and researchers to organize and optimize the structure and content of websites, applications, and other digital products. As an IA tool, PlaybookUX provides a systematic approach to organizing and labeling the information within a digital product to enhance its usability and accessibility. It involves creating a clear and logical structure for the content and ensuring that users can easily find and navigate through the information they need.

Pneumatic Tubes

Pneumatic Tubes, in the context of Information Architecture (IA), refer to a system of transporting physical objects or documents through a network of pressurized tubes using compressed air or a similar medium of propulsion. This system has been adapted for the purpose of transporting information, similar to how physical objects are transported in traditional pneumatic tube systems. In the digital world, pneumatic tubes serve as a metaphor for the efficient flow and exchange of data between different components or systems within an information architecture. They are used to facilitate the seamless transmission of information, enabling quick and secure communication between various nodes or channels of a complex system.

Principle

Information architecture (IA) refers to the practice of organizing, categorizing, and structuring information in a way that makes it easy for users to navigate and find what they need. It involves designing the underlying structure and organization of a website, application, or system to ensure that the information is logical, intuitive, and accessible. IA principles are the fundamental concepts and guidelines that guide the design and development of effective information architectures. These principles help ensure that the information is presented in a clear and coherent manner, improving the overall usability and user experience.

Progressive Disclosure

Progressive Disclosure in the context of Information Architecture (IA) refers to a design principle that aims to present information or functionality in a gradual and gentle manner. The concept focuses on revealing only the most relevant and necessary information to the user, while keeping the less important or advanced options hidden until needed. By implementing progressive disclosure, IA professionals can simplify complex interfaces, reduce cognitive load, and enhance user experience. Instead of overwhelming users with an abundance of choices or overwhelming information, the design gradually reveals additional options as the users engage with the interface.

Proto.Io

Proto.io is a web-based prototyping tool that enables designers and developers to create interactive and realistic prototypes of digital products. It is a powerful software that allows users to transform their ideas into functional visual designs, providing a high-fidelity representation of a user interface. With Proto.io, users can design and simulate various user interactions and experiences, making it an essential tool in the field of Information Architecture (IA). IA is concerned with the structure, organization, and navigation of information within a digital product, focusing on how users can easily find and interact with the content. Proto.io facilitates the prototyping phase of IA by allowing designers to create interactive wireframes and prototypes that showcase the proposed information structure and navigation.

Prototyping Tools

A prototyping tool in the context of Information Architecture (IA) refers to a software or application that helps designers create interactive and functional prototypes of a digital product or system. These tools enable designers to simulate the user experience and test the usability of their designs before they are implemented or developed. Prototyping tools are essential in the IA process as they allow designers to visualize and communicate their design ideas, structure, and functionality effectively. They help bridge the gap between conceptualizing and implementing digital products by providing a medium for designers to iterate and refine their designs based on user feedback and requirements.

Prott

Prott Definition Prott is a collaborative and interactive prototyping tool that visually expresses and connects the various components and interactions within a digital product or website. It allows designers and stakeholders to create and communicate the structure, layout, and functionality of the product. With Prott, information architects can define and organize the information hierarchy and navigation within a digital product. They can map out the different screens or pages and establish the relationships and flow between them. This helps to ensure a logical and user-friendly experience for the end-users.

Qualtrics

Qualtrics is a comprehensive research platform that allows users to design and distribute online surveys, collect and analyze data, and generate reports. In the context of Information Architecture (IA), Qualtrics can be utilized as a tool for conducting user research and gathering insights to inform the design and structure of digital information systems. Information Architecture refers to the organization and structure of information within a digital platform or system. It involves creating a framework that enables users to easily navigate and locate information, ensuring a seamless and intuitive user experience. With Qualtrics, IA professionals can collect data and feedback from users, allowing them to make informed decisions about the organization and presentation of content.

Quick And Dirty Testing

Quick and Dirty Testing refers to a rapid and informal method of evaluating the effectiveness and usability of a website's information architecture (IA). It involves quickly assessing the structure, organization, and navigation of a website to identify any potential issues or areas for improvement. This type of testing is typically conducted early in the development process, allowing designers and developers to quickly identify and address any IA problems before the website is launched. Quick and Dirty Testing does not require a formal testing plan or comprehensive user research, making it a cost-effective and time-efficient way to gather feedback on the website's IA.

Remote Usability Testing

Remote usability testing, within the context of Information Architecture (IA), refers to the evaluation and analysis of a website or digital product's usability and user experience remotely, without the need for in-person observation or testing. It allows researchers and designers to assess how well users are able to use and navigate through a website, identify any potential issues or points of friction, and gather valuable feedback and insights for improving the IA of the digital product. In remote usability testing, participants are typically asked to perform specific tasks or scenarios on the website or digital product while their interactions, behaviors, and comments are recorded. This can be achieved through various methods such as screen sharing, remote screen recording, or utilizing specialized usability testing tools. Researchers often provide participants with a set of instructions and tasks to complete, allowing them to observe how users navigate through the digital product, locate information, and accomplish their intended goals. The advantages of remote usability testing include its cost-effectiveness, as it eliminates the need for a physical testing facility or travel expenses for participants. It also allows for a larger pool of participants, providing a wider range of perspectives and insights. Remote usability testing provides flexibility in terms of participant locations, enabling researchers to engage with users from different geographical areas or target specific demographics. Additionally, conducting testing remotely allows participants to interact with the digital product in their natural environment, potentially providing more authentic feedback and user behaviors. Despite its advantages, remote usability testing also presents some challenges. Since researchers cannot directly observe participants during the testing session, it may be harder to capture non-verbal cues or subtle user reactions. Participants may also encounter technical difficulties or limitations due to their own devices or internet connections, which can potentially impact the overall testing experience. To mitigate these challenges, researchers should carefully plan and design the remote usability testing process, including appropriate technology setup, clear instructions for participants, and sufficient user support during the testing session.

Responsive Design IA

Responsive Design in the context of Information Architecture (IA) refers to the approach of designing and developing a website or application that automatically adjusts its layout and content depending on the screen size and device being used to access it. This allows the website or application to provide an optimal viewing experience, ensuring that users have easy access to all the information and functionality regardless of whether they are using a desktop computer, tablet, or smartphone. The primary goal of responsive design is to ensure that the content of a website or application is displayed in a clear and accessible manner, regardless of the device being used. This involves considering factors such as screen size, resolution, and input methods, and adapting the design accordingly. One of the key principles of responsive design is the use of flexible grid layouts. Instead of fixed-width layouts, responsive designs use fluid grids that adapt and change based on the available screen space. This allows the content to adjust and reflow, preventing horizontal scrolling or content getting cut off. In addition to flexible grids, responsive design also employs media queries. These are CSS rules that allow designers to specify different styles and layouts for different screen sizes or device types. For example, a media query could be used to adjust the font size or navigation menu layout for smaller screens, ensuring that the content remains readable and usable. Another important aspect of responsive design is the use of flexible images and media. Instead of fixed-size images, responsive designs use techniques such as CSS max-width to ensure that images resize and adapt to different screen sizes, preventing them from overflowing or causing layout issues. By implementing responsive design principles, websites and applications can provide a consistent and user-friendly experience across a wide range of devices. This enhances accessibility and usability, as users can easily interact with the content without the need for zooming or scrolling. Responsive design has become increasingly important in recent years with the rise of mobile devices and the diverse range of screen sizes and resolutions. By adopting a responsive design approach, information architects can ensure that their websites and applications are future-proofed and ready to adapt to the ever-changing landscape of technology and user preferences.

Responsive Navigation

A responsive navigation in the context of Information Architecture (IA) refers to a menu or set of links that adapt and adjust its layout, design, and functionality based on the screen size and device type for a better user experience. Responsive navigation is especially crucial in today's digital age where users access websites and applications through various devices such as desktops, laptops, tablets, and mobile phones. With the increasing range of screen sizes and resolutions, it is essential to provide a consistent and user-friendly navigation experience across all devices. To achieve a responsive navigation, HTML and CSS are used together to create a flexible and adaptable menu. The HTML structure typically consists of an unordered list (ul) containing list items (li) representing each navigation item. These list items are then styled using CSS to create an aesthetically appealing and functional navigation menu. CSS media queries play a significant role in making the navigation responsive. Media queries allow the CSS styles to be adjusted based on the screen size, allowing the navigation to adapt its layout and design accordingly. This ensures that the navigation remains accessible, readable, and usable on different devices. Responsive navigation can include different design patterns, such as hamburger menus, dropdown menus, or slide-out menus, depending on the desired user experience and the amount of content in the navigation. These patterns allow for more compact navigation layouts on smaller screens and expand to a full menu on larger screens. Overall, responsive navigation is crucial for effective Information Architecture as it improves the user's ability to navigate and access different sections and content of a website or application. By adapting to various device sizes, responsive navigation ensures that users can find what they're looking for easily, regardless of the device they're using. To summarize, responsive navigation in the context of Information Architecture refers to the use of HTML and CSS techniques to create a flexible and adaptable menu that adjusts its layout and design based on the screen size and device type. It enhances the user experience by providing a consistent and user-friendly navigation experience across different devices.

Responsive Web Design

Responsive Web Design (RWD) is an approach to web design that aims to create websites that provide an optimal viewing experience across a wide range of devices and screen sizes. It involves designing and coding websites in a way that ensures their layout and content adapt and respond to the user's device and screen resolution. The key principle of responsive web design is to use flexible grids and layouts, CSS media queries, and scalable images to create a fluid and flexible design that can automatically adjust and rearrange its elements based on the user's screen size. This ensures that the website is easily accessible and readable on any device, whether it is a desktop computer, laptop, tablet, or smartphone. Responsive web design plays a crucial role in information architecture (IA) as it ensures that information is organized and presented in a way that is easy to navigate and understand across different devices. With the increasing use of mobile devices to access the internet, it is essential for websites to provide a seamless and user-friendly experience on screens of various sizes. By adopting responsive web design, information architects can ensure that the website's IA is consistent and effective across different devices. They can design a single website that adapts to different screen sizes, eliminating the need for multiple versions of the website or separate mobile apps. This not only simplifies the management and maintenance of the website but also provides a consistent user experience across different devices. In conclusion, responsive web design is an integral part of information architecture (IA) that focuses on creating websites that can adapt and respond to different devices and screen sizes. It allows for a consistent and optimal user experience across a wide range of devices, enabling users to access and navigate the website easily regardless of the device they are using.

Responsive Wireframes

Responsive wireframes in the context of Information Architecture (IA) refer to a visual representation of a website or application's layout and functionality. They are created to demonstrate how the site or app will adapt and respond to different screen sizes and devices, ensuring a consistent user experience across platforms. Wireframes are low-fidelity sketches or blueprints that outline the basic structure and content placement of a digital product. They are typically black and white, devoid of colors, images, and detailed visual elements, allowing the focus to be on the layout and organization of information. Responsive wireframes take this a step further by illustrating how the design will respond to different devices, such as desktop computers, tablets, and mobile phones.

Reverse Card Sorting

Reverse Card Sorting is a method used in Information Architecture (IA) to gather insights and understand users' mental models when organizing and categorizing information. This technique involves presenting participants with a set of pre-defined content items and asking them to sort these items into categories that make sense to them. Unlike traditional Card Sorting, where participants create categories and place cards into them, Reverse Card Sorting flips the process by providing pre-defined categories and asking participants to assign the cards to these categories. This approach allows researchers to gain a deeper understanding of users' expectations and mental models of how information should be organized.

Reverse Tree Testing

Reverse Tree Testing is an analytical technique used in the field of Information Architecture (IA) to evaluate the effectiveness of an IA design in supporting user navigation and information retrieval. It involves examining the structure and organization of the IA from the user's perspective, specifically focusing on the hierarchy of categories and the relationship between different content nodes. In this testing approach, rather than starting from the top level and drilling down into the IA structure like traditional tree testing, reverse tree testing begins with a specific content node and asks users to find their way to that node. The goal is to identify any potential usability issues or limitations in the IA design that may hinder users' ability to find and access the desired content. To conduct reverse tree testing, the following steps are typically followed: 1. Define the research objective: Clearly articulate the specific content node or information that users need to find. 2. Select representative tasks: Identify a set of tasks that users might perform to find the target content node. These tasks should cover a range of scenarios and reflect the typical user journey. 3. Create a test scenario: Present users with a scenario or context to frame the task and provide some context for their navigation. This can help simulate a real-world situation and better understand how users would approach finding the content. 4. Conduct the test: Invite participants to perform the tasks and navigate through the IA structure to find the target content node. Observe their interactions and note any issues or challenges they encounter. 5. Analyze the results: Evaluate the success rate and efficiency of users in finding the target content node. Identify any recurring patterns or trends in the challenges faced by users. Use this information to make improvements to the IA structure if needed. Reverse tree testing helps uncover potential flaws in the IA's organization, labeling, and navigation hierarchy. It provides insights into how users perceive and understand the IA design, and highlights areas for improvement to enhance the user experience and ensure findability of content. Overall, reverse tree testing is a valuable technique in the IA field to evaluate the effectiveness of IA designs from a user-centric perspective. By starting from a specific content node and working backward, this approach can reveal crucial insights into the usability and navigational aspects of an IA structure, enabling iterative improvements to optimize user information retrieval and navigation experiences.

SEO Auditing

An SEO audit is a systematic evaluation of a website's performance and optimization in terms of search engine rankings and user experience. This process involves analyzing various on-page and off-page factors that can impact a website's visibility and accessibility on search engine result pages (SERPs). When conducting an SEO audit, the information architecture (IA) of a website plays a crucial role. IA refers to the structure and organization of content on a website, including navigation, categorization, and hierarchy. It ensures that users can easily find and access the information they are looking for, while also helping search engines understand the website's content and context. Within the context of IA, an SEO audit focuses on examining how the website's information is structured and presented. This involves evaluating the website's URL structure, internal linking, and categorization of content. A well-organized IA can enhance the visibility and accessibility of a website, making it easier for search engines to crawl and index its pages. In an SEO audit, the website's URL structure is assessed to ensure that it is clear, concise, and relevant to the content it represents. A clean URL structure not only improves the user experience but also helps search engines interpret the website's information architecture more effectively. The internal linking structure of a website is also evaluated during an SEO audit. Internal links help search engines navigate and understand the relationships between different pages on a website. By examining the internal linking structure, an SEO audit identifies any potential issues, such as broken links or orphaned pages, that may hinder the website's crawlability and indexability. Lastly, an SEO audit considers the categorization of content within the website's IA. The way content is organized and grouped can greatly impact how search engines perceive its relevance and importance. An effective categorization strategy helps search engines understand the website's overarching themes and topics, allowing them to provide more accurate search results.

Scapple

Scapple is a versatile software tool used in the field of Information Architecture (IA) that helps in the organization and visualization of ideas, thoughts, and connections. Developed by Literature and Latte, Scapple provides a simple and intuitive interface for creating and arranging digital sticky notes or "scaps" on a virtual canvas, enabling users to brainstorm, plan, and structure their information effectively. With Scapple, IA professionals and designers can easily map out the relationships between different concepts, break down complex information into smaller chunks, and identify patterns or themes. The software allows users to freely move and connect scaps, facilitating the creation of hierarchies, networks, or flowcharts that represent the underlying structure of a project or system.

Scenario-Based Design

Scenario-Based Design is an approach used in Information Architecture (IA) to create user-centric and contextually appropriate systems or websites. It involves understanding the needs, goals, and behaviors of the users through the creation of realistic scenarios or use cases that depict specific scenarios in which the system or website will be used.By focusing on scenarios, designers can gain insights into the various tasks users might perform and the context in which these tasks occur. This approach helps align the system or website's functionality, content, and structure with the users' requirements and expectations.

Screen Reader

A screen reader is a tool used to assist individuals with visual impairments in accessing and understanding digital content. Specifically in the context of Information Architecture (IA), screen readers play a critical role in ensuring that websites and applications are accessible to all users, including those who are blind or have low vision. A screen reader works by converting the text-based content displayed on a computer or device screen into synthesized speech or braille output, which is then presented to the user through an audio output or refreshable braille display. By analyzing the structure and markup of web pages, screen readers are able to provide an auditory or tactile representation of the content, enabling users to navigate, interact with, and consume digital information. In the field of IA, screen readers are essential for creating accessible and inclusive websites. Information architects design the structure, organization, and navigation of websites, and screen readers play a crucial role in ensuring that this information is effectively communicated to users with visual impairments. Screen readers rely on well-structured content, which is achieved using proper HTML markup and semantic elements. Elements such as headings (h1-h6), lists, and landmarks (such as nav, main, and footer) aid screen readers in understanding the hierarchy and organization of the content. In addition, alternative text descriptions (specified using the alt attribute) for images, icons, and other non-text elements provide important contextual information to screen reader users. By using a screen reader, individuals with visual impairments can navigate through a website using keyboard shortcuts or gestures, accessing headings, links, lists, and other interactive elements. Screen readers also provide users with information about their current location within the website, helping them understand the overall information structure and navigate between different sections. In conclusion, screen readers are assistive technologies that empower individuals with visual impairments to access and understand digital content. In the context of IA, screen readers are crucial for creating accessible websites by facilitating the navigation and consumption of information. By following best practices in HTML markup and ensuring the availability of alternative text descriptions, information architects can ensure that their websites are inclusive and provide a meaningful user experience for all.

Search Algorithms

Search algorithms in the context of Information Architecture (IA) refer to the methods used to retrieve relevant information from a collection of data or resources. These algorithms are designed to efficiently locate and present search results to users based on their search queries or criteria. Search algorithms in IA are responsible for analyzing and indexing the content of a website, database, or other information system in order to provide accurate and meaningful search results. They employ a variety of techniques to organize and categorize data, such as keyword extraction, metadata analysis, and semantic analysis.

Search Engine Optimization (SEO)

Search Engine Optimization (SEO) refers to the practice of improving a website's visibility and ranking in search engine results pages (SERPs). It is a crucial aspect of Information Architecture (IA) that focuses on enhancing the website's structure and content to make it more accessible and relevant to search engine algorithms. A well-optimized website is more likely to appear higher in search engine rankings, which in turn increases its chances of attracting organic traffic. This, in essence, means that implementing SEO techniques can help a website gain visibility and reach its target audience more effectively. SEO in the context of IA involves various strategies and best practices that aim to optimize the website's structure, URLs, metadata, content, and overall user experience. These techniques help search engines understand the website's content and relevance, allowing them to index and rank it appropriately in their search results. One important aspect of IA-related SEO is the proper organization and categorization of content. A well-structured website ensures that search engines can easily navigate and understand the hierarchy of information, leading to improved indexing and ranking. This involves using concise and descriptive headings, logical URL structures, and clear navigation menus. Additionally, optimizing the website's metadata, including title tags and meta descriptions, is crucial for IA-related SEO. These elements provide search engines with contextual information about the webpage's content and purpose, helping them accurately categorize and rank it. Well-written and keyword-rich metadata also plays a role in attracting users' attention in search engine result listings, increasing the likelihood of clicks. Furthermore, SEO in IA includes optimizing the website's content by incorporating relevant keywords and phrases that reflect the audience's search intent. This helps search engines understand the content's relevance to specific queries and improves the website's chances of appearing in relevant SERPs. However, it is important to use keywords naturally and avoid keyword stuffing, as search engines prioritize quality and user relevance. In conclusion, SEO in the context of Information Architecture involves implementing strategies and techniques to optimize a website's visibility and ranking in search engine results. By focusing on the website's structure, metadata, and content, IA-related SEO aims to improve search engine understanding and user relevance, leading to increased organic traffic and better user experience.

Semantic Search

Semantic search is a concept within the field of Information Architecture (IA) that aims to improve the relevance and accuracy of search results by understanding the meaning or intent behind a user's query, rather than simply matching keywords. It leverages various techniques and technologies to comprehend the context and semantics of the query and the content being searched, thereby providing more meaningful and personalized results to the user. Unlike traditional keyword-based search, semantic search goes beyond surface-level matching and takes into consideration the relationships between words, concepts, and entities. It utilizes natural language processing (NLP) algorithms and artificial intelligence (AI) techniques to analyze and interpret the user's query, understand its underlying intent, and connect it to relevant information within a given knowledge base or dataset. By understanding the semantics of the query, semantic search engines can generate more accurate results that align with the user's true informational needs. It enables them to take into account synonyms, related concepts, and contextual information, allowing for a more comprehensive and nuanced understanding of the user's query and the content being searched. One of the key advantages of semantic search is its ability to deliver personalized and context-aware results. It can tailor the search experience to individual users based on their preferences, past interactions, and demographic information. This personalization enhances the user's search experience, making it easier for them to find the information they are looking for in a faster and more efficient manner. In the context of IA, semantic search plays a vital role in enhancing the overall findability and discoverability of information within a digital ecosystem. It helps users navigate complex information landscapes by providing them with more accurate and relevant results, improving the overall usability and user experience of the system.

Semantic Web

Semantic Web is a concept in Information Architecture that aims to enhance the web by adding structure and meaning to the information available, allowing computers to understand and process the data in a more intelligent and automated way. It is built upon the concept of metadata, which provides additional context and definition to the content and relationships between different pieces of information. The Semantic Web relies on the use of standardized languages and technologies, such as Resource Description Framework (RDF), Web Ontology Language (OWL), and Uniform Resource Identifiers (URIs). These tools enable the representation of data in a structured and meaningful way, allowing for better integration and interoperability between different platforms and systems.

Serena Prototype Composer

Serena Prototype Composer, in the context of Information Architecture (IA), refers to a tool used for creating interactive prototypes of user interfaces. It allows designers and developers to efficiently visualize and test the structure, layout, and functionality of an application or website before actual development begins. With Serena Prototype Composer, IA professionals can define and organize the various elements of a user interface, such as pages, navigation menus, forms, and controls. The tool offers a range of pre-built UI components and templates, making it easy to create prototypes that closely resemble the final product. Additionally, it provides the ability to customize these components to match the specific design requirements.

SessionCam

SessionCam is an advanced session replay and website optimization tool that helps organizations understand user behavior, improve website usability, and optimize conversion rates. It provides valuable insights into how users interact with a website, identifying areas of improvement and enabling data-driven decision-making. As an information architecture (IA) tool, SessionCam plays a crucial role in organizing and structuring the digital information within a website. It captures user sessions and replays them, allowing designers and developers to observe and analyze user behavior in real-time. This helps in evaluating the effectiveness of the website's IA design and making informed decisions for its improvement.

Site Mapping

Site mapping is a crucial component of information architecture (IA), which involves the organization and structure of content within a website. It refers to the process of creating a visual representation or diagram of a website's structure, hierarchy, and navigation system. The primary purpose of site mapping is to provide a clear and intuitive roadmap for users to navigate through a website. It helps users understand how different pages or sections of a website are interconnected and allows them to easily browse and access the desired information or functionality. In addition, site mapping also aids in the planning, design, and development of a website by providing a high-level view of its structure.

SiteOrigin

SiteOrigin is a website design and development company that focuses on creating themes, plugins, and tools for WordPress. As an information architect (IA), SiteOrigin plays a crucial role in structuring and organizing the information of a website to enhance its usability and findability. Information architecture refers to the process of categorizing, organizing, and structuring content and information within a website or application. It involves creating a logical and intuitive navigation system, establishing a clear hierarchy of information, and defining the relationships between different pages and sections of a website. The primary objective of information architecture is to optimize the user's experience by making it easy for them to find the information they need quickly and efficiently.

Sitemap Generation

Sitemap Generation is the process of creating a structure or blueprint that outlines the organization and hierarchy of a website's content. It is an essential step in Information Architecture (IA), which focuses on designing and organizing information to enhance usability and user experience. A sitemap is a visual representation of a website's structure, displaying the pages and their relationships to each other. It provides a clear overview of the website's content and helps search engines and visitors navigate and understand the site's pages.

Sitemap Generator

A sitemap generator is a tool that is used in the field of Information Architecture (IA) to automatically create a structured representation of a website. This representation, referred to as a sitemap, serves as a blueprint of the website's structure, allowing both website owners and search engines to understand and navigate the site more effectively. By analyzing the website's internal links, a sitemap generator creates a hierarchical map that outlines the pages and sections of the website. This map can be organized in a way that aligns with the website's navigation structure, making it easier for users to find the information they are looking for. Additionally, search engines use sitemaps as a reference to crawl and index web pages, which can improve a website's visibility and ranking in search engine results.

Sitemaps & Spreadsheets

Sitemaps and spreadsheets are two essential tools used in the field of Information Architecture (IA) to organize and structure information effectively.A sitemap, in the context of IA, is a hierarchical diagram or representation of the various pages and content within a website. It provides an overview of the website's structure and shows how different pages are connected. Sitemaps typically depict the relationships between sections, sub-sections, and individual pages, helping users navigate and understand the overall organization of the website. They serve as a blueprint for the website's structure and are invaluable during the planning and design phase of a website.Spreadsheets, on the other hand, are tabular documents used to collect, store, and organize data and information. In the context of IA, spreadsheets are commonly used to manage and store large sets of information, such as content inventory or metadata. They provide a structured and systematic approach to organizing and categorizing data, making it easier to analyze, manipulate, and visualize information. Spreadsheets can be particularly useful in IA for tasks such as content auditing, content modeling, or information mapping.Both sitemaps and spreadsheets play a crucial role in the information architecture process. Sitemaps help designers and stakeholders visualize and understand the overall structure of a website, enabling them to make informed decisions about navigation and content organization. Spreadsheets, on the other hand, allow IA professionals to organize and manage complex sets of data, ensuring that information is structured and categorized in a meaningful way. By leveraging these tools effectively, IA practitioners can create well-organized and user-friendly digital experiences.

Sketch

Information Architecture (IA) refers to the organization, structure, and labeling of information within a system or website to facilitate effective navigation, findability, and understanding for users. It is a discipline that focuses on creating clear, intuitive, and user-centered designs that enable users to easily access and comprehend the information presented to them. IA encompasses various aspects, including the arrangement of content, the development of navigation systems, and the establishment of labeling conventions. Its principles aim to improve the user experience by ensuring that information is logically categorized, easily discoverable, and readily understandable. Effective IA involves the thoughtful grouping of related content and the systematic application of hierarchical structures. By organizing information into meaningful categories and subcategories, users can quickly locate the information they need. This may involve creating taxonomies, which are hierarchical systems of classification that assist in grouping similar content together. Navigation systems play a key role in IA by providing means for users to move between different sections or areas of a system or website. Well-designed navigation helps users understand the overall structure of the information and allows them to navigate effortlessly through the various levels of content. This may include using menus, breadcrumbs, or search bars to provide clear pathways. Labeling is another important aspect of IA. It involves the use of consistent and descriptive terminology to help users easily understand the purpose and context of the information. Labels should accurately represent the content they are attached to and be meaningful to the target audience. Effective labeling enhances the user's ability to locate and interpret information correctly. Overall, Information Architecture aims to create user-friendly systems and websites by effectively organizing and presenting information. It involves careful consideration of the users' mental models, information needs, and browsing behaviors. By implementing thoughtful IA strategies, designers can create intuitive interfaces, improve information findability, and enhance the overall user experience. Information Architecture (IA) refers to the organization, structure, and labeling of information within a system or website to facilitate effective navigation, findability, and understanding for users. IA involves the arrangement of content, development of navigation systems, and establishment of labeling conventions to create clear, intuitive, and user-centered designs that improve the user experience.

Sketch2React

Sketch2React is an innovative tool that facilitates the process of transforming design sketches into fully functional and interactive digital prototypes. It offers a streamlined workflow for designers and developers, enabling them to collaborate effectively and efficiently throughout the design and development stages. Driven by the principles of Information Architecture (IA), Sketch2React allows designers to organize and structure their design elements in a way that enhances user experience and promotes intuitive navigation. By implementing IA practices, designers can strategically arrange content, functionality, and interaction patterns, ensuring that users can easily find what they are looking for and accomplish their goals.

Sketchboard

The Sketchboard is an essential tool within the field of Information Architecture (IA). It serves as a visual representation of the IA process, allowing designers to sketch, map, and organize information in a structured and hierarchical manner. The Sketchboard is a physical or digital surface used to create, modify, and present information architecture diagrams. It provides a means for information architects and other stakeholders to collaboratively discuss, refine, and iterate on the structure and organization of information within a system or website.

Skeuomorphism

Skeuomorphism in the context of Information Architecture (IA) refers to the design technique that incorporates visual elements or metaphors from physical objects to improve the understanding and usability of digital interfaces and systems. Skeuomorphic design utilizes familiar and recognizable attributes, textures, shapes, and behaviors derived from the physical world to create a sense of familiarity and make digital experiences more intuitive for users. This design approach aims to bridge the gap between the physical and digital realms, leveraging users' pre-existing mental models to enhance usability.

Slickplan

Slickplan is an online tool used in the field of Information Architecture (IA) to visually map and outline website structures and content. It provides a user-friendly interface for creating sitemaps, flowcharts, and other IA deliverables, allowing designers and developers to efficiently plan and organize the structure and content of a website. With Slickplan, users can easily create and manage website structures, hierarchy, and relationships between different pages. The tool offers a drag-and-drop functionality, allowing users to rearrange and reorganize elements within the sitemap or flowchart easily. This helps in visualizing the overall structure of the website and making necessary adjustments to ensure optimal user experience and information flow. In addition to sitemaps and flowcharts, Slickplan also provides features for content management. Users can add descriptions, notes, and annotations to each page or element within the structure, helping to document and communicate the intended purpose and content of the website. This acts as a guide for designers, developers, and content creators to ensure consistency and clarity throughout the website. Collaboration is another key aspect of Slickplan. Users can invite team members to work on the same project, enabling multiple stakeholders to contribute to the website planning process. This promotes collaboration and communication between different disciplines, such as designers, developers, and content strategists, ensuring a cohesive and well-planned website structure. Slickplan also includes features for website content auditing and SEO planning. Users can analyze and review their website's existing content, identifying gaps, duplications, or outdated pages. This allows them to make informed decisions regarding content management and optimization for better search engine visibility and user engagement. In conclusion, Slickplan is an online tool designed for Information Architecture professionals and website planners. It offers a range of features for creating, managing, and organizing website structures and content. With its user-friendly interface and collaboration capabilities, Slickplan helps streamline the website planning and development process, ensuring a cohesive and well-structured website that aligns with user needs and business goals.

Slider Interaction

A slider interaction in the context of Information Architecture (IA) refers to a graphical user interface (GUI) element that allows users to select a value within a specified range by sliding a handle along a track. It is commonly used to control and manipulate numerical values, such as setting a volume level or selecting a value from a range of prices. The slider interaction is a key component in designing user-friendly and intuitive interfaces. It provides a visual representation of the available options and allows users to easily make selections or adjustments without requiring precise input. The slider typically consists of a horizontal or vertical track with a handle that can be dragged or clicked to move along the track.

Smartlook

Smartlook is a powerful tool used in the field of Information Architecture (IA) that allows website owners to understand and improve the user experience. With Smartlook, website owners can gain valuable insights into how visitors interact with their website. It tracks each user's mouse movements, clicks, and scrolling behavior, as well as records their entire session on the site. This allows website owners to see exactly what users are doing on their website and identify any potential issues or areas for improvement.

Social Proof

Social Proof in the context of Information Architecture (IA) refers to the concept of using evidence from the actions and behaviors of others to influence and guide user decisions and behaviors within a digital environment. By presenting social proof, IA aims to leverage the psychological tendency for individuals to conform to the actions and choices of others, and to rely on the collective wisdom of the crowd as a valuable indicator of trustworthiness, credibility, and relevance.

Solidify

Solidify is a term used in the context of Information Architecture (IA) to describe the process of refining and structuring the organization of information within a system or website. It involves creating a clear and logical framework that allows users to easily navigate and find the information they need. The solidify process typically begins with conducting user research and understanding the goals and needs of the target audience. This helps in identifying what information is most important and how it should be structured. Next, information architects use techniques such as card sorting, tree testing, and user testing to validate and refine the proposed structure. During the solidify process, information architects collaborate with stakeholders from different domains to ensure that the information architecture meets the objectives of both the users and the organization. They examine the relationships between different pieces of information, such as categories, subcategories, and individual content pages, and determine the most effective way to organize and present this information. One important aspect of solidifying IA is developing a clear and consistent labeling and navigation system. This involves coming up with descriptive and intuitive labels for different sections of the website or system, as well as creating a navigation hierarchy that allows users to easily move between different sections and levels of information. The solidify process also involves considering other aspects of IA, such as search functionality and metadata. Information architects ensure that there is a robust search feature that allows users to find information quickly and accurately. They also define and implement metadata, such as tags and categories, to enhance searchability and provide additional context to the information. Overall, solidify is a crucial step in IA that transforms initial ideas and research into a well-defined and structured information architecture. It ensures that the information is organized in a logical and user-friendly manner, making it easier for users to find what they are looking for and improving the overall user experience.

Sound Feedback

Sound feedback in the context of Information Architecture (IA) refers to the auditory cues or audio signals that are used to provide feedback or confirmation to users during their interaction with a digital system or interface. Sound feedback can play a crucial role in enhancing the user experience by providing additional sensory information that complements the visual or textual feedback. It can help users in better understanding and interpreting the system's response to their actions, thus improving the overall usability and user satisfaction.

Split.Io

Split.io is an Information Architecture (IA) tool that allows for effective organization and categorization of digital information. It is designed to improve the usability and findability of information within a website or application. Split.io utilizes various IA techniques, such as taxonomy development and controlled vocabularies, to structure and label information in a logical and intuitive manner. This enables users to navigate and search for relevant content easily. With Split.io, IA professionals can create a hierarchical structure for organizing information, defining categories and subcategories that align with user needs and goals. The tool also allows for the creation of metadata, which provides additional context and descriptive information about the content. One of the key features of Split.io is its ability to facilitate user-centered design. It enables IA professionals to conduct user research, gather insights, and incorporate user feedback into the IA design process. This ensures that the resulting IA structure meets user expectations and supports their information-seeking behaviors. Split.io also offers features for content organization and management. It allows IA professionals to create content models, defining the structure and relationships between different types of content. This helps in maintaining consistency and coherence across the digital ecosystem. Additionally, Split.io provides features for content testing and optimization. IA professionals can track user interactions and behavior within the information architecture to identify areas for improvement. This data-driven approach allows for continuous refinement and optimization of the IA structure. In summary, Split.io is an IA tool that empowers professionals to create effective and user-centric information architectures. It enables the organization and categorization of digital information, improving usability and findability. The tool offers features for taxonomy development, metadata creation, content organization, and user research. With Split.io, IA professionals can create, test, and optimize IA structures that meet user needs and goals.

Storytelling In Design

Storytelling in Information Architecture (IA) refers to the practice of using narrative techniques and structures to organize and present information in a way that creates a meaningful and engaging user experience. It involves designing and arranging content in a way that tells a coherent and compelling story, guiding users through the information and helping them make sense of it. Storytelling in IA draws on principles from traditional storytelling and applies them to the design of information systems. It recognizes that humans have an innate ability to understand and remember information better when it is presented in a narrative form, with a clear beginning, middle, and end. By incorporating storytelling techniques, IA practitioners can create a more intuitive and memorable user experience.

Sympli

Information architecture (IA) in the context of web design refers to the organization and structure of a website or application to facilitate easy navigation and efficient access to information. It focuses on creating a logical and intuitive system of categorizing and labeling content. IA involves the design and arrangement of information elements such as menus, navigation bars, page layout, and search functionalities. The goal is to create a clear and understandable structure that helps users find what they are looking for quickly and easily. The process of information architecture starts with understanding the target audience and their needs. This involves conducting user research and gathering information about their preferences, habits, and expectations. Based on this information, information architects can develop a user-centered design that aligns with users' mental models and goals. IA also considers the content of the website or application. It involves organizing the content into categories, subcategories, and hierarchies that make sense to the users. This is often done through the creation of site maps, which provide an overview of the website's structure. In addition to organization, IA also focuses on navigation. It involves designing clear and intuitive navigation systems that guide users through the website or application. This may include primary navigation menus, bread crumbs, and search functions. The navigation should be consistent across the website to prevent confusion and enhance usability. Usability testing is an important part of the information architecture process. It helps identify issues and gather feedback from users to refine the IA. Based on the feedback, adjustments can be made to improve the structure, labels, and navigation. Overall, information architecture plays a crucial role in creating a user-friendly and efficient website or application. It helps users find information easily, enhances their overall experience, and contributes to the success of the digital product.

Synonym Ring

The term "Synonym Ring" refers to a concept in the field of Information Architecture (IA). It is a technique used to improve search relevance and user experience by connecting related terms or words within a system or website. By creating associations between synonyms, the aim is to ensure that users can find the information they are looking for, even if they use different terms or vocabulary.A synonym ring consists of a collection of synonymous terms, all pointing to the same concept or topic. These terms are carefully selected to cover different variations, spellings, or alternative names that users might use when searching for a particular item. For example, in an e-commerce website, a synonym ring for the term "smartphone" could include synonyms such as "mobile phone," "cellphone," or "handset."When implementing a synonym ring, IA professionals take into account the goals and objectives of the system or website, as well as the needs and expectations of the target users. They conduct thorough research to identify common synonyms and variations that users are likely to use in their search queries. By mapping these synonyms to the appropriate concept or topic, IA professionals establish a connection that helps bridge the gap between different ways of expressing the same idea.Utilizing a synonym ring can have several benefits for both users and the website owners. From a user perspective, it enhances the search experience by increasing the chances of finding relevant information, even when using different terminologies. For instance, if a user searches for "movie," but the website uses the term "film," the synonym ring ensures that results for both terms are displayed. This avoids frustrating situations where users cannot find what they are looking for due to terminology differences.From a website owner's standpoint, incorporating a synonym ring improves the overall user experience, leading to increased satisfaction and engagement. By accommodating different vocabularies and search preferences, the chances of users successfully finding the desired information are heightened, resulting in higher conversions and customer retention.In conclusion, a synonym ring is a valuable tool in IA that bridges the gap between different user vocabularies and improves search relevance. By connecting related terms and synonyms, the goal is to enhance the user experience and increase the likelihood of finding the desired information, regardless of the terminology used.

Tagging System

A tagging system in the context of Information Architecture (IA) is a method of categorizing and organizing information using tags or labels. Tags are short keywords or phrases that are assigned to content to describe its topic, theme, or subject. These tags serve as metadata, providing additional information about the content and enabling users to easily find and navigate related information. Tags are usually added by content creators or system administrators, but in some cases, users may also be allowed to add their own tags to content. The tags are usually displayed in a tag cloud or list format, allowing users to click on a tag to view all content associated with that tag. The tagging system is a flexible and dynamic way of organizing information, as tags can be easily added or removed as needed. It allows for a more organic and user-centric approach to categorization, compared to traditional hierarchical or folder-based structures. One of the main advantages of using a tagging system in IA is that it allows for a more granular and detailed way of categorizing information. Instead of being limited to a single category or folder, content can be assigned multiple tags, allowing for more nuanced connections and relationships between pieces of information. Another advantage is that tags can be easily modified or updated over time, as the content evolves or new topics emerge. This flexibility helps to ensure that the IA remains relevant and adaptable to changing user needs. In summary, a tagging system in IA is a method of categorizing information using tags or labels. It allows for a more flexible and user-centric approach to organizing information, enabling users to easily find and navigate related content.

Tagging And Labeling

Tagging and labeling are two key concepts in the field of Information Architecture (IA) that aid in organizing and categorizing information to improve findability and user experience. Tagging refers to the process of assigning metadata or keywords to a piece of information, such as a document, image, or webpage. These tags describe the content, subject matter, or characteristics of the information. Tags can be generated by content creators, users, or automated systems. They help in classifying information and making it more searchable. For example, a blog post about gardening tips can be tagged with keywords like "gardening," "tips," "plants," "flowers," etc. Tagging enables users to find related information by clicking on or searching for specific tags. Labeling, on the other hand, involves creating clear and concise names or labels for categories or groups of information. Labels provide a high-level overview and help users understand the content hierarchy and structure. They are often displayed as headings, menu items, or navigation links. In IA, effective labeling contributes to a logical and intuitive information organization, allowing users to quickly locate and access the desired information. For instance, a website may have labels like "Home," "About Us," "Products," and "Contact" to guide users through the site's content.

Task Analysis

Information Architecture (IA) refers to the practice of structuring and organizing information in a way that allows users to easily find and navigate through content on a website or application. It involves the planning, designing, and implementation of a website's structure, labeling, and navigation system. The main goal of IA is to create a logical and intuitive information hierarchy that supports users' needs and goals, and helps them quickly and efficiently find the information they are looking for. This involves various activities, such as content analysis, user research, and usability testing. One key aspect of IA is the creation of a site map, which visually represents the structure and organization of a website's content. The site map typically includes the main categories, subcategories, and individual pages within the website. It helps stakeholders understand the overall information flow and hierarchy, and serves as a planning tool for developers. Another important element of IA is navigation design, which determines how users move through a website and find the information they need. This includes the placement and design of menus, links, and search functionality. A well-designed navigation system should be easy to understand, consistent across all pages, and provide clear labels and cues for users. IA also involves the creation of metadata, which is information about the content of a website. This includes attributes such as page titles, descriptions, keywords, and tags. Metadata helps search engines understand and index the content, and also provides context and relevance to users when they are navigating through the website. Furthermore, IA considers the organization and labeling of content. This includes creating categories and subcategories that are meaningful to users, and using clear and consistent labeling to describe the content. Effective labeling helps users understand what they can expect to find within different sections of a website. In summary, Information Architecture is the practice of structuring and organizing information in a way that enhances usability and findability. By carefully planning and designing the structure, labeling, and navigation system of a website, IA aims to improve the user experience and help users easily find the information they need.

Task-Centered Design

p.indent{ padding-left: 30px; text-indent: -30px; } Task-centered design is an approach in Information Architecture (IA) that focuses on understanding user tasks and designing user interfaces based on these tasks. It involves analyzing the activities and goals of users to create effective and usable websites or applications. This design approach begins with conducting research to identify the tasks that users need to accomplish when interacting with a website or application. This research may include user interviews, surveys, and observations to gather data about user behaviors and goals. By collecting this information, designers can gain insights into the specific tasks that users expect to perform within the system. Once the tasks are identified, designers can then organize the information architecture of the website or application to support these tasks. This involves structuring the content and navigation in a way that allows users to easily find and complete their intended tasks. The goal is to minimize the number of clicks or steps required to complete a task, enhancing user efficiency and satisfaction. Task-centered design also considers the context in which users are performing their tasks. This includes factors such as the user's environment, goals, and constraints. For example, if users are accessing a website on a mobile device with limited screen space, the design should prioritize the most important tasks and minimize clutter. Throughout the design process, usability testing and feedback from users play a crucial role in refining the task-centered design. By observing users interacting with the interface and gathering their feedback, designers can identify any issues or usability obstacles that hinder task completion. This iterative process allows for continuous improvement of the interface and ensures that it aligns with the needs and expectations of the users.

Taxonomy Classification

Taxonomy Classification refers to the process of organizing and categorizing information based on a predefined set of criteria. In the context of Information Architecture (IA), taxonomy classification is a crucial aspect of designing and structuring information systems to facilitate efficient navigation and retrieval of information. A taxonomy is a hierarchical framework that groups related concepts and topics together, allowing for easier organization and discovery of information. It provides a system for classifying content in a logical and meaningful way, making it easier for users to navigate and find the information they need. Taxonomy classification involves defining a set of categories and subcategories that accurately represent the content and ensure consistency in the organization of information.

Taxonomy Design Tools

Taxonomy design tools in the context of Information Architecture (IA) refer to software or tools that assist in the creation, management, and organization of taxonomies. Taxonomies are hierarchical structures that categorize and classify information based on their relationships and characteristics. These tools provide a range of functionalities to facilitate the design process of taxonomies. They typically offer features such as taxonomy creation, editing, and visualization. Users can define and customize taxonomy structures, including adding or modifying categories, subcategories, and associated metadata. These tools often include various hierarchical and relationship-building capabilities to reflect the complex relationships between different taxonomy elements.

Taxonomy Development

Taxonomy development is a process within the field of Information Architecture (IA) that involves organizing and categorizing content in a structured and systematic manner. It aims to create a classification system that helps users find and navigate information effectively within a website or other digital platform. At its core, taxonomy development is the practice of creating a hierarchical framework that groups similar items together based on their shared characteristics. This framework not only assists users in locating specific information but also helps them understand the relationships and connections between different pieces of content.

Taxonomy Facets

Taxonomy facets are a key component of information architecture (IA) that help organize and categorize information in a structured manner. They are a set of attributes or characteristics that are used to classify and filter information, allowing users to navigate and find relevant content more easily. In the context of IA, taxonomy facets are used to create a hierarchical structure for organizing and classifying information. They provide a consistent framework for categorizing and labeling content, ensuring that it is logically arranged and easily accessible to users.

91

Taxonomy Governance

Taxonomy Governance refers to the process of managing and maintaining a taxonomy within the context of Information Architecture (IA). It involves establishing and implementing guidelines, policies, and procedures to ensure the accuracy, consistency, and relevance of the taxonomy. The taxonomy in IA is a structured classification system that organizes and categorizes content and information. It enables users to navigate and find the desired information efficiently and effectively. However, without proper governance, taxonomies can become disorganized, inconsistent, and outdated, leading to confusion and frustration for users. Taxonomy governance encompasses several key components to ensure the taxonomy remains accurate and useful. First, it involves defining and documenting the purpose and scope of the taxonomy. This includes identifying the intended user groups, their needs, and the specific content or information that the taxonomy will cover. Second, taxonomy governance includes establishing a clear and consistent naming convention for the taxonomy terms. This helps to ensure that the terms are descriptive, concise, and easily understandable for users. It also facilitates the mapping of terms across different systems and platforms, promoting interoperability and information consistency. Third, taxonomy governance involves setting up a process for adding, modifying, and retiring taxonomy terms. This includes defining roles and responsibilities for taxonomy management, such as who is responsible for creating and maintaining the taxonomy and who has the authority to approve changes. Additionally, taxonomy governance includes ongoing monitoring and quality control to ensure the taxonomy remains accurate and up-to-date. This may involve regular reviews and audits of the taxonomy, user feedback and testing, and addressing any issues or inconsistencies that arise.

Themify Builder

Themify Builder is an efficient tool used in the context of Information Architecture (IA) to design and construct websites. It is a drag-and-drop page builder that allows users to create visually appealing and responsive web pages without the need for extensive coding knowledge or skills. With its user-friendly interface, Themify Builder simplifies the website development process and provides a flexible and customizable platform for designers and developers. By utilizing Themify Builder, IA experts can easily organize and structure the content of a website to ensure optimal usability and accessibility for users. The builder provides various modules and elements that can be placed and arranged on the web page according to the information hierarchy and user flow. These modules include text, images, videos, call-to-action buttons, sliders, and more, enabling the IA professional to create intuitive and engaging interfaces. Themify Builder offers a range of design options, allowing for the customization of fonts, colors, backgrounds, and layouts. This flexibility ensures that the website design aligns with the brand identity and visual aesthetics of the organization or individual. The builder also supports responsive design, ensuring that the website adapts seamlessly to different screen sizes and devices, further enhancing the user experience. In addition to its design capabilities, Themify Builder incorporates best practices for IA by providing features that improve the navigation and organization of content. Users can create menus, breadcrumbs, and site maps to guide visitors through the website's structure and facilitate easy access to relevant information. The builder also supports the creation of landing pages and custom post types, giving IA professionals the ability to segment and organize content based on user needs and preferences. In conclusion, Themify Builder is a powerful tool in the realm of Information Architecture, empowering users to design and build visually appealing, user-friendly, and accessible websites. Its intuitive drag-and-drop interface, customization options, support for responsive design, and IA-focused features make it a valuable asset for IA professionals and web developers alike.

Thesaurus

Information Architecture (IA) refers to the organization, structure, and labeling of information within a system or website to improve usability and findability for users. It encompasses the design and planning of the information hierarchy, navigation, and categorization in a way that allows users to easily locate and access the desired information. IA aims to create a logical and intuitive framework that guides users through the content by presenting information in a clear and meaningful manner. It involves understanding the users' needs and expectations, and strategically arranging and connecting the various components of the system to facilitate efficient information retrieval.

Think-Aloud Testing

Think-Aloud Testing is a usability testing method commonly used in the field of Information Architecture (IA). It involves asking participants to verbalize their thoughts as they navigate through a website or application, providing insights into their decision-making processes and level of understanding. In this testing method, participants are given specific tasks to perform on a website or application while sharing their thoughts and reactions out loud. The goal is to understand their experience and identify any usability issues or areas for improvement within the IA design.

Thrive Architect

The Thrive Architect is a software tool specifically designed for creating visually appealing and highly functional websites. It is a powerful tool that allows users to easily design and build websites without any coding knowledge. Thrive Architect is part of the broader field of Information Architecture (IA), which focuses on organizing, structuring, and labeling content in a way that is intuitive and user-friendly. Thrive Architect's main goal is to improve the user experience by optimizing the way information is presented on a website. It helps designers and developers create effective information architectures by providing them with a wide range of tools and features. By using Thrive Architect, users can design and create well-structured websites that are easy to navigate and understand. One of the key features of Thrive Architect is its drag-and-drop interface, which allows users to easily place and arrange elements on their websites. This feature simplifies the process of designing and organizing web content, as users can simply drag and drop elements like headings, paragraphs, images, and videos onto their pages. Users can also easily resize and reposition elements to create the desired layout. In addition to the drag-and-drop interface, Thrive Architect offers a variety of pre-designed templates and content blocks. These templates and blocks can be used as a starting point for creating web pages, allowing users to quickly and easily build professional-looking websites. Thrive Architect also includes a wide range of customization options, allowing users to personalize their websites to match their branding and design preferences. Overall, Thrive Architect is a powerful tool for creating visually appealing and user-friendly websites. Its drag-and-drop interface, pre-designed templates, and customization options make it a popular choice among web designers and developers. By using Thrive Architect, users can easily design and build websites that are not only aesthetically pleasing but also logically structured and intuitive to navigate.

Top-Down Card Sorting

Top-down card sorting is a method in the field of Information Architecture (IA) that involves organizing, categorizing, and structuring information at a high-level before diving into specific details. This technique is used to develop an initial information architecture framework for a website or application, and it helps to establish a hierarchical structure for the content. In top-down card sorting, an IA team or UX designer begins by creating a set of predefined categories or high-level labels that represent the broad topics or themes of the content. These labels or categories are usually based on the organization's goals, user needs, or existing knowledge of the subject matter.

Touch Target

A touch target refers to an area on a digital interface, typically on a touchscreen, that is designed to be tapped or touched by a user's finger or stylus. In the context of Information Architecture (IA), touch targets play a crucial role in ensuring the usability and accessibility of a website or application on touch-enabled devices. The size and placement of touch targets are essential considerations in IA. The target should be large enough to be easily tapped without accidentally touching nearby elements, while also being small enough to avoid triggering actions unintentionally. The ideal touch target size is around 9-10mm, which allows for effective interaction and minimizes user errors.

Touchscreen IA

Touchscreen IA refers to the organization and structure of information and content on a touchscreen device. It focuses on designing the layout and navigation of the touchscreen interface to ensure that users can easily interact with and access the desired information or perform tasks efficiently. The goal of touchscreen IA is to create a seamless and intuitive user experience on touchscreen devices, such as smartphones, tablets, and interactive kiosks. The primary objective of touchscreen IA is to organize information in a way that is logical and easy to understand for users. This involves categorizing and grouping related content, creating hierarchies, and establishing clear paths for navigation. By structuring the information effectively, touchscreen IA helps users find what they are looking for quickly and easily, improving overall usability. Another important aspect of touchscreen IA is the placement and positioning of interactive elements and controls on the touchscreen interface. These elements include buttons, icons, menus, and input fields. Touchscreen IA considers factors such as the size and positioning of these elements relative to the size of a user's finger, as well as the ease of touch interaction. It ensures that these elements are easily reachable and sufficiently sized to avoid accidental touches or errors. Touchscreen IA also involves the consideration of device-specific capabilities and constraints. For example, the IA for a smartphone touchscreen may differ from that of a larger tablet touchscreen, taking into account the available screen real estate and orientation. It also considers the limitations of touch inputs compared to traditional mouse or keyboard inputs and adapts the IA accordingly. Overall, touchscreen IA plays a crucial role in the design and development of touchscreen interfaces. It aims to create an intuitive and user-friendly experience by organizing information effectively, optimizing touch interactions, and considering device-specific constraints. By implementing effective touchscreen IA, designers and developers can enhance the usability and user satisfaction of their touchscreen applications and devices.

Tree Testing

Tree testing, also known as reverse card sorting, is a research method used in the field of Information Architecture (IA) to evaluate the findability and usability of a website's navigation structure. This method involves testing the organization and labeling of the website's content hierarchy without the visual distractions of the interface or design elements. The main objective of tree testing is to assess the effectiveness of the website's navigation system in terms of helping users locate specific pieces of information. By conducting tree testing, IA professionals can identify potential issues or areas for improvement in the website's structure, hierarchy, labeling, and categorization.

Treejack

Treejack is a tool used in the field of Information Architecture (IA) to evaluate the effectiveness and usability of website structures and navigational hierarchies. It helps in conducting tree testing, which is a research method that aims to assess the findability and discoverability of content within a hierarchical structure. With Treejack, researchers can create and administer tasks to participants, who are presented with a simplified website structure known as a tree or tree diagram. This tree represents the information hierarchy of a website, where each node represents a page or category, and the connections between nodes represent the navigational links. The participants then need to find and select the most appropriate location within the tree to perform the given task. Their selections are recorded and analyzed to determine the effectiveness of the website's structure. Treejack provides quantitative data such as success rates, time taken, and the paths chosen by participants, which can be used to identify areas of improvement for the information architecture. This method allows researchers to measure the intuitiveness and efficiency of different navigational paths, identify potential pitfalls or confusion points, and validate or redesign the website's tree structure accordingly. By analyzing the data collected through Treejack, IA professionals can make informed decisions to optimize the organization and labeling of website content, enhancing the user experience and ensuring that users can easily find the information they are looking for.

TryMyUI

Information Architecture (IA) refers to the organization and structure of information within a system, website, or application. It involves designing and planning the navigation, labeling, and hierarchy of information to enhance user experience and facilitate efficient access to content. IA aims to create a clear and intuitive structure that helps users easily locate and understand information. This involves categorizing information into logical groups, defining relationships between different pieces of content, and determining how users can navigate through the system.

UX Copywriting

UX Copywriting in the context of Information Architecture (IA) refers to the process of designing and crafting concise, clear, and engaging written content that guides and informs users within a digital product or website. Information Architecture is concerned with organizing, structuring, and labeling content in a way that enables users to find and navigate information effectively. UX Copywriting plays a vital role in IA by providing user-friendly and contextually relevant text that enhances the overall user experience.

UX Design Framework

A UX design framework in the context of Information Architecture (IA) refers to a systematic approach or set of principles and guidelines that help designers organize and structure the information and interaction within a digital product or website, with the ultimate goal of enhancing the user experience. This framework is used to create a blueprint for the overall navigation, layout, and organization of content, ensuring that it is intuitive, efficient, and user-friendly. It helps designers analyze and understand the needs and expectations of the target users, and guides them in making informed design decisions to meet those requirements.

UX-App

An UX-App is a software application that is designed to provide a user-friendly and intuitive experience for its users, focusing on usability, interaction design, and visual aesthetics.It involves a combination of information architecture, user interface (UI) design, and user experience (UX) design principles to create a seamless and enjoyable user experience.

UXPin

UXPin is a collaborative design platform that enables designers to create and iterate on user interfaces, with a specific focus on information architecture (IA). Information architecture involves organizing and structuring information in a way that makes it easy for users to navigate and find what they are looking for. UXPin provides designers with the tools and functionality to create clear and intuitive information architectures for their digital products.

Ultimate Addons For Elementor

The Ultimate Addons for Elementor is a plugin designed to enhance the functionality and capabilities of the Elementor page builder for WordPress websites. As an Information Architecture (IA) component, the Ultimate Addons adds a set of powerful and feature-rich elements that can be used to create and customize web pages. These elements include advanced widgets, templates, and extensions that help in enhancing the user experience and improving the overall design of the website.

Unbounce

Unbounce is a software platform that enables businesses to create and optimize landing pages for their websites. It falls under the realm of Information Architecture (IA), which focuses on the organization, structure, and labeling of information within a website or digital product. Specifically, Unbounce helps users design and develop landing pages - standalone web pages that are created for a specific marketing campaign or objective. These landing pages are designed to capture visitor's attention, provide relevant information, and encourage them to take a specific action, such as making a purchase or filling out a form. Unbounce provides a range of features and tools to aid in the creation and optimization of landing pages. Users can choose from a variety of pre-designed templates or create their own custom designs using a drag-and-drop interface. The platform also allows for easy integration with other marketing tools, such as email marketing software and CRM systems. One of the key benefits of Unbounce is its ability to A/B test landing pages. This means that users can create variations of a landing page and test them to see which one performs better in terms of conversions or other desired outcomes. This enables businesses to continuously optimize their landing pages and improve their overall marketing strategy. Overall, Unbounce plays a crucial role in the field of Information Architecture by helping businesses create effective landing pages that deliver a seamless user experience and drive desired actions. It combines user-centric design principles with powerful technology to enable businesses to optimize their marketing efforts and achieve their goals.

Usability Benchmarking

Usability benchmarking is a method used in Information Architecture (IA) to evaluate the effectiveness and efficiency of a system or interface. It involves comparing the usability of a website, application, or digital product against established usability standards or criteria. During the usability benchmarking process, key tasks and scenarios are identified based on user goals and objectives. These tasks represent common actions that users would typically perform on the system. A group of representative users is then selected to participate in the benchmarking study. Participants are usually given a set of predefined tasks to complete while using the system. Their interactions and behaviors are recorded and analyzed to determine the overall usability and user experience. Usability measures, such as task completion time, errors, and user satisfaction, are collected and compared to established benchmarks or industry standards. The results of the usability benchmarking study provide valuable insights into the strengths and weaknesses of the system or interface. It helps identify areas for improvement and guides the iterative design process. By identifying usability issues early on, IA professionals can make informed decisions to improve the user experience and refine the design. Usability benchmarking is an essential part of the IA process as it allows designers and stakeholders to evaluate the success of the information architecture in meeting user needs and goals. It helps ensure that users can easily find and access information, navigate the system efficiently, and complete tasks effectively. In conclusion, usability benchmarking in the context of Information Architecture is a method used to assess the usability and user experience of a system or interface. It involves comparing the system's performance against established usability standards and criteria. The results provide valuable insights for improving the design and meeting user needs.

Usability Evaluation

Usability Evaluation in the context of Information Architecture (IA) refers to the process of assessing the effectiveness, efficiency, and satisfaction of a website or digital product in terms of its usability. During a usability evaluation, various techniques and methods are employed to gather data and insights into how users interact with the website or digital product, with the goal of identifying any usability issues or improvements that can be made to enhance the user experience.

Usability Goals

Usability goals in the context of Information Architecture (IA) refer to specific objectives that aim to enhance the overall usability and user experience of a website or digital product. Usability goals encapsulate the desired outcomes and criteria for evaluating the effectiveness, efficiency, and satisfaction of users when interacting with an IA system. These goals are crucial in guiding the design and development process to ensure that the IA solution meets the needs of its intended users.

Usability Heuristic

The usability heuristic is a set of principles used in information architecture (IA) to evaluate the usability and effectiveness of a website or application. It provides a framework for identifying and addressing potential issues that can impact the user experience. These heuristics, originally proposed by Jakob Nielsen, are a set of guidelines that help designers and developers create intuitive and user-friendly interfaces. They are based on observations of common patterns and practices that have been found to enhance usability.

Usability Metrics

Usability metrics in the context of Information Architecture (IA) refer to quantitative and qualitative measures used to assess the effectiveness, efficiency, and user satisfaction of a system's usability. These metrics provide insights into how well an IA design meets the needs

96

and expectations of its users. They help evaluate the usability of a website or application, identify areas for improvement, and inform design decisions.

Usability Sciences

Usability Sciences is a field of study that focuses on enhancing the usability and user experience of digital platforms, products, and services through the application of scientific methods and principles. In the context of Information Architecture (IA), Usability Sciences plays a crucial role in designing and structuring information in a way that allows users to easily find, understand, and interact with the content. Information Architecture is the practice of organizing and structuring information in a clear and intuitive manner. It involves creating a logical and efficient framework that enables users to navigate and access information effectively. The goal of Information Architecture is to provide a user-friendly and user-centric experience by organizing content in a way that aligns with user expectations and mental models.

Usability Standards

Usability standards in the context of Information Architecture (IA) refer to guidelines or principles that aim to ensure that a system, website, or application is easy to use, efficient, and effective for its intended users. These standards are used to guide the design and development process, helping IA practitioners make informed decisions that contribute to a positive user experience. Usability standards are based on research, expert knowledge, and best practices in the field of user-centered design.

Usability Test Plan

The usability test plan is a formal document that outlines the approach, objectives, and methodologies for evaluating the usability of an information architecture (IA) system. It provides a structured framework for conducting usability tests and collecting data to assess the effectiveness, efficiency, and satisfaction of users interacting with the IA. The usability test plan typically begins with an introduction that provides an overview of the IA system being tested, its purpose, and the objectives of the usability testing. This section also defines the target audience, which may be specific user groups, such as novices or experts, and outlines any specific tasks or scenarios that will be used during the tests. The plan then details the methodology and tools used in the usability testing process. This includes information on the test environment, equipment, and any software or monitoring tools that will be employed. It also outlines the data collection methods, such as observation, video recordings, and questionnaires, and explains how the data will be analyzed and interpreted. Additionally, the plan includes a schedule that outlines the timeline for the different phases of the usability testing, including participant recruitment, testing sessions, and data analysis. It also defines the roles and responsibilities of the team members involved in the testing process, such as the test facilitators, note-takers, and data analysts. Finally, the usability test plan includes a section on reporting and communicating the findings. This outlines how the test results will be documented and presented, whether through written reports, presentations, or other means. It also specifies the target audience for these reports, such as project stakeholders or development teams, and how the findings will be used to inform design decisions and improvements to the IA system.

Usability Testing Methods

"Usability Testing Methods" refer to the various techniques used in Information Architecture (IA) to evaluate the effectiveness, efficiency, and satisfaction of a user interface or website. These methods focus on assessing how easily and intuitively users can interact with the system and accomplish their goals. One common usability testing method is the "Think-Aloud Protocol" where participants are asked to verbalize their thoughts and actions while performing tasks on the interface. This method provides insight into users' decision-making processes, difficulties encountered, and overall satisfaction. By observing the users' verbalizations, IA professionals can identify areas for improvement and refine the design accordingly.

Usability Testing Script

Information architecture (IA) refers to the organization, structure, and labeling of information within a website or application. It focuses on designing an effective and intuitive system to help

97

users navigate and find the information they need. IA is crucial in creating a user-friendly experience by ensuring that content is logically organized and easily accessible. In the context of usability testing, IA plays a vital role in assessing the effectiveness of the information structure and navigation within a website or application. Usability testing is a method used to evaluate the ease of use and efficiency of a product by observing real users completing specific tasks. By conducting usability tests, designers can uncover any usability issues or bottlenecks in the IA and make improvements accordingly. Usability testing for IA involves observing participants as they interact with the system and complete tasks or find information. The aim is to gather qualitative data about how effectively users navigate the content and whether the IA meets their expectations. The testing process typically follows a script that outlines the tasks the participants need to perform and the specific areas of the IA that need evaluation. During the test session, the moderator guides the participants through the tasks while taking notes on their interactions, difficulties, and feedback. This data is then analyzed to identify any areas of improvement in the IA. Usability testing can reveal insights such as confusing navigation labels, ineffective categorization of information, or unclear hierarchy within the IA. The findings from usability testing can be used to inform design decisions and optimize the IA. Iterative testing and refinement help ensure that the IA supports users in achieving their goals efficiently and effectively. The ultimate goal is to create a clear and intuitive information structure that enables users to find the desired information quickly, enhancing their overall user experience. Overall, usability testing is a critical part of the IA design process, as it helps designers identify and address any issues that may hinder users' ability to find and navigate information. By conducting usability tests, designers can optimize the IA, leading to a better user experience and increased user satisfaction.

Usability Testing For IA

Usability testing for Information Architecture (IA) refers to the process of evaluating the effectiveness and efficiency of a website's organization, navigation, and labeling, with the goal of improving its usability. IA encompasses the structure and organization of information within a website, including content categorization, hierarchies, and navigation design. Usability testing involves observing users as they interact with a website or prototype, with the aim of identifying any issues or challenges they encounter while trying to find information or complete tasks. It helps to uncover usability problems that may arise due to poor IA, such as confusing navigation, inconsistent labeling, or lack of clear hierarchy.

Usability Testing With Clickable Models

Usability testing with clickable models is a method used in information architecture (IA) to evaluate the effectiveness and efficiency of interactive designs before they are implemented. It involves creating interactive prototypes or models that simulate the user interface and functionality of a digital product or system. Clickable models are often developed using HTML, CSS, and JavaScript to replicate the intended user experience. They can include various elements such as navigation menus, buttons, forms, and content placeholders. The models typically allow users to interact with these elements by clicking or tapping on them, triggering predefined actions or transitions.

Usability Testing With Interactive Prototypes

Usability Testing With Prototypes

A usability testing with prototypes is a systematic and controlled process conducted during the information architecture (IA) phase of a design project to evaluate the efficiency, effectiveness, and satisfaction of the intended users interacting with a prototype of the proposed IA solution. Usability testing with prototypes involves observing and gathering qualitative and quantitative data on users' interactions with the IA prototype. The purpose is to identify any usability issues, understand user behavior and preferences, and validate design decisions to ensure the IA design meets the needs and expectations of the target users.

Usability Testing With Wireframes

Usability testing with wireframes is a technique employed in the context of Information Architecture (IA) to evaluate the effectiveness and efficiency of a website or application design before its development. Wireframes are simplified visual representations of the proposed user interface, presenting the structure and layout of the interface elements, without focusing on aesthetics or graphical details. The goal of usability testing with wireframes is to gather user feedback and identify potential usability issues early in the design process, allowing for iterative improvements and refinements before investing time and resources into the actual development phase. This method helps in aligning the design with user needs and expectations, enhancing user satisfaction and overall usability of the final product.

UsabilityHub

Information Architecture (IA) is a practice in the field of user experience design that focuses on organizing, structuring, and labeling information in a way that makes it easy for users to find and navigate through a digital product or website. IA involves the creation of a clear and logical information structure, ensuring that information is presented in a way that is intuitive and meaningful to the user. It aims to improve the usability of a digital product by providing users with a cohesive and coherent experience.

User Behavior Analysis

User behavior analysis in the context of Information Architecture (IA) refers to the process of studying and understanding how users interact with a website or digital platform. It involves analyzing various aspects of user behavior, such as their navigation patterns, search queries, and interactions with content, to inform the design and organization of information within the IA. Through user behavior analysis, IA professionals aim to gain insights into how users perceive and navigate a website or application. This information helps them make informed decisions about the placement, labeling, and hierarchy of information elements, ultimately improving the user experience.

User Experience (UX) Design

The User Experience (UX) Design, in the context of Information Architecture (IA), refers to the process of creating a design that focuses on improving the overall experience of users when interacting with a website or application. UX Design aims to enhance user satisfaction by improving the usability, accessibility, and overall desirability of a digital product or service. It involves understanding the needs and behaviors of the target audience, conducting user research, and translating those insights into a design that meets users' expectations.

User Flow Diagram

A User Flow Diagram, in the context of Information Architecture (IA), is a visual representation that illustrates the path a user takes to navigate through a website or application. It provides a logical flow of how the user interacts with the various components and pages within the system. The diagram aims to show the user journey from the initial point of entry to the ultimate goal or desired outcome. User Flow Diagrams are essential in the IA process as they help to map out the user experience and identify any potential issues or areas of improvement. By visually representing the sequence and connections between screens, pages, and actions, designers can gain a better understanding of the user's perspective and how they interact with the system. The diagram typically consists of different shapes and lines to represent the various components of the user flow. Rectangles or squares are used to signify pages or screens, with arrows indicating the direction the user takes from one page to another. Labels and annotations can be added to explain the purpose or action associated with each element. By analyzing the User Flow Diagram, IA designers can identify bottlenecks or points where users may get confused or lost. This allows for proactive adjustments to be made, such as optimizing the navigation structure, improving the clarity of calls to action, or simplifying the user interface to enhance the overall user experience. User Flow Diagrams also play a critical role in collaboration among designers, developers, and stakeholders. They serve as a common visual language, facilitating communication and ensuring that everyone involved in the project is aligned with the intended user journey. This shared understanding helps to streamline the design and development process, leading to a more efficient and effective final product. Overall, User Flow Diagrams are a valuable tool in IA, providing a clear and concise representation of the user experience. They help designers identify and address potential usability issues, improve communication between team members, and ultimately create a more user-friendly digital product.

User Flow Diagrams

A User Flow Diagram is a visualization tool used in the field of Information Architecture (IA) to depict the path a user takes while navigating through a website or application. It helps in understanding and improving the user experience by mapping out the different steps, interactions, and decision points that occur during a user's journey. User Flow Diagrams provide a visual representation of the different paths users can take within a website or application. They typically consist of a series of interconnected boxes or shapes that represent the different screens or pages the user encounters. The arrows between these boxes indicate the flow of information or the path the user follows. The primary purpose of User Flow Diagrams is to help designers, developers, and other stakeholders visualize and understand the user journey. They provide a shared language for discussing and addressing user needs, goals, and pain points. By mapping out the user flow, IA professionals can identify areas where users may encounter difficulties or confusion, allowing them to make informed design decisions. User Flow Diagrams can be used in the early stages of the design process to plan and define the IA of a website or application. They allow designers to anticipate and address potential user issues before they become problems. Once a website or application is launched, User Flow Diagrams can also be used to monitor user behavior and identify areas for improvement. In conclusion, User Flow Diagrams are an essential tool in the field of Information Architecture. They provide a clear visualization of the user journey, helping stakeholders understand and improve the user experience. By mapping out the different pathways and decision points, User Flow Diagrams assist in creating intuitive and user-friendly designs.

User Flow Prototyping

User Flow Prototyping in the context of Information Architecture (IA) refers to the process of creating a visual representation of the flow of interactions that a user will experience when navigating through a website or a digital product. It is a method used to outline the sequence of screens, pages, or steps that a user will encounter while completing a specific task or achieving a particular goal. A user flow prototype is typically created using a combination of wireframes, screen layouts, and annotations. It allows designers, developers, and stakeholders to visualize and understand the logical progression of actions that a user will take to accomplish their objectives. The purpose of user flow prototyping is to identify and address any usability issues or bottlenecks in the user journey early in the design process, before investing significant time and resources in development. In IA, user flow prototyping helps to establish the hierarchy and organization of information within a website or application. It aids in determining the most intuitive and efficient routes for users to access the content they need. By outlining the steps and decision points in a user's journey, user flow prototypes enable designers to optimize the overall user experience and ensure that users can easily find and complete their desired tasks. Creating user flow prototypes can involve various techniques, such as using flowcharts, diagrams, or storyboards. These visual representations provide a clear overview of the different paths a user may take, including alternative routes and potential decision points. By simulating user interactions, designers can anticipate user behavior, identify potential pain points, and iterate on the design accordingly. User flow prototyping is an essential part of the IA process as it allows designers to validate and refine their initial assumptions about user behavior. By testing and iterating on user flow prototypes, designers can gather feedback, make informed design decisions, and ultimately create intuitive, user-centered digital experiences. In short, user flow prototyping in the realm of IA involves creating visual representations of the sequential steps and interactions that a user will go through when navigating a website or digital product. These prototypes help designers optimize the user experience, identify and address any usability issues early on, and ensure that the information hierarchy and user journeys are intuitive and efficient.

User Flows

User flows refer to the visualization of the steps that a user takes to accomplish a specific task or goal on a website or application. It is an essential aspect of Information Architecture (IA) as it helps designers understand the logical sequence of actions that users need to perform to complete a particular task. In the context of IA, user flows provide a structural representation of the paths users take within a digital product. They outline the various screens, interactions, and decision points that occur throughout the user journey. By mapping out these paths, designers can identify potential pain points, optimize the user experience, and ensure that users can easily achieve their goals. User flows typically begin with a user's entry point, such as the homepage or a specific landing page, and depict the subsequent steps required to accomplish a task. These steps may include filling out forms, navigating through menus, selecting options, reviewing information, or even making a purchase. Each action or decision point leads to a different screen or interaction, and the user flow visually represents the connections between these screens. Designers often use diagrams or wireframes to create user flows, providing a visual representation of the website or application's structure. These visualizations allow designers to communicate and collaborate with stakeholders, developers, and other team members effectively. When creating user flows, designers should consider the various user personas and their specific needs. This approach helps ensure that the user flow accommodates different user behaviors, preferences, and skill levels. Additionally, designers should aim to keep the user flow as simple and intuitive as possible, avoiding unnecessary steps or complexity that may confuse or frustrate users. Overall, user flows play a critical role in the IA process by enabling designers to strategically plan and organize the information and interactions within a digital product. By analyzing and understanding the user's journey, designers can create clear, efficient, and user-centric experiences that align with the goals and objectives of the website or application.

User Interface (UI) Design

User Interface (UI) design, in the context of Information Architecture (IA), involves the arrangement and presentation of user interactive elements within a digital application or website. It focuses on creating an intuitive and visually appealing interface that allows users to efficiently navigate, interact, and accomplish their goals within the system. The UI design encompasses various aspects such as layout, visual elements, typography, color schemes, and interactive components. The primary goal is to enhance user experience by providing a seamless and aesthetically pleasing interface that aligns with the overall brand identity and the user's mental model. To achieve effective UI design, it is necessary to consider the principles of IA. This involves understanding the user's needs and behaviors, organizing and structuring information in a logical manner, and creating clear and meaningful labels and navigation. The UI design should support the underlying IA by enabling easy access to relevant information and functionality. The layout of the UI design should be well-structured, with a clear hierarchy that guides users through the content and actions. This can be achieved through the use of grids, columns, and consistent spacing. Visual elements, such as icons and imagery, should be used purposefully to enhance understanding and communicate information. Typography plays a crucial role in UI design as it contributes to the overall readability and accessibility of the interface. Clear and legible fonts should be employed, with appropriate font sizes and spacing, to ensure that users can easily read and understand the content. Color schemes should be chosen carefully to create a visually appealing interface that also supports usability. Colors can be used to differentiate elements, provide feedback, and establish a visual hierarchy. However, it is important to ensure that the chosen colors are accessible to all users, including those with visual impairments. Interactive components, such as buttons, forms, and menus, should be designed to be easily recognizable and usable. They should respond to user actions in a timely manner and provide clear feedback to indicate their state or outcome. In conclusion, UI design in the context of IA focuses on creating a user-friendly and visually appealing interface that supports efficient navigation and interaction within a digital application or website. It involves considering principles of IA, such as information organization and structuring, and employing design elements, such as layout, typography, color, and interactivity, to enhance the overall user experience.

User Interface (UI) Framework

A User Interface (UI) Framework, in the context of Information Architecture (IA), refers to a collection of standardized components, guidelines, and tools that enables the creation and implementation of consistent and intuitive user interfaces for digital products or applications. These frameworks provide a structured approach to designing and developing user interfaces by offering pre-defined templates, reusable components, and a set of design principles that promote usability, accessibility, and overall user experience. UI frameworks are typically created to streamline the design and development process, ensure consistency across different parts of the interface, and enhance collaboration between designers and developers.

User Interface (UI)

User Interface (UI) refers to the visual elements and components that allow users to interact with a website, application, or system. In the context of Information Architecture (IA), the UI plays a crucial role in facilitating effective communication between users and the underlying information. As an important element of IA, the UI serves as the bridge between the user and the content. It encompasses the layout, design, and presentation of information, aiming to enhance usability and user experience. The UI design should be intuitive, efficient, and visually appealing to engage users and enable them to access and interact with information effortlessly. The UI in IA focuses on organizing and presenting information in a logical and hierarchical manner, making it easily accessible and understandable for users. It includes elements such as navigation menus, search bars, buttons, forms, and visual representations like images, graphs, and charts. These elements should be thoughtfully designed and strategically placed to guide users through the information and help them find what they need quickly and conveniently. The IA principles influence the UI design by influencing the organization and structure of information. A well-designed IA ensures that the UI effectively supports users in finding, understanding, and using the information. For instance, the categorization and labeling of content in the IA should align with the UI design, allowing users to navigate and locate information with ease. The UI design in IA should also provide consistency and coherence throughout the system. Consistent visual elements, fonts, color schemes, and interactions across different pages or sections of the platform contribute to a seamless and cohesive user experience. Consistency in the UI design prevents confusion and reduces cognitive load, enabling users to focus on the content rather than deciphering different interface elements. In conclusion, the UI in the context of IA refers to the visual representation and design of information that enables users to interact with digital platforms. It incorporates principles of usability, accessibility, and aesthetics to optimize the user's ability to navigate, consume, and engage with the underlying information. A well-designed UI aligns with the IA structure, provides effective organization and presentation of content, and ensures consistency and coherence throughout the entire system.

User Journey Map

A User Journey Map in the context of Information Architecture (IA) is a visual representation that helps designers and developers understand the flow of user interactions with a system or website. It provides a holistic view of the user experience, illustrating the various touchpoints, actions, and emotions that a user may experience while navigating through the system. User Journey Maps are typically created by conducting user research, such as interviews or observations, to gain insights into user behaviors, motivations, and pain points. This research helps designers identify the different stages and tasks that users may go through when interacting with the system. The map then visualizes these stages and tasks in a sequential and structured manner. The goal of a User Journey Map is to highlight the user's perspective and their overall experience with the system. It helps designers and developers align their efforts to create a user-centered design by identifying potential pain points, areas of improvement, and opportunities for innovation. A User Journey Map typically includes several key elements. It starts with the user's goal or intent, followed by the various touchpoints or interactions they have with the system. These touchpoints can include actions such as searching for information, completing a form, making a purchase, or contacting customer support. Each touchpoint is depicted along with the user's emotional state or satisfaction level, which helps to understand their overall experience. Additionally, a User Journey Map may include insights or observations from the user research, such as user expectations, pain points, or opportunities for improvement. This helps designers and developers to gain a deeper understanding of the user's needs and goals. Overall, a User Journey Map is a powerful tool in IA as it helps stakeholders visualize and empathize with the user's experience. It aids in identifying pain points and opportunities for improvement, ultimately leading to the creation of a user-centered design that optimizes the user's experience with the system. A User Journey Map in the context of Information Architecture (IA) is a visual representation that helps designers and developers understand the flow of user interactions with a system or website. It provides a holistic view of the user experience, illustrating the various touchpoints, actions, and emotions that a user may experience while navigating through the system. User Journey Maps are typically created by conducting user research, such as interviews or observations, to gain insights into user

102

behaviors, motivations, and pain points. This research helps designers identify the different stages and tasks that users may go through when interacting with the system. The map then visualizes these stages and tasks in a sequential and structured manner.

User Persona

Information Architecture (IA) is the practice of organizing and structuring information to enable efficient navigation, effective searching, and meaningful discovery of content within a system. It involves designing the organization, labeling, and categorization of information in a way that is intuitive and easy for users to understand and interact with. IA aims to create a cohesive and logical structure for content within a system, such as a website or app, by considering the needs and goals of both the users and the organization. It involves understanding the relationships between different pieces of information and designing pathways for users to find the content they are looking for.

User Profile Modeling

A user profile in the context of Information Architecture (IA) refers to a representation of an individual user within a system or platform. It encompasses various attributes, characteristics, preferences, and behaviors of the user, which are stored and utilized to provide personalized experiences and tailored content. A user profile acts as a central repository of user information that helps in understanding and predicting user needs, interests, and motivations. It can include both explicit information, such as demographic data, contact details, and user-generated content, as well as implicit data, such as browsing history, search queries, and interactions with the system.

User Research Methods

User research methods in the context of Information Architecture (IA) refer to the various techniques and processes used to gather insights and obtain a deeper understanding of users' needs, behaviors, and preferences. These methods help IA professionals make informed decisions in the design and optimization of digital information environments. One common user research method used in IA is interviews. Interviews involve direct conversations with users to gather qualitative data about their experiences, goals, and challenges. Through open-ended questions, IA professionals can gain insights into users' mental models and information needs, which can inform the organization and structure of information within an IA.

User Research

Information architecture (IA) refers to the art and science of organizing and structuring information to facilitate effective navigation, findability, and usability. It involves designing the structure, labeling, and organization of different types of content in a way that allows users to easily understand and interact with the information. IA encompasses several key components and principles to ensure a seamless user experience. It involves defining the information hierarchy, which determines the relationships and priority of different pieces of content. This hierarchy aids in guiding users through the information, allowing them to navigate from broader categories to more specific details. Another important aspect of IA is taxonomy development, which involves creating a classification system that organizes information into logical categories and subcategories. This system helps users locate and retrieve information based on their specific needs and preferences. IA also involves creating intuitive navigation systems that enable users to move through the information easily. This can include menus, links, breadcrumbs, and search functionality. By designing effective navigation, IA ensures that users can quickly and efficiently find the information they are looking for. Additionally, IA focuses on the labeling and organization of content to ensure clarity and consistency. This involves creating clear and concise titles, headings, and descriptions that accurately describe the content. Consistent labeling and organization help users understand the relationship between different pieces of information and make informed decisions about which content to engage with. Overall, the goal of information architecture is to create a user-centered structure and organization of information that enhances the usability and findability of a system or website. By applying IA principles, designers can improve the overall user experience, making it easier for users to navigate, understand, and interact with the information they need.

User Scenario

Information Architecture (IA) refers to the practice of organizing, structuring, and labeling content in a way that facilitates seamless navigation and findability for users. It is a discipline that focuses on designing the information and content organization within a website, application, or digital platform. The main goal of Information Architecture is to create a clear and intuitive structure that enables users to easily understand and navigate through the information. This involves categorizing and arranging content in a logical and meaningful way, ensuring that users can easily find what they are looking for and understand the relationships between different pieces of information. Information Architecture takes into account various factors such as user needs, business goals, and technological constraints to create an effective information structure. It involves determining the appropriate taxonomy, hierarchy, and labeling of content elements to create a coherent and user-friendly experience. One of the key aspects of Information Architecture is the development of a navigation system that allows users to move through the content hierarchy and explore different sections of a website or application. This navigation system can include menus, breadcrumbs, search functionality, and other elements that enable users to easily locate and access the desired information. Furthermore, Information Architecture also considers the organization and labeling of individual content elements, such as pages, articles, images, and documents. This involves creating consistent and meaningful labels, metadata, and tagging that facilitate content discovery and retrieval. Overall, Information Architecture plays a crucial role in enhancing the usability and user experience of digital platforms. By creating a well-structured and intuitive information framework, it enables users to navigate effortlessly, find relevant information, and complete their desired tasks efficiently.

User Scenarios

Information Architecture (IA) is a discipline that focuses on organizing and structuring information to facilitate its effective retrieval and use. IA aims to create logical and intuitive information structures that support the goals of users and businesses. User Scenario 1: A user is visiting an e-commerce website to purchase a new laptop. They want to find information about different laptop models, compare their features, and make an informed decision. The website's IA needs to ensure that relevant information about laptop models is easily accessible, allowing the user to navigate through different categories, filter and sort the available options. The IA should also provide clear paths to product details, customer reviews, and purchase options, ensuring a seamless experience for the user. The e-commerce website's IA is organized into clearly defined categories, such as brand, price range, and specifications, allowing users to narrow down their search based on their preferences. Within each category, the IA provides options for sorting the results by price, popularity, and other relevant factors, helping users compare and evaluate different laptop models easily. User Scenario 2: A student is researching a specific topic for their assignment. They want to find reliable information from various sources, including academic journals, research papers, and online articles. The IA of a digital library platform needs to assist the student in easily discovering relevant resources, filtering them by publication date, author, and relevance. The IA should also provide clear paths for accessing full-text versions, citing references, and saving resources for later use. The digital library's IA offers a search bar prominently placed on the homepage, allowing users to enter keywords related to their research topic and retrieve relevant resources. The IA provides advanced search options, enabling users to refine their search results by selecting specific publication types, authors, or date ranges, facilitating more targeted and efficient research. In conclusion, Information Architecture plays a crucial role in organizing and structuring information to enhance user experience and achieve business goals. By creating logical and intuitive information structures, IA helps users navigate through complex information systems, find relevant content efficiently, and accomplish their tasks effectively.

User Stories

User stories are brief, narrative descriptions of the requirements and tasks that a user would like to accomplish when interacting with a website or application. In the context of Information Architecture (IA), user stories provide a structured way of capturing the needs and expectations of users, which helps in designing the structure and organization of information within a website or application. Each user story consists of three essential components: a user role, a goal or task, and a benefit. The user role represents the persona or type of user who will be using the website or application. The goal or task represents the specific action or objective the user wants to achieve. The benefit explains why the user wants to accomplish the goal or task, usually highlighting the value or advantage it brings to them. The user stories capture the user's perspective and act as a bridge between the development team and the end-users. They help in understanding the users' needs, motivations, and expectations and guide the decision-making process for creating an effective information architecture. By using user stories for IA, designers can identify the key tasks and goals users have, prioritize and organize information accordingly, and create a user-centered structure. It allows for a more intuitive and seamless navigation experience, enabling users to find the desired information or complete tasks efficiently. User stories also provide a foundation for conducting user testing and gathering feedback to validate and refine the information architecture. Overall, user stories in the context of Information Architecture contribute to a user-centric design process, ensuring that the structure and organization of information meet the needs and expectations of the intended users, ultimately leading to a more successful and engaging website or application.

User Story Mapping

User story mapping is a technique used in information architecture (IA) to visually organize and prioritize the functionality and user experience of a digital product or application. It involves the creation of a user-centric narrative that represents the flow of tasks and actions required to achieve specific goals within the system. The process of user story mapping starts by identifying the primary user roles or personas, along with their respective goals and motivations. These goals are then broken down into smaller, manageable tasks or user stories that describe specific actions or interactions that the user would perform within the system. Each user story is represented as a sticky note or card on a physical or virtual board, ordered according to their priority and any dependencies between them. By visualizing the user journey through a sequential arrangement of user stories, user story mapping enables IA professionals to gain a holistic understanding of the overall structure and flow of the system. It allows them to identify any gaps or inconsistencies in the user experience, as well as potential opportunities for improvement or innovation. The process of user story mapping also helps in identifying and prioritizing features and functionalities based on user needs and goals, rather than personal biases or assumptions. It fosters collaboration and alignment among stakeholders by providing a shared understanding of the system's purpose and the value it delivers to its users. User story mapping can also be used to facilitate iterative and incremental development, as it allows for the identification and prioritization of the minimum viable product (MVP) features. By focusing on delivering the most valuable functionality to users early on, user story mapping helps reduce the risk of developing unnecessary or unwanted features. In conclusion, user story mapping is an essential technique in IA that enables the organization and visualization of user-centric narratives. It helps prioritize functionality, identify gaps in the user experience, and align stakeholders around a shared understanding of the system's purpose. By focusing on user needs and goals, user story mapping promotes iterative development and the delivery of value to users.

User Task Analysis

Information Architecture (IA) is a discipline that focuses on the organization and structure of information within a system, such as a website or application. It involves designing and arranging information in a way that is easy to navigate and understand for users. IA aims to create a clear and logical structure for information, ensuring that users can find what they need quickly and efficiently. This involves organizing information into categories, subcategories, and other hierarchical structures, as well as creating intuitive navigation systems.

User-Centered Content

A user-centered content refers to the approach of designing and organizing information in a way that prioritizes the needs and expectations of the users. It focuses on creating content that is tailored to the users' goals, preferences, and behaviors, ensuring that they can easily find, understand, and engage with the information they are seeking. When implementing user-centered content in the context of Information Architecture (IA), the goal is to structure and present content in a logical and intuitive manner, taking into consideration the users' mental models and cognitive processes. This involves understanding the target audience and their specific needs, as well as conducting user research and testing to validate and refine the IA.

User-Centered Design Principles

User-Centered Design Principles prioritize the needs, goals, and preferences of the users in the design and development of information architecture (IA). Utilizing user-centered design principles allows for the creation of intuitive and efficient IA that optimizes the user experience. These principles include: 1. User Focus: The user is the primary focal point throughout the IA design process. Their needs, behavior, goals, and preferences are considered and prioritized to ensure the IA effectively caters to their requirements. 2. Inclusive Design: IA should be inclusive and accessible to all users, regardless of their abilities, languages, or cultural backgrounds. Design elements such as font size, color contrast, and navigation should be considered to accommodate diverse user groups. 3. Clear and Consistent Navigation: Intuitive and coherent navigation is essential to help users locate information quickly and effortlessly. Consistent placement, terminology, and visual cues guide users through the IA seamlessly. 4. Information Organization: IA should be structured in a logical and intuitive manner, enabling users to easily find and comprehend information. Grouping related content and providing clear headings and categories enhances the organization of information. 5. Contextual Relevance: IA should present information in context, meaning the user understands the purpose and relevance of the content within the broader context of their needs and goals. Providing clear context helps users make informed decisions and take appropriate actions. 6. Flexibility and Customization: IA should accommodate user preferences and offer customization options, allowing users to adjust the structure or layout based on their specific requirements. This personalization enhances user satisfaction and engagement. 7. Feedback and Guidance: The IA should provide timely feedback and clear guidance to users, validating their actions and informing them of system responses. Feedback can be in the form of visual cues, error messages, or confirmation notifications to enhance usability. By adhering to these user-centered design principles, IA can be optimized to align with user needs, facilitating efficient information retrieval, enhancing overall user satisfaction, and promoting the usability of the system.

User-Centered Design Process

User-Centered Design Process is a systematic approach that focuses on understanding the needs, goals, and behaviors of users to create meaningful and effective information architecture (IA) solutions. It aims to ensure that the IA is intuitive, user-friendly, and aligns with the behaviors and expectations of the target audience. The process begins with conducting user research, which involves gathering data through methods such as interviews, surveys, and observation. This helps in understanding the users' needs, goals, and preferences, as well as identifying any pain points or challenges they might face when interacting with the IA. The research findings serve as the foundation for the design decisions that follow. Based on the insights gained from the research, the next step is to define user personas and scenarios. Personas are fictional representations of different user types, while scenarios depict the tasks and goals that users might have when interacting with the IA. These personas and scenarios provide a clear understanding of the target audience and help in designing an IA that caters to their specific needs. The design phase involves creating prototypes and iteratively refining them based on user feedback. Wireframes and mockups are used to visualize the structure and layout of the IA, while interactive prototypes allow users to test the navigation and functionality. User feedback is invaluable at this stage, as it helps in identifying areas of improvement and refining the IA based on actual user behavior. Once the design is finalized, the IA is implemented, and usability testing is conducted to ensure that the IA performs as intended and meets the users' needs. This involves observing users as they interact with the IA, noting any difficulties they encounter, and making necessary adjustments to enhance the user experience. In summary, the User-Centered Design Process for Information Architecture involves understanding user needs, defining personas and scenarios, designing prototypes, incorporating user feedback, implementing the final design, and conducting usability testing. This iterative process ensures that the IA is user-friendly, intuitive, and aligned with the needs and behaviors of the target audience.

User-Centered Design (UCD)

User-Centered Design (UCD) is an approach to Information Architecture (IA) that focuses on

106

creating designs and experiences that meet the needs and goals of the users. It involves understanding and empathizing with the target audience, considering their perspectives and preferences, and involving them throughout the design process. In a UCD approach, the IA team conducts research to gain insights into the users' needs, goals, and behaviors. This research may involve interviews, surveys, observations, and other methods to gather data and understand the target users better. The team analyzes this data to form a clear understanding of the users and their requirements. Based on the insights gained from research, the IA team creates user personas, which represent the archetypal users of the system or website. These personas help the team to keep the end-users in mind throughout the design process and make decisions that align with their needs and goals. In the UCD approach, the IA team also creates user scenarios or user stories, which describe the typical tasks or interactions that users may have with the system or website. These scenarios help the team to design intuitive and user-friendly information structures and navigation systems that support the users' tasks and expectations. Prototyping and user testing are integral parts of UCD. The IA team creates prototypes or mock-ups of the design and conducts usability testing sessions with representative users. This allows the team to evaluate the design's effectiveness, identify any usability issues, and make iterative improvements based on the feedback received. Throughout the UCD process, the IA team collaborates closely with stakeholders, including users, clients, developers, and other relevant parties. This collaboration ensures that the final IA solution aligns with the users' needs and goals while also considering any constraints or requirements from the business or organizational perspective. In conclusion, User-Centered Design is an approach to Information Architecture that prioritizes the users' needs, goals, and perspectives. It involves researching and understanding the users, creating personas and user scenarios, prototyping and testing the design, and collaborating closely with stakeholders. By putting users at the center of the design process, UCD aims to create effective and user-friendly information architectures.

User-Centered Development

User-Centered Development is an approach in Information Architecture (IA) that prioritizes the needs and preferences of the end user during the process of designing and developing digital products or services. It aims to create intuitive and user-friendly experiences by placing the user at the center of the design process. In user-centered development, extensive research is conducted to gain a deep understanding of the target users, their goals, and their expectations. This research typically includes methods such as user interviews, observations, surveys, and usability tests. By gathering insights from real users, designers can identify their pain points, needs, and motivations, enabling them to create solutions that meet those needs effectively. Once the user research phase is complete, the information obtained is used to inform the design decisions. This includes creating user personas, which are fictional representations of the target users based on the research findings. Personas help designers empathize with users and make decisions that align with their goals and preferences. During the design phase, user-centered development emphasizes iterative prototyping and testing. Multiple versions of the design are created and tested with real users to gather feedback and make improvements. This iterative process allows designers to identify any usability issues early on and make necessary adjustments before the final implementation. Collaboration is a key aspect of user-centered development. Design teams often work closely with stakeholders, developers, and other professionals to ensure that all aspects of the product or service align with the users' expectations. This collaborative approach helps to create a holistic and seamless user experience. In conclusion, user-centered development in the context of Information Architecture involves conducting user research, creating user personas, iterating on design prototypes, and fostering collaboration to create digital products or services that prioritize the needs and preferences of the end user.

User-Centered Evaluation

User-centered evaluation refers to the process of systematically gathering and analyzing data to assess the effectiveness and usability of an information architecture (IA) from the perspective of its intended users. It involves evaluating how well the IA supports user tasks, goals, and needs, and identifying any areas for improvement. The primary goal of user-centered evaluation is to ensure that the IA is user-friendly, efficient, and intuitive. By involving users in the evaluation process, designers and developers can gain valuable insights into how the IA is perceived and used in real-world scenarios. This feedback can then be used to make informed decisions and adjustments to enhance the overall user experience. User-centered evaluation methods typically involve the collection of both qualitative and quantitative data. Qualitative data can be gathered through techniques such as user interviews, focus groups, and usability testing. These methods allow researchers to directly observe and listen to users as they interact with the IA, providing insights into their thoughts, feelings, and behaviors. Quantitative data, on the other hand, is often collected through surveys, questionnaires, and analytics tools. This data can help measure user satisfaction, efficiency, and performance metrics. The evaluation process typically follows a structured approach, starting with the identification of evaluation goals and objectives. This includes determining what aspects of the IA will be assessed and what specific questions will be answered. Next, appropriate evaluation methods and techniques are selected and implemented. Data is then collected, analyzed, and interpreted to identify patterns, trends, and areas for improvement. Finally, the findings are documented and communicated to stakeholders, such as designers, developers, and decision-makers, who can then take action based on the insights provided. By conducting user-centered evaluations, organizations can ensure that their IA meets the needs and expectations of their target users. This iterative process of evaluation and refinement leads to the creation of more effective and usable information architectures, ultimately enhancing user satisfaction, engagement, and productivity.

User-Centered Navigation

User-Centered Navigation is an approach in Information Architecture (IA) that focuses on designing and structuring a website or digital platform's navigation system based on the needs, behaviors, and expectations of its users. This approach ensures that users can easily find, understand, and navigate through the content or features they are looking for, enhancing their overall user experience. In User-Centered Navigation, the navigation system is designed to align with the mental models and mental processes of the target users. This requires understanding the users' goals, tasks, and preferences, as well as considering factors such as their level of expertise, familiarity with the domain, and technological proficiency. The design of the navigation system involves organizing and labeling website content or features in a way that is intuitive and meaningful to the users. This includes grouping related items together, providing clear and concise labels, and using navigational elements that are familiar and consistent with users' expectations. User-Centered Navigation also emphasizes the importance of providing multiple navigation paths or options to accommodate users' diverse needs and preferences. This can be achieved through strategies such as hierarchical menus, search functionality, breadcrumb trails, contextual links, or a combination of these. Additionally, User-Centered Navigation considers the usability principles of simplicity, consistency, and predictability. The navigation system should be straightforward and easy to use, with a consistent layout and interaction patterns across different pages or sections of the website. It should also provide visual cues or feedback to indicate users' current location within the site's structure, enabling them to understand their position and easily backtrack if needed. Overall, User-Centered Navigation aims to create a seamless and efficient user experience by ensuring that users can effortlessly navigate through a website or digital platform, find the content or features they seek, and accomplish their goals with minimal effort or frustration.

User-Centered Prototyping

The user-centered prototyping in the context of Information Architecture (IA) refers to a design approach that focuses on creating prototypes of a system or interface that incorporate the needs and requirements of end users. It is a process where designers and architects develop prototypes that closely simulate the final product, allowing users to interact with it and provide feedback. The goal is to gather valuable insights and refine the design based on user input, ensuring that the final product meets their needs and expectations.

User-Centered Requirements

A user-centered requirement refers to a specific need or expectation that is derived from the perspectives, goals, and tasks of the target user group in the context of information architecture (IA). It emphasizes the importance of placing the user at the center of the design process, ensuring that the IA meets their needs and supports their goals effectively. User-centered requirements in IA are essential for creating an intuitive and usable information structure. To identify these requirements, the IA designer must conduct thorough user research, including user interviews, surveys, and user testing. This helps in gaining insights into their requirements, preferences, and behaviors when interacting with the information system. By prioritizing user needs, the IA designer can focus on organizing and structuring the information in a way that makes it easily accessible and meaningful to the users. This includes considering factors such as content hierarchy, navigation design, and labeling conventions that best align with the users' mental models and expectations. User-centered requirements also play a crucial role in determining the overall user experience (UX) of the IA. It ensures that the information is presented in a clear and understandable manner, minimizing cognitive load and helping users find what they need efficiently. Additionally, a user-centered approach allows for iterative design and evaluation, incorporating user feedback and making necessary adjustments to enhance the IA over time. In summary, user-centered requirements in the context of IA refer to the needs and expectations of the target users, which are used to guide the design and organization of information in a way that optimizes usability and supports the users' goals and tasks effectively.

User-Centered Testing

User-Centered Testing is a method used in Information Architecture (IA) to evaluate the effectiveness and efficiency of a website or application in meeting the needs and goals of its users. It is a systematic approach that involves gathering feedback and insights from real users to inform the design and organization of content and functionality. During User-Centered Testing, a variety of techniques may be used, such as usability testing, interviews, surveys, and card sorting. Usability testing involves observing users as they perform specific tasks on the website or application, while interviews and surveys gather qualitative and quantitative data about user preferences, expectations, and satisfaction. Card sorting, on the other hand, allows users to group and categorize content in a way that makes sense to them. The goal of User-Centered Testing is to uncover any usability issues and identify opportunities for improvement in the IA. By involving real users in the testing process, designers and developers can gain valuable insights about how well the IA aligns with user expectations, mental models, and workflows. This data can then be used to make informed decisions and refinements that lead to a more user-friendly and efficient digital experience. User-Centered Testing is an iterative process that is typically conducted throughout the design and development lifecycle. By testing early and often, designers can validate their assumptions and gather feedback at different stages of the IA's development. This allows for early detection and resolution of usability issues, leading to a more robust and user-centric IA.

User-Centered Web Design

User-Centered Web Design is an approach that prioritizes the needs and goals of the users in order to create effective and intuitive web interfaces. It is a fundamental principle of Information Architecture (IA), which focuses on organizing, structuring, and labeling information in an understandable and accessible manner. In user-centered design, the website's architecture is designed around the users' mental models, behaviors, and expectations. This involves conducting user research, such as interviews, surveys, and usability testing, to better understand the target audience and their preferences. By understanding the users' needs, designers can create navigation systems, interaction patterns, and content layouts that align with users' expectations, providing them with a seamless and satisfying browsing experience. User-centered design also emphasizes the importance of usability, ensuring that the website is easy to use and navigate. This includes streamlining the navigation structure, minimizing cognitive load, and providing clear and concise labels and instructions. By focusing on usability, designers can eliminate obstacles and frustrations that users may encounter, enhancing their overall satisfaction with the website. Furthermore, user-centered design takes into consideration the accessibility of the web interface. It aims to ensure that all users, regardless of their abilities, can access and navigate the website effectively. This involves following web accessibility guidelines, such as using proper headings, descriptive link texts, and alternative text for images, as well as providing options for font sizes and color contrasts. Overall, user-centered web design in the context of Information Architecture is an iterative process that places the users at the center of the design decisions. It considers their needs, behaviors, and abilities to create websites that are intuitive, usable, and accessible. By adopting this approach, designers can create web interfaces that meet the users' expectations, enhance their browsing experience, and ultimately achieve the goals of the website owner or organization.

109

User-Centric Navigation

User-Centric Navigation refers to the design and implementation of an intuitive and user-friendly navigation system within the context of Information Architecture (IA). It focuses on creating a seamless and efficient browsing experience for users, allowing them to easily navigate and find the desired information on a website or application. In user-centric navigation, the navigation system is designed with the needs, mental models, and expectations of the target users in mind. It takes into account their preferences, goals, and behavior patterns to create a navigation structure that is intuitive and easy to understand.

User-Experience Design (UXD)

User-Experience Design (UXD) is a discipline within the field of Information Architecture (IA), focused on creating meaningful and effective experiences for users while they interact with digital products or systems. It encompasses all aspects of a user's interaction with a product, including visual design, information architecture, usability, and accessibility. The goal of UXD is to enhance the user's satisfaction and improve the usability and usefulness of a digital product or system. It seeks to understand the user's needs, goals, and motivations in order to design intuitive interfaces that meet those needs and provide a seamless and enjoyable experience. UXD involves conducting user research to gain insights into user behavior and preferences. This research helps inform the design decisions and ensures that the end product meets the needs and expectations of the target users. User research methods may include interviews, surveys, usability testing, and user journey mapping. Information architecture plays a key role in UXD, as it focuses on organizing and structuring information in a way that facilitates easy navigation and retrieval. It involves creating a clear and logical structure for the content, ensuring that the information hierarchy is well-defined, and implementing effective navigation patterns. UX designers also pay close attention to the visual design of a product, ensuring that it is visually appealing and aligns with the brand's identity. They use visual elements such as color, typography, and imagery to create engaging and aesthetically pleasing interfaces. Usability testing is another important component of UXD, where designers evaluate the usability of a product by observing users as they interact with it. This helps identify any usability issues or pain points and allows designers to make iterative improvements based on user feedback. In addition, accessibility is a key consideration in UXD, as it ensures that digital products can be used by people with disabilities. UX designers strive to create inclusive designs that are usable and accessible to users with different abilities, by adhering to accessibility guidelines and standards.

User-Experience Goals

User-Experience Goals, in the context of Information Architecture (IA), refer to the specific outcomes or objectives that are desired for the overall experience of users interacting with a digital product or website. These goals are based on understanding the needs, motivations, and expectations of the target audience and strive to deliver a positive and meaningful experience. User-Experience Goals are key considerations in IA as they directly influence the design and structure of information. They guide the organization and presentation of content, navigation systems, and interactions, ensuring that users can easily find what they need and accomplish their goals efficiently.

User-Experience Map

An User-Experience Map is a visual representation or diagram that illustrates the overall user experience with a particular product or service. It is an essential tool in Information Architecture (IA) that helps designers and architects to understand and analyze the user's journey, emotions, and interactions throughout their experience. The purpose of creating a User-Experience Map is to gain insights into the user's needs, pain points, and motivations, allowing the IA team to design an effective and user-centered information structure. The map provides a holistic view of the user's touchpoints, enabling the team to identify both positive and negative aspects of the experience and make informed decisions to improve it.

User-Experience Prototyping

User experience prototyping refers to the process of creating a representative model or simulation of a proposed digital interface or system, with the aim of evaluating its usability and effectiveness. In the context of Information Architecture (IA), it involves the creation of interactive prototypes that mimic the functionality and user interactions of the final product. The primary goal of user experience prototyping is to understand how users interact with a system and identify potential usability issues or design flaws early in the development process. By simulating the user experience, designers can gather feedback, test different design alternatives, and refine the IA based on user insights. Prototyping in the IA domain typically involves the construction of low-fidelity or high-fidelity prototypes. Low-fidelity prototypes are quick and simple representations of the intended user interface, often created using pen and paper, or digital wireframing tools. These prototypes focus on the basic structure and layout, allowing designers to test the organization and labeling of information without investing significant time or resources. High-fidelity prototypes, on the other hand, aim to closely mimic the final product, often utilizing interactive tools or programming languages to replicate user interactions and functionality. These prototypes provide a more realistic representation of the user experience and allow designers to evaluate the effectiveness of the IA in a more accurate context. User testing is a crucial aspect of user experience prototyping in IA. By observing and analyzing how users interact with the prototype, designers can gain valuable insights into navigation patterns, information retrieval, and overall user satisfaction. This feedback can then be used to inform design decisions and iterate on the IA to create a more user-centered and efficient system. In conclusion, user experience prototyping in the context of IA involves the creation of interactive models or simulations that simulate the user experience of a proposed digital system. By testing and evaluating these prototypes, designers can identify usability issues, gather user feedback, and refine the IA to improve the overall user experience.

User-Experience Research

User-Experience Research in the context of Information Architecture (IA) is a systematic approach to understanding and improving how users interact with and perceive an information system or website. It involves gathering and analyzing data about user behavior, preferences, and needs to inform the design and organization of digital information. To conduct User-Experience Research for Information Architecture, a variety of qualitative and quantitative methods can be employed. These methods typically include user interviews, surveys, usability testing, card sorting, and analytics analysis. The primary goal is to gain insights into user perceptions, preferences, and usage patterns, and to align the IA with user needs and expectations. User interviews provide an opportunity to gather in-depth qualitative data about user goals, expectations, and experiences. Through open-ended questions, researchers can uncover user mental models and information seeking behaviors, which can inform the structuring and labeling of information within the IA. Surveys are an efficient way to collect quantitative data from a larger sample of users. They can help identify trends, patterns, and preferences related to content organization and navigation, enhancing the IA design decisions. Usability testing involves observing users as they interact with a prototype or a live system. This method helps researchers identify usability issues, pain points, and potential improvements within the IA. It also provides insight into the effectiveness and efficiency of the IA design, allowing for iterative improvements. Card sorting is a method in which participants categorize and organize information into groups according to their mental models. This technique helps to understand how users conceptually organize and relate information, providing valuable input for structuring and grouping content within the IA. Analytics analysis involves leveraging data from tools like Google Analytics to gain insights into user behavior, such as popular pages, user flow, and search queries. This data can inform IA decisions, such as prioritizing content, optimizing navigation, and improving search functionality. By employing User-Experience Research methods in the context of Information Architecture, designers can create user-centric IA designs that effectively organize and present information to users. This approach fosters intuitive navigation, efficient information retrieval, and overall user satisfaction.

User-Experience Testing

User-Experience Testing in the context of Information Architecture (IA) refers to the process of evaluating and measuring the effectiveness, efficiency, and satisfaction of users when interacting with an IA system or website. It involves conducting experiments, gathering insights, and collecting feedback from users to improve the design and functionality of the IA. This type of testing is essential for IA development as it helps ensure that the design is user-centered, intuitive, and easy to navigate. By testing the IA, designers can identify potential usability issues, understand user behaviors and preferences, and make informed decisions to enhance the overall user experience. User-Experience Testing can be conducted through various methods, including: 1. Usability Testing: This method involves observing users as they perform specific tasks using the IA system. Test participants are given a series of tasks to complete, while their interactions with the system are closely monitored. The goal is to identify any difficulties, errors, or confusion encountered during the process. This direct observation helps designers gain insights into the usability and effectiveness of the IA. 2. A/B Testing: This method involves comparing two different versions of an IA system or webpage to determine which one performs better in terms of user experience. Users are randomly assigned to either version, and their interactions and behaviors are measured and analyzed. A/B testing allows designers to understand user preferences, optimize the IA, and make data-driven decisions. 3. Surveys and Questionnaires: These tools are used to gather feedback and opinions from users about their experiences with the IA system. Surveys can provide valuable insights into user satisfaction, ease of use, and overall perceptions of the IA. By collecting quantitative and qualitative data through surveys, designers can identify areas for improvement and prioritize future enhancements. 4. Eye Tracking: This method involves using specialized hardware and software to monitor and record the eye movements and gaze patterns of users as they navigate the IA system. Eye tracking provides valuable data on where users focus their attention, what elements they overlook, and how they visually explore the IA. This information helps designers optimize the placement and visual hierarchy of elements within the IA. In conclusion, User-Experience Testing is a crucial component of Information Architecture development. By testing and evaluating the IA system with real users, designers can ensure that the system is intuitive, user-friendly, and meets the needs and expectations of its intended audience.

User-Experience Wireframe

A User-Experience Wireframe, within the context of Information Architecture (IA), refers to a visual representation of a website or application's structure and layout. It is a low-fidelity design that showcases the fundamental elements, functionalities, and content of the digital product, allowing stakeholders to gather feedback and make informed decisions before proceeding to higher-fidelity designs. A wireframe serves as a blueprint for the user interface (UI), presenting a skeletal framework that focuses on the arrangement of elements, such as navigation menus, content sections, and interactive components, without concerning itself with aesthetics or detailed visual design. It helps shape the hierarchy, flow, and organization of information, guiding designers and developers in creating an intuitive and seamless user experience. The primary goal of creating wireframes is to ensure clarity and effective communication of ideas among project teams. By using simple shapes, lines, and placeholders, a wireframe outlines the overall structure and functionality of the website or application, enabling stakeholders to visualize the user journey and understand the core functionalities without being distracted by visual design elements. Wireframes also play a crucial role in user testing and obtaining user feedback. By presenting a simplified representation of the digital product, testers can focus on evaluating the usability and functionality of the interface, providing valuable insights early in the design process. This iterative approach allows for adjustments and optimizations to be made prior to investing significant time and resources into higher-fidelity designs. When creating wireframes, it is important to consider the target audience and their needs. IA practitioners should prioritize the clarity of information and navigational paths, ensuring that the wireframe effectively communicates the intended user flow and interactions. Furthermore, wireframes should align with the overall information architecture strategy, reflecting the established IA principles and best practices.

User-Feedback Analysis

Information Architecture (IA) is a discipline within the field of user experience design that focuses on the organization, structure, and labeling of information in digital products and services. It involves the creation and maintenance of clear and logical pathways for users to navigate through information, ensuring that the content is presented in a way that is intuitive, accessible, and meets the needs of the target audience. IA aims to provide users with a seamless and meaningful user experience by effectively organizing and categorizing information. This involves understanding the users' mental models, information needs, and goals in order to create a structure that supports efficient and effective information retrieval. IA helps users find what they are looking for quickly and easily, reducing cognitive load and frustration.

User-Feedback Gathering

Information Architecture (IA) is a discipline that involves the design and organization of information to support effective user experiences. It focuses on structuring, labeling, and categorizing information in a way that helps users easily navigate and find what they need within a website, application, or other digital platform. IA plays a crucial role in creating intuitive and user-centered interfaces, ensuring that users can understand the content and functionality available to them. It considers the overall structure of the information and its relationships, as well as the presentation and layout of navigational elements.

User-Friendly Design

User-Friendly Design, within the context of Information Architecture (IA), refers to the practice of creating digital interfaces and systems that are intuitive, efficient, and enjoyable for users to navigate and interact with. The main goal of user-friendly design is to ensure that users can easily find and access the information or functionality they need, without encountering unnecessary complexity or confusion. A user-friendly design incorporates various principles and techniques to enhance the overall user experience. One important aspect is the organization and structure of information. This involves arranging content in a logical and meaningful way, grouping related items together, and providing clear labels and headings. By implementing a consistent and intuitive navigation system, users can easily locate and move between different sections of a website or application. Another key consideration is the use of visual cues and feedback. User-friendly interfaces make effective use of color, typography, and imagery to guide users and draw attention to important elements. Providing visual indications of interactive elements, such as buttons or links, helps users understand how to interact with the interface. Additionally, providing feedback to user actions, such as changes in color or animation, helps users understand their progress and confirms that their actions have been successfully executed. Usability is a fundamental aspect of user-friendly design. It involves considering the abilities, needs, and limitations of users when designing interfaces. User research, testing, and feedback play important roles in identifying potential usability issues and improving the overall design. By incorporating user feedback throughout the design process, designers can iteratively enhance the user experience and address any pain points or difficulties encountered by users. In conclusion, user-friendly design in the context of Information Architecture (IA) focuses on creating interfaces and systems that are intuitive, efficient, and enjoyable for users to navigate and interact with. Through effective organization, clear visual cues, and consideration of usability principles, user-friendly design strives to provide users with a seamless and satisfying experience.

User-Interface Design Tools

User-interface design tools, in the context of Information Architecture (IA), are software or applications that support the creation and development of visually appealing and user-friendly interfaces for digital products or websites. These tools enable designers and developers to efficiently organize and present information, content, and functionality in a way that maximizes usability, accessibility, and overall user experience. By utilizing user-interface design tools, IA professionals can effectively plan and structure the layout, navigation, and interaction elements of a digital interface. These tools often provide a range of features such as wireframing, prototyping, and visual design capabilities, allowing designers to iterate and refine their designs before implementation.

User-Interface Design (UID)

User-Interface Design (UID) is a discipline within the field of Information Architecture (IA) that focuses on the visual design and layout of the user interface (UI) of a digital product or system. It involves creating a visually appealing and intuitive interface that allows users to easily interact with the information and functionality of the product. UID encompasses various aspects, including the arrangement of elements on the screen, the use of color and typography, the consistency of design throughout the system, and the overall user experience. It aims to enhance the usability and accessibility of the product by providing clear and logical navigation, intuitive controls, and informative feedback. In the context of Information Architecture (IA), UID plays a crucial role in organizing and presenting information in a way that aligns with the user's mental model and enables efficient information retrieval. It focuses on creating a coherent and structured visual representation of the information architecture, facilitating the user's understanding and interaction with the content. Effective user-interface design is essential for a successful digital product or system. It enables users to quickly grasp the purpose and functionality of the system, reducing the learning curve and increasing user satisfaction. By providing an aesthetically pleasing and visually coherent interface, UID also helps establish a positive brand impression and builds trust with the users. To achieve a well-designed user interface, designers apply various principles and techniques, such as visual hierarchy, balance, contrast, and proximity. They also consider factors such as user goals, cognitive load, and contextual factors to create an interface that meets the needs and expectations of the target audience. In conclusion, User-Interface Design (UID) in the context of Information Architecture (IA) is the discipline that focuses on creating visually appealing and intuitive interfaces for digital products or systems. It aims to enhance usability and accessibility by organizing and presenting information in a coherent and structured manner. Effective UID plays a crucial role in facilitating user interaction, reducing cognitive load, and increasing user satisfaction.

User-Interface Elements

User-interface elements refer to the components and features that make up the visual and interactive aspects of a website or application. These elements are designed to facilitate user interaction and enhance the overall user experience (UX). In the context of Information Architecture (IA), user-interface elements play a crucial role in organizing, structuring, and presenting information in a way that is intuitive, accessible, and engaging. They help users navigate through the digital space, locate relevant content, and interact with the system effectively. User-interface elements can include a wide range of components, such as navigation menus, buttons, forms, search bars, sliders, tabs, icons, and images. Each of these elements serves a specific purpose and contributes to the overall functionality and usability of the interface. Navigation menus allow users to move between different sections or pages of a website, enabling them to find the desired information quickly. Buttons are interactive elements that trigger specific actions when clicked or tapped. Forms are used to collect user input, such as personal information, feedback, or search queries. Search bars facilitate searching for specific content within a website or application. Sliders and tabs are often used to display and navigate through different sets of information or media. Icons are visual symbols that represent a particular action, concept, or entity, enhancing the visual communication and guiding user interactions. Images help convey information, set the mood, or provide visual interest. Each user-interface element should be designed with careful consideration of its placement, size, color, and other visual attributes to ensure optimal user comprehension and engagement. Consistency and coherence in the design and placement of these elements throughout the interface are essential for creating a cohesive and intuitive user experience. In summary, user-interface elements are the various components and features that form the visual and interactive aspects of a website or application. In the context of Information Architecture, these elements are designed to organize and present information in a user-friendly and intuitive way, enhancing navigation, interaction, and overall user experience.

User-Interface Guidelines

User interface guidelines in the context of Information Architecture (IA) are a set of principles and recommendations that help designers and developers create intuitive, consistent, and user-friendly interfaces for digital products. These guidelines ensure that the interface elements and interactions are easily understandable, accessible, and efficient for the target audience. IA focuses on organizing, structuring, and labeling information to support findability and usability. User interface guidelines in IA consider how the information architecture is presented to users through the interface design.

User-Interface Patterns

User-Interface patterns are pre-established, commonly accepted solutions to user interface design problems. Evidenced through repeated use in various applications, these patterns provide effective ways to solve recurring design problems. They serve as guidelines or best practices in information architecture (IA) to improve the usability and user experience of digital products. User-Interface patterns in IA help designers and developers to design and implement consistent and predictable user interfaces. These patterns can be applied to navigation, layout, interaction, and content organization. By following these patterns, designers can create intuitive interfaces that users are familiar with, reducing the learning curve and promoting efficient navigation. Navigation patterns in IA include the use of menus, breadcrumbs, and tabs. These patterns provide users with clear and consistent ways to move through the information space, making it easier for them to find the desired content. Menu patterns, such as dropdown menus or mega menus, allow users to access a wide range of options in a hierarchical structure, ensuring efficient access to all available content. Breadcrumbs patterns indicate the user's current location within the website's hierarchy, helping them understand the overall structure and providing a clear path for navigation. Tab patterns allow users to switch between different sections or categories of information without losing their place, improving the overall usability of the interface. Layout patterns in IA help designers organize and present content in a clear and visually appealing manner. Grid layouts, card layouts, and magazine layouts are commonly used patterns that provide a consistent structure for presenting information. Grid layouts use a system of rows and columns to align and organize content, ensuring a visually balanced interface. Card layouts break down information into digestible chunks, making it easier for users to scan and locate specific content. Magazine layouts create a visual hierarchy by using different-sized and differently-arranged content elements, guiding users through the content in a natural flow. Interaction patterns in IA guide the way users interact with the interface. Input patterns, such as forms or search boxes, provide a consistent way for users to input information or perform searches. Feedback patterns, such as tooltips or progress indicators, keep users informed about the status or result of their actions, improving the overall user experience. Modal patterns, such as pop-ups or overlays, provide focused interactions by temporarily taking control of the user's attention, reducing cognitive load and enhancing task completion. Content organization patterns in IA help designers structure and categorize information in a logical and meaningful way. These patterns include hierarchical structures, tag-based structures, and alphabetical structures. Hierarchical structures use parent-child relationships to organize content, allowing users to drill down into specific categories or topics. Tag-based structures allow users to filter and discover content based on specific tags or labels, facilitating personalized content exploration. Alphabetical structures provide users with a familiar order for accessing and locating information, especially in content-heavy interfaces. In conclusion, User-Interface patterns in the context of Information Architecture are pre-established design solutions that help designers and developers create intuitive, consistent, and user-friendly interfaces. By applying these patterns, IA professionals can enhance the usability and user experience of digital products, ultimately leading to higher user satisfaction and improved business outcomes.

User-Interface Principles

User interface principles in the context of Information Architecture (IA) refer to the guiding rules and principles that dictate the design and organization of the elements within a digital interface to enhance user experience and facilitate effective interaction with the system or website. These principles help to ensure that the interface is intuitive, user-friendly, and visually appealing, enabling users to navigate and access information easily. One important principle is consistency, which entails presenting information and interface elements in a uniform manner throughout the system. Consistency allows users to develop mental models and expectations, making it easier for them to understand and use the interface efficiently. This principle is achieved by using standardized design components, such as headings, buttons, menus, and icons, that are consistently placed and styled across all pages. Another principle is simplicity, which emphasizes the need for clear and concise design with minimal complexity. A simple interface avoids overload and confusion, making it easier for users to focus on the main tasks and objectives. Simplicity can be achieved by removing unnecessary elements, reducing cognitive load, and organizing information in a logical and intuitive manner. Clarity is another vital principle that focuses on the use of clear and unambiguous language, labels, and instructions. Clear communication helps users understand the purpose and functionality of different interface elements. It involves using plain and simple language that is easily comprehensible to a wide range of users, avoiding jargon or technical terms that may be unfamiliar to some users. Effective navigation is another essential principle of user interface design in IA. It involves providing users with clear and consistent navigation options that enable easy exploration and access to different sections or pages within the system. Effective navigation can be achieved through the use of clear menu structures, breadcrumbs, and sitemaps, allowing users to understand their current location and easily navigate backward or forward within the system. Lastly, responsiveness is a crucial principle that focuses on designing interfaces that adapt and respond to user interactions and different device capabilities. A responsive interface ensures that the system is accessible and usable across various devices and screen sizes, providing a consistent experience to users regardless of the platform they are using. By adhering to these user interface principles in the context of Information Architecture (IA), designers can create interfaces that are intuitive, user-friendly, aesthetically pleasing, and efficient, ultimately enhancing the user experience and improving overall system usability.

User-Interface Prototyping

User-Interface Prototyping is a technique used in Information Architecture (IA) to create visual representations of the user interface of a digital product before it is developed. It involves the creation of low-fidelity or high-fidelity prototypes that simulate the user interface, allowing designers, stakeholders, and users to interact with and provide feedback on the proposed design. Prototyping is an essential part of the IA process as it helps to validate and refine the design concepts, ensure usability, and gather valuable user feedback early in the development cycle. The goal of user-interface prototyping is to create a tangible representation of the proposed user interface that closely resembles the final product, allowing for a realistic evaluation of its functionality, usability, and overall user experience. User-interface prototypes can range from simple paper sketches to interactive digital prototypes, depending on the level of fidelity required at each stage of the design process. Low-fidelity prototypes are often used in the early stages of design to quickly explore different design concepts and gather initial feedback. These prototypes are usually created using sketching tools or mockup software and focus on the structural layout and flow of the user interface. High-fidelity prototypes, on the other hand, provide a more advanced representation of the user interface, often including visual design elements, interactive elements, and realistic content. These prototypes are typically created using specialized software or web development tools and are used to simulate the actual user experience more closely. User-interface prototyping allows designers to iterate and refine the design based on user feedback, usability testing, and stakeholder requirements. It helps to identify potential design flaws, usability issues, or areas for improvement before the development phase begins, saving time, effort, and resources. In conclusion, user-interface prototyping is a vital technique in Information Architecture that allows designers to create visual representations of the proposed user interface. Through the use of low-fidelity and high-fidelity prototypes, designers can gather valuable feedback and refine the design before development, ultimately leading to a more usable and successful digital product.

User-Interface Testing

User-Interface Testing, within the context of Information Architecture (IA), refers to the evaluation and assessment of the visual and interactive elements of a website or application. It focuses on ensuring that these components align with the intended user experience and conform to established design guidelines. User-Interface Testing aims to validate the effectiveness, usability, and accessibility of the interface, as well as identify any potential usability issues or inconsistencies that may hinder optimal user engagement and satisfaction. During User-Interface Testing, IA professionals carefully examine the design elements, layout, and functionality of the interface. They evaluate how users interact with the interface, the ease of navigation, and the clarity of information presented. This type of testing involves both visual inspection and interactive exploration, and may employ various testing techniques, such as heuristic evaluations, usability testing, or expert reviews.

User-Interface Wireframe

A User-Interface Wireframe is a visual representation that outlines the structure and functionality of a digital interface. It is a skeletal framework that depicts the various elements and their placement within the interface, allowing designers and stakeholders to understand the overall layout and interaction flow. Wireframes are created during the initial stages of the design process and serve as a blueprint for the user interface. They provide a clear and concise representation of the intended design, without getting into the specifics of colors, typography, or visual elements. Instead, wireframes focus on the arrangement and hierarchy of the interface elements, such as buttons, form fields, navigation menus, and content areas. The primary purpose of a wireframe is to establish the information architecture (IA) of a digital product, ensuring that the layout and organization of content are intuitive and user-friendly. By mapping out the structure of the interface, designers can easily identify potential usability issues and make necessary adjustments before proceeding to the visual design stage. Wireframes are typically created using low-fidelity tools like pen and paper, or digital equivalents such as wireframing software or graphic design tools. They are intentionally kept simple and devoid of visual distractions to emphasize the UX/UI framework. This allows designers to quickly iterate and test different design ideas without investing too much time and effort into detailed visual elements. Wireframes can be categorized into several types, including: 1. Low-Fidelity Wireframes: These are basic, grayscale representations that focus solely on the core layout and content structure. They are quick to create and ideal for early concept validation and user testing. 2. Mid-Fidelity Wireframes: These wireframes add more detail to the low-fidelity version by including annotations, labels, and basic styling. They provide a clearer representation of the interface without compromising flexibility. 3. High-Fidelity Wireframes: These wireframes closely resemble the final design, incorporating visual elements like color, typography, and images. They are typically used for detailed design evaluations, presenting a more realistic experience to stakeholders. In conclusion, user-interface wireframes are essential tools in the information architecture process. They help designers and stakeholders visualize the structure of a digital interface, facilitating effective communication and decision-making. By focusing on layout and functionality, wireframes lay the foundation for a well-organized and user-centric user interface design.

User-Research Analysis

Information Architecture (IA) is a discipline that involves the organization and categorization of information to enhance the usability, accessibility, and findability of digital products and services. IA focuses on structuring information in a logical and intuitive manner so that users can easily navigate and understand the content. The primary goal of IA is to create a clear and coherent structure that allows users to efficiently locate and interact with information. This involves several key activities, including content analysis, user research, and the development of navigation systems and metadata schemas. One of the main aspects of IA is the creation of a well-defined and intuitive navigation system. This involves designing menus, links, and other navigation elements that guide users through different sections of a website or application. The navigation system should be consistent, predictable, and reflect the overall structure of the information. Another crucial aspect of IA is the development of a comprehensive metadata schema. Metadata refers to descriptive information about the content, such as titles, tags, and descriptions. A well-designed metadata schema enables efficient searching and filtering of information, allowing users to quickly find what they are looking for. The process of IA also involves conducting user research to understand the needs, goals, and mental models of users. This can be done through various methods, such as interviews, surveys, and usability testing. By gaining insights into user behaviors and preferences, IA professionals can make informed decisions about the organization and presentation of information. In conclusion, Information Architecture is a discipline that focuses on the organization and categorization of information to improve the usability and accessibility of digital products and services. By creating clear and logical structures, designing effective navigation systems, and incorporating user research, IA professionals ensure that users can easily locate, understand, and interact with information.

User-Research Findings

User research findings refer to the results and insights obtained from conducting research with users in order to understand their needs, behaviors, and preferences. As part of the information architecture (IA) process, user research findings are used to inform the design and organization of information within a system or website. The goal of user research is to gather data and insights directly from users through various qualitative and quantitative research methods. These methods can include interviews, surveys, usability testing, card sorting, and observation. By engaging with users, IA practitioners can gather a deep understanding of their goals, motivations, and challenges when interacting with information systems. Once user research is conducted and the findings are analyzed, IA practitioners can use the insights to make informed decisions about how to structure and organize information. These findings can help identify key

117

user tasks, content priorities, and user mental models. By understanding users' mental models and information-seeking behaviors, IA practitioners can design systems that are intuitive and user-friendly. User research findings also play a crucial role in validating and refining IA designs. By involving users throughout the design process and continuously testing and gathering feedback, IA practitioners can ensure that the information architecture meets users' needs and expectations.

User-Research Methods

User research methods in the context of Information Architecture (IA) refer to the systematic approaches used to gather and analyze insights about users, their behaviors, needs, and preferences. These methods aim to inform the design and development of IA, ensuring that it aligns with user expectations and goals. The goal of user research in IA is to create a user-centered information structure that organizes and presents content in a way that is intuitive, efficient, and meets the needs of the target audience. By understanding users' mental models, their expectations, and their information-seeking behaviors, IA practitioners can create a structure that enables users to easily find, comprehend, and navigate through information.

User-Research Planning

Information Architecture (IA) is a field within the larger discipline of user experience design that focuses on organizing and structuring information in a way that is intuitive and user-friendly. It involves the systematic organization, labeling, and navigation of digital content, such as websites, applications, and databases, to make it accessible and understandable for users. The goal of IA is to design coherent and meaningful structures that allow users to find and understand information quickly and easily. This is achieved by analyzing user needs and behaviors, conducting research, and applying principles of organization, categorization, and navigation. IA professionals use various techniques and tools, such as card sorting, user interviews, surveys, and usability testing, to gather insights and feedback from users and stakeholders.

User-Research Reporting

User research reporting in the context of Information Architecture (IA) refers to the process of documenting and presenting the findings, insights, and recommendations derived from user research activities carried out during the IA design process. This reporting allows IA professionals to communicate the results of their user research efforts to stakeholders, such as clients, designers, developers, and other team members involved in the IA project. It serves as a means to share the knowledge gained from engaging with users, understanding their needs, and evaluating the effectiveness of the IA design solutions.

User-Task Analysis

Information Architecture (IA) refers to the practice of organizing, structuring, and labeling content in a way that promotes effective information retrieval and navigation. It involves designing and implementing the structure and organization of a website, application, or other digital product to ensure that users can easily find and access the information they need. The goal of IA is to create a logical and intuitive system that allows users to understand the relationships between different pieces of information and navigate through them efficiently. This is achieved through the use of various techniques, such as creating clear and consistent navigation menus, organizing content into categories or hierarchies, and defining meaningful labels and metadata.

User-Task Flow

An information architecture (IA) user-task flow is a representation of the steps and interactions that a user goes through to complete a specific task or achieve a particular goal on a website or application. It presents the sequence of actions and the relationships between those actions, providing a clear and structured path for users to follow. The IA user-task flow helps designers and developers understand the user's journey by visually mapping out the different steps, from the initial entry point to the final outcome. It aims to optimize the user experience by identifying potential hurdles or inefficiencies in the task flow and finding ways to streamline or improve the process.

User-Task Flowchart

The User-Task Flowchart is a visual representation in Information Architecture (IA) that illustrates the sequence of actions and interactions between a user and a system to accomplish a specific task. It provides a structured overview of the steps and decision points involved in completing a task, helping to identify potential user challenges and improve the overall user experience. Within the User-Task Flowchart, the user's goals and actions are depicted alongside the system's responses and outputs, creating a comprehensive understanding of the task flow. It encompasses the various paths, branches, and outcomes that can occur during the user's interaction, allowing designers and developers to anticipate and address user needs and pain points.

User-Task Mapping

Mapping user tasks to information architecture involves the process of aligning the tasks that users need to accomplish with the corresponding structure and organization of information within a website or application. This mapping is crucial in ensuring that users can easily find and access the information they need in order to complete their tasks effectively and efficiently. The user-task mapping process typically begins with a thorough understanding of the users and their goals. This involves conducting user research, such as interviews, surveys, and usability testing, to gain insights into the tasks that users commonly perform and the information they seek. By understanding users' goals and behaviors, designers can create an information architecture that supports these tasks and facilitates a smooth user experience. The next step in user-task mapping is to analyze and categorize the information that needs to be presented to users. This involves organizing and structuring the content in a logical and intuitive manner, taking into consideration the relationships between different pieces of information. Designers may use techniques such as card sorting or tree testing to help determine the most effective and logical ways to organize the information. Once the information has been organized, designers can then map specific user tasks to the corresponding sections or areas within the information architecture. This involves identifying the pathways or navigation paths that users would most likely take to accomplish their tasks. By aligning the tasks with the structure of the information architecture, users can easily locate the relevant information and navigate through the website or application without confusion or frustration. Throughout the user-task mapping process, designers should continuously validate their decisions through user testing and feedback. This iterative approach allows for refinement and optimization of the information architecture to better meet the needs and expectations of the target users.

User-Task Modeling

User-Task Modeling is an approach used in Information Architecture (IA) to identify and understand the tasks that users need to accomplish while interacting with a system, and to develop a structured representation of these tasks for design and organization purposes. It involves the systematic analysis and documentation of the actions, goals, and workflows that users undertake within a given system or platform. User-Task Modeling aims to capture the user's perspective and mental model of how they expect to interact with the system, rather than focusing solely on the technical aspects of the system. By mapping out the user's goals, actions, and workflows, it helps designers and developers gain insight into the user's needs, behaviors, and motivations, thus enabling them to create user-centered designs that are intuitive and efficient. During the user-task modeling process, various techniques and tools can be employed, such as user interviews, task analysis, personas, and scenario mapping. By gathering data through these methods, IA professionals can identify key tasks, prioritize them based on user goals, and create a hierarchical structure that reflects the relationships between different tasks and subtasks. The outcome of user-task modeling is often represented visually using diagrams, such as flowcharts or task trees. These diagrams provide a clear overview of the system's functionality and enable designers and stakeholders to identify potential gaps, redundancies, and areas of improvement. Additionally, user-task models can inform the development of navigation systems, information hierarchies, and content organization strategies within a website or application. In conclusion, user-task modeling is a fundamental practice in Information Architecture that allows designers and developers to understand the user's perspective, define their tasks and goals, and create effective and user-centered digital experiences. It plays a crucial role in ensuring that systems are designed in a way that meets the needs and

119

expectations of the intended users.

User-Task Performance

User-task performance refers to the effectiveness and efficiency with which users are able to achieve their goals and complete tasks within a given information architecture (IA) system. In the context of IA, user-task performance is crucial for ensuring that users can easily and successfully navigate and interact with the information presented to them. Effective user-task performance means that the IA system is designed in a way that allows users to quickly and accurately find the information or complete the tasks they are seeking. Efficiency, on the other hand, refers to the speed and ease with which users can accomplish their goals within the IA system.

User-Task Scenarios

The concept of User-Task Scenarios in the context of Information Architecture (IA) refers to a method that is used to describe and analyze the various tasks or actions that users can perform on a website or digital platform. These scenarios are created to understand the user's goals and needs, and to design the information architecture in a way that supports and facilitates these tasks. User-Task Scenarios serve as a tool for IA practitioners to gain insights into how users interact with a website or application, and to identify the information structure and navigation paths that would best support their tasks. By envisioning and documenting specific scenarios, designers can better understand the user's perspective and provide a user-centered design. In an IA context, User-Task Scenarios involve the following steps: 1. Identify User Goals: Firstly, the designer must identify the main goals that users would have when visiting the website or platform. These goals can vary depending on the nature of the website and the target audience. 2. Define Scenarios: Based on user goals, designers create specific scenarios that reflect the tasks or actions users would perform. These scenarios should be realistic, representative, and cover a variety of user types and situations. 3. Detail User Actions: In this step, the designer outlines the specific steps or actions that users would need to take to accomplish each task. This includes the interactions, input, and navigation paths required to complete the task successfully. 4. Analyze and Iterate: Designers then analyze the user-task scenarios to identify any potential issues or challenges that users might face. This analysis helps to improve the information architecture by addressing any usability or accessibility concerns. By following these User-Task Scenarios, IA practitioners are able to design information architectures that are intuitive, user-friendly, and aligned with the user's needs and goals. The scenarios provide a framework for understanding the user's perspective and enable designers to make informed decisions about the organization and structure of information on the website or platform. In summary, User-Task Scenarios in Information Architecture involve identifying user goals, defining specific scenarios, detailing user actions, and analyzing and iterating to create an effective information structure that supports user tasks. This approach ensures that users can easily navigate, find relevant information, and accomplish their goals on a website or digital platform. User-Task Scenarios in Information Architecture involve identifying user goals, defining specific scenarios, detailing user actions, and analyzing and iterating to create an effective information structure that supports user tasks. This approach ensures that users can easily navigate, find relevant information, and accomplish their goals on a website or digital platform.

User-Task Sequences

User-task sequences in the context of Information Architecture (IA) refer to the logical order or flow in which users interact with a system or website to accomplish specific tasks or goals. It involves understanding the steps that users take to complete a task and optimizing the design and organization of information to support their journey. The first step in creating user-task sequences is to identify the different tasks that users need to perform on the website or system. This can be done through user research, such as interviews, surveys, or observation. Once the tasks are identified, the next step is to determine the most efficient and intuitive way for users to accomplish them. A user-task sequence typically consists of a series of steps or actions that users need to take to complete a task. These steps should be organized in a logical order that makes sense to the users. For example, if a user wants to purchase a product online, the sequence may include steps such as browsing the product catalog, adding items to the cart, entering shipping and billing information, and completing the payment process. It is crucial to understand the context and goals of users when designing user-task sequences. This involves considering factors such as their prior knowledge, expectations, and preferences. By aligning the sequences with the users' mental models and providing clear and concise instructions, it becomes easier for users to navigate through the tasks. User-task sequences also need to consider the information architecture of the system. This entails organizing information in a way that is intuitive and easy to navigate. Key elements of information architecture, such as categorization, labeling, and navigation, should be optimized to support the user-task sequences. Regular testing and evaluation of user-task sequences is essential to ensure their effectiveness. This may involve usability testing, where users are observed while completing tasks, and feedback is collected to identify areas for improvement. Iterative refinement based on user feedback can lead to improved user experiences and increased task completion rates.

User-Task Simulation

Information Architecture (IA) refers to the structural design and organization of information within a system, website, or application. It is a practice that focuses on designing intuitive and effective ways to organize, navigate, and retrieve information, in order to enhance user experience and facilitate access to relevant content. IA involves the process of categorizing and organizing information in a logical and meaningful way, ensuring that users can easily find what they are looking for. This is achieved by creating clear and consistent navigation menus, organizing content into hierarchies, and developing effective search functionalities.

User-Task Steps

Information Architecture (IA) is the discipline of organizing and structuring information to enhance the usability and findability of digital products and services. It involves the careful planning and design of the information component and navigational structure of a website or application. The goal of IA is to create a clear and intuitive structure that allows users to easily find and access the information they need. IA encompasses several key principles and techniques that help designers and developers create effective information structures. One of the fundamental principles is categorization, which involves grouping similar information and resources together based on their attributes or characteristics. Categorization helps users understand the relationships between different pieces of information and makes it easier for them to navigate through the content. Another important technique in IA is navigation design. This includes designing menus, links, and other navigation elements that allow users to move between different sections or pages of a website or application. Effective navigation design ensures that users can easily locate and access the information they need, regardless of their location within the site. IA also involves creating hierarchical structures, such as taxonomies and hierarchies, to organize information in a logical and intuitive manner. These structures help users understand the relationships between different categories or topics and provide a clear path for information exploration. Furthermore, IA considers the use of labeling and metadata to provide additional context and description for different pieces of information. This helps users understand the content and ensures that it is accurately represented in search results or navigation menus. In conclusion, Information Architecture plays a crucial role in designing user-friendly and intuitive digital experiences. By carefully organizing and structuring information, IA enhances the usability and findability of websites and applications, allowing users to quickly and efficiently access the information they need.

User-Task Workflow Analysis

User-Task Workflow Analysis refers to the systematic examination and documentation of the steps and interactions involved in a specific user task within a given information architecture (IA) context. It involves the identification and understanding of the workflow followed by users as they accomplish a particular task, with the aim of improving the usability and effectiveness of the IA. The analysis begins by defining the scope and purpose of the task, as well as the users involved. This helps in creating a clear context and understanding of the task at hand. The next step involves mapping out the workflow, which includes identifying the sequence of steps performed by users, the decisions they make, and the interactions they have with the IA. This mapping process helps in visualizing the entire task flow and identifying potential bottlenecks, confusion points, or areas of improvement. During the analysis, it is essential to identify any external systems, tools, or interfaces that users interact with while completing the task. These external factors can significantly impact the workflow and need to be taken into account when making IA recommendations. Additionally, understanding the goals and objectives of the task is crucial in assessing the effectiveness of the IA in supporting users in achieving their desired outcomes. The analysis also considers the user's mental model and expectations for completing the task. This involves examining how users perceive the task and the IA, which helps in identifying any discrepancies or mismatches between the user's mental model and the actual IA structure. By understanding the user's perspective, IA designers can make informed decisions about how to structure and present information in a more intuitive and user-friendly way. Overall, User-Task Workflow Analysis is a key component of IA design, as it provides insights into the user's journey and helps in identifying opportunities for improvement. By documenting and understanding the user's workflow, IA designers can optimize the IA structure, navigation, and presentation to enhance usability, efficiency, and user satisfaction.

User-Task Workflow Continual Improvement

A user-task workflow is a series of steps that a user takes to complete a specific task within a digital system or application. It involves the user's actions, interactions with the interface, and the system's response to these interactions. User-task workflows are designed to be efficient, intuitive, and user-friendly. In the context of Information Architecture (IA), user-task workflows are an important aspect of designing effective information structures within a website or application. IA focuses on organizing, categorizing, and labeling information to enhance usability and user experience.

User-Task Workflow Design

User-task workflow design refers to the process of creating a structured and intuitive flow of tasks and actions that a user follows to accomplish their goals within a digital environment. This design approach aims to enhance the user experience by providing a clear and logical path for users to navigate, perform tasks, and achieve their objectives. In the context of Information Architecture (IA), user-task workflow design involves organizing and structuring information in a way that supports the user's tasks and goals. It requires a deep understanding of the users' needs and objectives, as well as the content and functionality of the digital system being designed.

User-Task Workflow Diagram

Information Architecture (IA) is a discipline that focuses on organizing, structuring, and labeling content in a way that facilitates effective and intuitive user experiences. User-task workflow diagrams are graphical representations commonly used in IA to depict the sequence of steps or interactions between a user and a system in order to accomplish a specific task or achieve a particular goal. These diagrams typically consist of a series of connected nodes or boxes that represent different stages or actions within the user-task workflow. The nodes are linked by arrows or lines to illustrate the flow and direction of the user's interactions. Each node may include additional information such as inputs, outputs, decision points, or conditions that shape the progression of the workflow. By visualizing the user's journey through a series of steps, user-task workflow diagrams help designers, developers, and stakeholders gain a better understanding of the user's perspective and provide insights into potential pain points, bottlenecks, or opportunities for improvement in the overall user experience. They serve as a means of communication and collaboration among various stakeholders, ensuring a shared understanding of the intended user flow and system behavior. Furthermore, user-task workflow diagrams can assist in identifying dependencies, exceptions, or alternative paths that users may encounter. This enables designers to anticipate and cater to different user scenarios, ensuring a robust and adaptable information architecture that meets the needs and expectations of a diverse range of users. In summary, user-task workflow diagrams play a vital role in information architecture by visually representing the sequence of steps or interactions required to accomplish a specific task. They help facilitate effective communication, collaboration, and understanding among stakeholders, while also providing insights into the user's perspective and potential areas for improvement in the overall user experience.

User-Task Workflow Enhancement

An enhanced user-task workflow in the context of Information Architecture (IA) refers to a more efficient and user-friendly process that allows users to accomplish their tasks and goals effectively within a digital product or system. It focuses on optimizing the sequence of steps, interactions, and information presentation to enhance the overall user experience. This enhancement involves several key aspects: 1. Clear task understanding: An improved user-task workflow begins with a thorough understanding of the users' tasks and goals. IA professionals conduct user research and analysis to identify the core tasks and prioritize them based on their importance and frequency. This ensures that the workflow meets the users' needs and aligns with their mental models. 2. Simplified navigation and structure: IA plays a crucial role in creating a logical and intuitive structure for content and features. Enhancing the user-task workflow involves organizing information in a way that aligns with users' mental models and reduces cognitive load. This includes creating clear navigation menus, intuitive labels, and consistent categorization, enabling users to locate and access relevant information easily. 3. Streamlined interactions and flows: An enhanced user-task workflow minimizes unnecessary steps and interactions, reducing friction and complexity. This involves optimizing user interfaces, eliminating redundant actions, and incorporating contextual cues to guide users through the process. By simplifying and streamlining interactions, users can complete tasks more efficiently and with fewer errors. 4. Responsive and adaptive design: As users interact with digital products across various devices and screen sizes, it is crucial to ensure a consistent and seamless user-task workflow. An enhanced workflow considers the responsive and adaptive design principles, enabling the system to adapt and provide optimal experiences on different devices. This involves optimizing layouts, interactions, and content presentation to accommodate varying screen sizes and input methods. Overall, an enhanced user-task workflow in the context of IA aims to improve the usability and effectiveness of digital products by prioritizing user needs, simplifying navigation and interactions, and ensuring a seamless experience across devices. By focusing on optimizing the flow of tasks, users can accomplish their goals efficiently, leading to increased satisfaction and engagement.

User-Task Workflow Evaluation

User-task workflow evaluation is a crucial aspect of the Information Architecture (IA) design process. It involves assessing the effectiveness and efficiency of the workflows that users follow when interacting with a digital system or platform. This evaluation aims to identify any issues or challenges that users might face during their tasks and workflows, in order to make improvements and enhance the overall user experience. The evaluation process typically begins by defining the specific tasks that users need to perform within the digital system or platform. This can include actions such as searching for information, completing a transaction, or navigating through different sections of the website. Once the tasks are defined, the next step is to observe and analyze how users actually perform these tasks, collecting data on their interactions, behaviors, and pain points. During the evaluation, various techniques and methods can be employed. These include usability testing, where users are asked to perform specific tasks and provide feedback on their experience. It can also involve conducting interviews or surveys to gather qualitative data about users' preferences, needs, and frustrations. Quantitative data may be collected as well, such as task completion times or error rates. The data collected during the evaluation phase is then analyzed, interpreted, and used to inform the design and optimization of the user-task workflows. It helps identify areas where the design can be improved, such as simplifying complex tasks, reducing unnecessary steps, or improving the discoverability of key features or functions. By addressing these issues, the overall user experience can be enhanced, leading to increased user satisfaction, improved task completion rates, and higher conversion rates. User-task workflow evaluation is an iterative process that should be conducted throughout the development cycle of a digital system or platform. By regularly evaluating and refining the workflows, IA professionals can ensure that the system meets the needs and expectations of the users, aligns with business goals, and ultimately drives user engagement and success.

User-Task Workflow Implementation

Information Architecture (IA) is the practice of organizing and structuring information to facilitate effective navigation, findability, and usability within a digital environment. It involves designing and implementing user-task workflows, which establish a step-by-step sequence of actions that users need to take to accomplish specific tasks or goals. A user-task workflow describes the path that a user follows to complete a particular task within a system or application. It outlines the series of steps, actions, and interactions required to achieve a desired outcome. The implementation of a user-task workflow in the context of IA involves creating a logical and intuitive flow of information that supports seamless and efficient user experiences.

User-Task Workflow Improvement

Information Architecture (IA) refers to the structural design and organization of information within a system or website to facilitate effective and efficient user-task workflows. It involves the arrangement and categorization of content, features, and functionalities in a logical and intuitive manner, helping users navigate and find the information they seek easily. IA aims to optimize the user experience by improving the findability, usability, and accessibility of information.In the context of user-task workflows, IA focuses on streamlining the process by which users interact with a system to accomplish their goals. It involves understanding the tasks that users need to perform and designing the information structure in a way that supports these tasks. By mapping out the user journey and identifying key touchpoints, IA allows for the creation of a seamless and efficient workflow.

User-Task Workflow Interactive Prototype

A user-task workflow interactive prototype refers to a visual representation of the flow and interactions that occur between a user and a system while completing specific tasks or activities. In the context of Information Architecture (IA), it is a valuable tool that helps in designing and testing the usability of a digital product or service. The user-task workflow interactive prototype is based on the principles of user-centered design and allows designers and stakeholders to understand and evaluate how users will interact with the system. It provides a practical way to validate concepts, gather feedback, and make iterative improvements to the user experience. The prototype typically consists of a series of screens or wireframes that depict the system's interface, user interface elements, content, and interactive elements such as buttons, menus, forms, and controls. Each screen represents a specific stage or step in the user's journey, and users can navigate between screens to simulate actual usage scenarios. The user-task workflow interactive prototype is designed to simulate the intended functionality of the system, allowing users to interact with the interface and perform tasks as they would in a real-world scenario. It provides an opportunity to test the effectiveness and efficiency of the system's interactions, user flows, and information organization. Information architecture plays a crucial role in the development of the user-task workflow interactive prototype. IA principles help ensure that the prototype is structured, intuitive, and easy to navigate. It involves organizing and categorizing information, defining navigation paths, and determining how the system will present content and functionality to users. An effective user-task workflow interactive prototype aligns with the overarching IA strategy, ensuring that the system's structure and organization meet users' needs and expectations. It helps designers and stakeholders identify potential usability issues, uncover areas for improvement, and refine the IA strategy in an iterative manner. In conclusion, a user-task workflow interactive prototype is a visual representation of the flow and interactions between users and a digital system while completing specific tasks. It is an essential tool in the field of Information Architecture for testing and improving the usability of digital products and services.

User-Task Workflow Iteration

The user-task workflow iteration refers to the process of refining and improving the sequence of steps or actions that a user needs to take to accomplish a specific task or goal within a system or application. In the context of Information Architecture (IA), this typically involves analyzing and optimizing the structure and organization of information and content within a website or software interface. During the user-task workflow iteration, the IA team examines the current user flow and identifies any pain points, inefficiencies, or inconsistencies that may hinder the user's ability to complete their desired task. This may include analyzing the navigational structure, labeling, and categorization of information, as well as considering the overall information hierarchy and relationships between different pieces of content. After identifying areas for improvement, the IA team iteratively designs and tests different versions of the user-task workflow to address these issues. This may involve creating wireframes or prototypes to visualize the proposed changes and gather feedback from users or stakeholders. The team then incorporates this feedback to

124

refine the workflow further, repeating the design and testing process as necessary. The goal of user-task workflow iteration is to create an optimal user experience by streamlining the task completion process, reducing cognitive load, and increasing user satisfaction. By iteratively reviewing and refining the workflow, the IA team can uncover opportunities for simplification, clarification, and personalization, ensuring that the system or application meets the needs and expectations of its users.

User-Task Workflow Maintenance

User-task workflow maintenance in the context of Information Architecture (IA) refers to the ongoing management and optimization of the flow of tasks and actions that users perform while interacting with a website or application. It involves ensuring that the user's journey through the system is seamless, intuitive, and aligned with their goals and needs. This practice involves analyzing and understanding the user's behavior, preferences, and expectations in relation to the tasks they want to accomplish. By gaining insights into the user's workflow, IA professionals can identify areas of improvement and implement changes to enhance the overall user experience.

User-Task Workflow Mapping

User-Task Workflow Mapping is a process within Information Architecture (IA) that involves organizing and mapping the user's tasks and actions to the overall structure and flow of a system or website. It focuses on defining and designing the sequences of steps that users take to complete their goals or tasks while using a digital interface. The purpose of User-Task Workflow Mapping is to create a clear and intuitive user experience by aligning the system's functionalities and content with the user's needs and expectations. It involves understanding the goals, motivations, and behaviors of the target users and translating them into a logical and efficient workflow. By mapping the user's tasks and actions, the IA professional can develop an information structure that supports the user's mental model and allows them to easily navigate and find the information they need. During the User-Task Workflow Mapping process, the IA professional identifies the main tasks and actions that users perform within the system or website. This could include actions such as searching for information, completing a form, making a purchase, or interacting with various features or functions. The IA professional then analyzes and organizes these tasks into a logical and sequential order, ensuring that the workflow aligns with the user's goals and expectations. Once the tasks and actions are identified and organized, the IA professional creates a visual representation or diagram that illustrates the flow of the user's activities. This could be in the form of a flowchart, a sitemap, or a wireframe. This visual representation helps the IA professional and other stakeholders understand the overall structure and flow of the system, and allows for iterative refinement and improvement of the user experience. User-Task Workflow Mapping is an essential step in the IA process as it ensures that the system or website is designed with the user in mind. By aligning the user's tasks and actions with the information structure, the IA professional can ensure that the system is user-friendly, intuitive, and efficient. This ultimately leads to increased user satisfaction, improved task completion rates, and a more successful digital interface overall.

User-Task Workflow Modeling

User-task workflow modeling in the context of Information Architecture (IA) refers to the process of understanding and representing the sequence of activities or steps undertaken by users to accomplish their goals within a given information system or interface. The primary objective of user-task workflow modeling is to analyze and document how users interact with an information system, identifying the different stages, actions, and decisions made during the user's journey. By representing this workflow, IA professionals can gain insights into the user's mental model, understand the context in which tasks are performed, and identify areas for improvement or optimization.

User-Task Workflow Monitoring

User-Task Workflow Monitoring is a process in Information Architecture (IA) that involves systematic observation, analysis, and evaluation of user interactions during the execution of tasks within a digital system or application. It focuses on capturing and assessing user behavior, performance, and satisfaction in order to gain valuable insights and improve the overall user experience. The goal of User-Task Workflow Monitoring is to gather data and generate meaningful feedback about how users interact with a system, identify potential issues or bottlenecks, and make informed decisions to optimize the design and functionality of the system. This monitoring process allows IA professionals to gain a better understanding of user needs, preferences, and patterns of interaction, which in turn helps in making informed decisions for designing an effective user interface. User-Task Workflow Monitoring typically involves the use of various techniques such as usability testing, task analysis, user feedback, and analytics data. Usability testing involves observing users as they perform specific tasks within the system, recording their actions, and collecting their feedback. This provides insights into how users navigate through the system, understand instructions, and accomplish their goals. Task analysis helps in identifying the steps and actions involved in completing a specific task, allowing IA professionals to identify potential issues and streamline the workflow. User feedback, through surveys or interviews, provides additional insights into user perceptions and satisfaction levels. Analytics data, such as click-through rates, completion rates, and time on task, can provide quantitative information about user behavior and performance. By monitoring user-task workflows, IA professionals can identify areas of improvement, determine if the system meets user expectations, and uncover potential usability issues that may hinder user productivity or satisfaction. This information can be used to make data-driven decisions and guide the iterative design process, ensuring that the digital system or application is continuously evolving and meeting the needs of its users. In conclusion, User-Task Workflow Monitoring plays a crucial role in ensuring an optimal user experience and driving the success of digital products and services.

User-Task Workflow Optimization

User-Task Workflow Optimization is a process in the field of Information Architecture (IA) that aims to improve the efficiency and effectiveness of user interactions with digital systems. It involves streamlining and enhancing the flow of tasks performed by users, with the ultimate goal of providing a seamless and intuitive user experience. The optimization process typically consists of several key steps. First, it is important to fully understand the users and their tasks within the specific context of the digital system. This involves conducting user research, analyzing user behavior and interactions, and identifying pain points or areas of improvement. Based on this initial understanding, the next step is to restructure the information architecture of the system to better align with user needs and preferences. This may involve reorganizing content, simplifying navigation, or creating new pathways for users to find and access information or complete tasks more efficiently. The goal is to create a logical and coherent structure that reflects how users think and how they expect to interact with the system. Once the information architecture is optimized, the next step is to design and implement user interfaces that facilitate effortless navigation and interaction. This involves considering factors such as visual hierarchy, clear labeling, well-designed menus and buttons, and intuitive workflows. The aim is to provide users with clear cues and guidance, helping them effortlessly navigate through the system and complete their tasks with minimal effort or confusion. Throughout the optimization process, it is crucial to continuously test and gather feedback from users. This allows for iterative improvements and adjustments based on real user insights and preferences. Usability testing, user feedback surveys, and other user research methods can provide valuable data for further refining and enhancing the user-task workflow. In summary, User-Task Workflow Optimization is a crucial component of Information Architecture (IA). By understanding user needs, restructuring the information architecture, and designing intuitive interfaces, the optimization process aims to maximize user efficiency and satisfaction. Through continuous testing and refinement, the digital system can evolve to better align with user expectations and deliver a superior user experience.

User-Task Workflow Prototyping

Workflow prototyping in the context of Information Architecture (IA) refers to the process of visually representing and evaluating the sequence of user tasks within a system or website. It involves creating a simplified version of the user interface and interaction flow to test and refine the structure and organization of content and functionality. Through the use of prototyping, IA professionals can explore different design options and identify potential issues or areas for improvement before implementing the final user interface. It enables them to gather feedback from users and stakeholders early in the design process, ensuring that the final system meets the needs and expectations of its intended audience.

User-Task Workflow Redesign

Information Architecture (IA) is the practice of organizing, structuring, and labeling information in a way that allows users to find and navigate through it efficiently and effectively. It involves the design and implementation of a user-task workflow, which is a systematic representation of the steps involved in completing a specific task or achieving a specific goal within a digital system. User-task workflow redesign in the context of IA refers to the process of reevaluating and modifying the existing workflow to improve its usability and overall user experience. It involves analyzing how users interact with the system, identifying pain points and areas for improvement, and making changes that streamline the flow of information and enhance task completion. The first step in user-task workflow redesign is conducting user research to gain insights into the needs, goals, and behaviors of the target audience. This may involve methods such as interviews, surveys, and usability testing. The findings from this research help inform the redesign process by providing a deep understanding of user expectations and preferences. Once the user research is complete, the next step is to analyze the existing workflow and identify areas that need improvement. This could include removing unnecessary steps, simplifying complex processes, or reorganizing information to make it more intuitive and easily accessible. The goal is to create a workflow that allows users to accomplish their tasks with minimal effort and confusion. After identifying the areas for improvement, the redesign phase begins. This involves creating a new workflow that incorporates the insights gained from the user research and addresses the identified issues. The new workflow should be visually and conceptually coherent, easy to understand and use, and align with the overall goals and objectives of the digital system. Finally, the redesigned workflow is implemented and tested. This involves creating prototypes or wireframes that illustrate how the new workflow will work in practice. Usability testing is conducted to gather feedback from users and validate the effectiveness of the redesign. Based on the results of testing, further iterations and refinements may be made to ensure that the redesigned workflow meets the needs and expectations of the users.

User-Task Workflow Simulation

In the context of Information Architecture (IA), user-task workflow simulation refers to the process of modeling and evaluating the flow of tasks that users perform within a digital system or website. It involves identifying the steps, actions, and interactions that users need to undertake in order to achieve specific goals or complete tasks within the system. The simulation of user-task workflows is a crucial aspect of IA as it allows designers and architects to understand and improve the overall user experience. By examining the sequence of actions and interactions, designers can identify potential issues, bottlenecks, or usability problems that could hinder users from achieving their objectives efficiently and effectively. The simulation process involves several steps. First, designers identify the primary tasks and goals that users are expected to perform within the system. This could include actions such as searching for information, making a purchase, or completing a form. Once the tasks are defined, designers map out the steps and interactions required to complete each task. During the simulation, designers can use various techniques and tools to visualize and assess the user-task workflows. This can include creating flowcharts, diagrams, or prototypes that showcase the sequence of steps and interactions. These visual representations help designers identify any potential gaps, redundancies, or areas of confusion within the workflow. Designers can also conduct usability testing or heuristic evaluations to assess the effectiveness of the simulated workflows. By observing real users or experts interacting with the system, designers can gather valuable insights and feedback about the usability, efficiency, and overall user experience of the workflow. Based on the findings from the simulation and evaluation, designers can then make informed decisions and modifications to the IA of the system. This could involve rearranging or restructuring the navigation, revising the information hierarchy, or simplifying the user interfaces to better accommodate the identified user tasks and workflows. In conclusion, user-task workflow simulation is a critical part of the IA process. It helps designers understand how users interact with the system and enables them to improve the overall user experience. By modeling, visualizing, and evaluating the flow of tasks, designers can optimize the system's IA to ensure users can accomplish their goals efficiently and effectively.

User-Task Workflow Usability Testing

User-Task Workflow Usability Testing in the context of Information Architecture (IA) refers to a methodological process of evaluating the efficiency, effectiveness, and user-friendliness of a digital system or website in relation to how users complete specific tasks. This testing aims to identify potential usability issues, gather user feedback, and make evidence-based recommendations for improving the overall user experience. The workflow involved in User-Task Workflow Usability Testing consists of several key stages. The first stage is planning and defining the objectives of the usability test. This includes determining the specific tasks that users will be asked to perform, setting clear success criteria, and selecting appropriate metrics to measure task completion rates, error rates, and user satisfaction. Next, participants are recruited for the usability test. Typically, a diverse group of representative users are selected based on specific demographics, such as age, gender, or technical expertise. These users are then provided with pre-defined tasks to perform on the website or digital system being tested. During the test, participants are observed and their interactions with the system are recorded. This can be done through methods such as screen recording, eye-tracking, or think-aloud protocols. Usability testers may also ask participants to provide feedback on their experience and highlight any difficulties or confusion they encountered while completing the tasks. Once the usability testing phase is completed, the collected data is analyzed. This involves quantitatively assessing task completion rates, error rates, and user satisfaction scores. Additionally, qualitative analysis is performed to identify common themes or patterns in user feedback. Finally, based on the analysis of the data, a report is generated that outlines the findings and recommendations for improving the user experience. This report is typically shared with stakeholders, including designers, developers, and product managers, who can then use the insights to make informed decisions and implement necessary changes to the digital system.

User-Task Workflow Usability

User-Task Workflow Usability refers to the measure of how easily and efficiently users can complete their tasks within a system or platform, focusing on the overall experience and effectiveness of the user's workflow. In the context of Information Architecture (IA), it pertains to the usability of the organization and structure of information and content, ensuring that it supports users in achieving their goals. A well-designed user-task workflow provides users with a clear and intuitive path to accomplish their objectives. It considers the logical flow of tasks, the navigation structure, and the arrangement and labeling of information within the interface. By optimizing the workflow, IA aims to minimize cognitive load, frustration, and errors while enhancing user satisfaction and task completion rates. Effective user-task workflow usability in IA involves several key elements. Firstly, it necessitates a comprehensive understanding of the users and their specific goals and tasks within the system. This user-centered approach enables designers to align the structure and organization of information with user expectations and mental models. Secondly, an efficient information architecture should offer clear and concise navigation. Users should be able to locate and access relevant information and functionalities effortlessly. This can be achieved through well-structured menus, breadcrumbs, search functionality, and contextual links that guide users through the system and provide orientation at all times. Additionally, user-task workflow usability involves effective labeling and categorization of content. Clear and consistent terminology should be used to ensure users can easily understand and interpret the information presented. Logical grouping and hierarchical structures can assist users in finding the desired information promptly. Lastly, a successful user-task workflow takes into account the interplay between different tasks and user journeys. It should facilitate the completion of complex workflows and support users in progressing seamlessly between related tasks. Providing visual cues, progress indicators, and allowing for flexible interaction patterns contribute to an efficient and effective user experience. In summary, user-task workflow usability in the context of IA addresses the ease and efficiency with which users can complete their tasks within a system. By considering user goals, providing clear navigation, effective labeling, and supporting complex workflows, IA can optimize the user experience and enable users to accomplish their objectives with minimal effort and frustration.

User-Task Workflow User Feedback

User-Task Workflow User Feedback refers to the process of capturing and analyzing feedback from users regarding their experiences with the user-task workflow in an information architecture

(IA) system. It involves gathering insights and opinions from users who have interacted with the system and identifying areas for improvement. User feedback plays a critical role in the iterative design process of an information architecture. It helps designers and developers understand how users perceive and navigate through the user-task workflow, allowing them to identify pain points, areas of confusion, and opportunities for enhancing the overall user experience. The feedback collection process can take various forms, including surveys, interviews, usability testing, and analytics data analysis. Surveys are often used to collect quantitative data, such as user ratings and rankings of different aspects of the user-task workflow. Interviews, on the other hand, provide an opportunity for qualitative insights, allowing users to express their opinions, preferences, and suggestions. Usability testing is another valuable method for gathering feedback. It involves observing users as they perform tasks within the IA system, and collecting their thoughts and reactions in real-time. This method provides valuable insights into the actual user experience and can uncover usability issues that may not be apparent through other methods. Analyzing analytics data, such as user behavior metrics and patterns, can also provide valuable feedback on how users interact with the user-task workflow. This data can shed light on common user paths, drop-off points, and areas of high engagement, which can inform IA decisions and improvements. Once the feedback is collected, it needs to be carefully analyzed to identify patterns, common issues, and suggestions. The feedback should be categorized based on relevant themes and used to inform the design decisions and optimization efforts for the user-task workflow. Overall, User-Task Workflow User Feedback is a crucial aspect of information architecture, helping to identify areas for improvement and ensuring that the user-task workflow is optimized for a seamless and engaging user experience.

User-Task Workflow User Testing

User-Task Workflow User Testing is a process within Information Architecture (IA) that involves evaluating and refining the design and usability of a website or application. It focuses on how users interact with the system and aims to identify any pain points, usability issues, or areas for improvement. This testing method involves observing users as they perform specific tasks or workflows, allowing designers and developers to gain insights into the user experience and make informed design decisions. During User-Task Workflow User Testing, a group of representative users is selected to participate in the testing process. These users are given specific tasks to complete on the website or application, simulating real-world scenarios. The testers are then observed and their interactions with the system are recorded, both qualitatively and quantitatively. The information gathered during the testing process helps designers and developers understand how users navigate through the interface, how they interpret visual cues and labels, and how they interact with different features and functionalities. It provides valuable insights into how users perceive the system's usability, efficiency, and effectiveness. The findings from User-Task Workflow User Testing can be used to make improvements to the information architecture and user interface design. It may uncover issues such as confusing navigation, unclear labels, or cumbersome workflows that hinder users from completing their tasks efficiently. By identifying these pain points, designers and developers can make informed design decisions to enhance the overall user experience. User-Task Workflow User Testing is an essential component of the iterative design process. It allows designers and developers to validate their design choices, gather valuable feedback, and make data-driven improvements to the system. By involving users in the testing process, IA professionals can create user-centered designs that align with user needs and expectations, ultimately leading to a more intuitive and enjoyable user experience.

User-Task Workflow User-Centered Design

User-Task Workflow User-Centered Design aims to create Information Architecture (IA) that takes into consideration the needs and goals of the users, while facilitating the efficient completion of tasks. It involves a user-centered approach that focuses on the users' mental models, goals, and behaviors, and designs information structures that support their workflow. This design approach starts by understanding the target audience and their tasks. It involves gathering user requirements through research methods such as interviews, usability testing, and surveys. The insights gained from these activities help define the user personas, which represent the different types of users and their characteristics. Once the users and their tasks are defined, the design team creates user flows that outline the steps and actions required to accomplish each task. These user flows provide a visual representation of the users' journey through the information architecture, highlighting key touchpoints and decision points. The next step is to create wireframes and prototypes that reflect the envisioned IA. These visual representations serve as a blueprint for the final design, illustrating the content organization, hierarchy, and navigation structure. Iterative feedback and testing are crucial during this phase to ensure that the IA effectively supports user tasks and workflows. The IA design should prioritize usability and efficiency. It should make it easy for users to find information, understand its relevance, and complete their tasks with minimal cognitive load. The design team focuses on organizing content into meaningful categories and labeling them appropriately, ensuring that the information is easily discoverable and accessible. User-Task Workflow User-Centered Design also emphasizes the importance of context in IA design. It considers the different platforms and devices that users may interact with, as well as the constraints and opportunities presented by these contexts. This ensures that the IA is adaptable and responsive, providing a consistent and seamless user experience across various devices and channels.

User-Task Workflow Validation

User-task workflow validation in the context of Information Architecture (IA) refers to the process of evaluating the effectiveness and efficiency of a system or application in supporting user tasks and workflows. It involves assessing whether the system's structure, organization, and interactions align with the users' goals, needs, and mental models, ensuring a seamless user experience. The validation of user-task workflows is crucial in IA as it helps identify potential usability issues and design flaws that can hinder users from achieving their objectives efficiently. By validating the workflows, IA professionals ensure that the system's navigation, content organization, and functionality align with users' expectations and facilitate their interactions with the system.

User-Task Workflow Visualization

A user-task workflow visualization in the context of Information Architecture (IA) refers to the representation of the sequential steps and interactions involved in accomplishing a specific task within a system or application. It is a visual diagram that depicts the flow of actions and decisions that a user takes while completing a particular task. The purpose of a user-task workflow visualization is to provide a clear and intuitive visual representation of the user's journey, enabling designers and stakeholders to understand and analyze the user experience. By mapping out the steps involved in a task, it helps identify potential bottlenecks, inefficiencies, and areas of improvement in the user interface and interaction design.

User-Task Workflow Wireframing

User-task workflow wireframing in the context of Information Architecture (IA) refers to the process of visually representing the steps a user takes to complete specific tasks or goals within a digital product or system. It involves mapping out the sequence of actions and interactions that a user will go through to achieve their desired outcome. The purpose of user-task workflow wireframing is to create a clear and intuitive blueprint of the user's journey through the system, allowing designers and stakeholders to understand and evaluate the flow of information and interactions. It helps identify potential pain points, inconsistencies, and areas for improvement in order to enhance the user experience. The wireframes used in user-task workflow wireframing typically consist of simple sketches or diagrams that outline the different screens, elements, and interactions necessary to complete a task. These wireframes focus on the overall structure and flow of the user interface, rather than the visual design or aesthetics. By visualizing the user's path, user-task workflow wireframing allows designers to make informed decisions about the organization and placement of content, as well as the sequencing of tasks. It helps ensure that the system provides a logical and intuitive experience for users by aligning their mental models with the system's structure and functionality. User-task workflow wireframing is an essential step in the IA process as it helps bridge the gap between user needs and system requirements. It enables designers to iteratively refine and optimize the user experience, leading to more efficient and effective task completion. In summary, user-task workflow wireframing is the practice of visually mapping out the user's journey through a digital product or system, aiming to create a clear and intuitive path for users to achieve their desired outcomes. It helps designers identify and address potential issues, enhancing the overall user experience and ensuring the system's effectiveness in meeting user needs.

User-Task Workflow

A user-task workflow, in the context of Information Architecture (IA), refers to the sequence of steps or actions undertaken by a user to accomplish a specific task or goal within a digital system or interface. It involves the interaction between the user and the system, as well as any necessary inputs and outputs. Understanding and designing user-task workflows is integral to effective IA, as it enables designers to create intuitive and efficient interfaces that support users in achieving their objectives. By mapping out the sequence of steps, designers can identify potential usability issues, optimize the flow, and ensure a seamless user experience.

UserBob

Information architecture (IA) refers to the organization and structure of information within a system or website. It involves the design and organization of information, data, and content to enhance usability, findability, and accessibility for the users. IA aims to create a clear and intuitive navigation system that allows users to easily find and understand the information they are seeking. It involves the categorization, labeling, and organization of information in a logical and meaningful way. IA also includes the creation of navigation menus, sitemaps, and other elements that support the user's journey through the system or website.

UserFeel

Information Architecture (IA) is the practice of structuring and organizing information to facilitate efficient and effective navigation and retrieval. It involves designing the information hierarchy and categorization, as well as the labeling and organization of content within a system or website. The goal of IA is to create a logical and intuitive structure that allows users to easily find and access the information they need. This is achieved through the use of clear and consistent navigation menus, site maps, and search functionality. IA also encompasses the design of taxonomies and metadata to provide meaningful and relevant information about the content and aid in its discoverability. IA is a multidisciplinary field that draws from information science, cognitive psychology, design, and user experience. It requires understanding the needs and mental models of the users and aligning the structure of the information to match those mental models. This involves conducting user research, such as user interviews and usability testing, to inform the design decisions. Effective IA enhances the user experience by reducing cognitive load and allowing users to quickly and easily navigate and access information. It improves findability by organizing content in a logical and intuitive manner, making it easier for users to discover relevant information. IA also supports scalability, as a well-designed information architecture can accommodate future growth and expansion of the system or website. In conclusion, Information Architecture plays a crucial role in the design and organization of information. It focuses on structuring and categorizing information to improve navigation and findability. By understanding user needs and mental models, IA aims to create a logical and intuitive structure that enhances the user experience.

UserReport

Information Architecture (IA) is a discipline that focuses on organizing and structuring information in a way that enables users to find and understand it easily. It involves the design and arrangement of information in systems, websites, and other digital and physical spaces, with the goal of creating intuitive and efficient navigation. The main purpose of IA is to improve the user experience by making information accessible, coherent, and meaningful. It aims to create a clear and logical structure that allows users to navigate through complex information landscapes without feeling overwhelmed or lost. IA also plays a crucial role in facilitating information retrieval and search, ensuring that users can quickly find the information they are looking for. IA encompasses various principles and techniques for organizing information, such as categorization, labeling, hierarchy, and navigation systems. It involves analyzing the content and context of information to determine the most appropriate ways to structure and present it. This can include creating taxonomies, classifying information into meaningful categories, and developing metadata schemas to enhance search and discoverability. IA is a multidisciplinary field that draws on elements from user experience (UX), interaction design, content strategy, and information science. It requires a deep understanding of user needs, cognitive processes, and information behavior, as well as an awareness of technological constraints and capabilities.

Effective IA is essential for creating user-friendly and efficient digital products, websites, and applications. It enhances the findability and usability of information, leading to improved user satisfaction and task completion. By applying IA principles, designers and information architects can ensure that information is organized in a logical and intuitive manner, promoting seamless navigation and enhancing the overall user experience.

UserZoom

Information Architecture (IA) refers to the practice of organizing and structuring information to enhance usability and findability within a digital system. It involves the planning and design of how information is organized, labeled, and presented to users. IA aims to create intuitive and efficient navigation schemes that enable users to quickly find the content they need. IA encompasses various principles and techniques that help create a logical and coherent structure for information. This includes designing clear and meaningful labels and categories, establishing a hierarchical structure to organize information, and defining relationships between different pieces of content. IA also involves considering user mental models and cognitive processes to ensure the information is presented in a way that matches users' expectations and helps them understand and interpret the content.

VWO (Visual Website Optimizer)

VWO (Visual Website Optimizer) is a tool used in the field of Information Architecture (IA) that allows designers and developers to perform A/B testing and multivariate testing on their websites. A/B testing involves creating multiple versions of a webpage and randomly presenting them to users to determine which version performs better in terms of user engagement and conversions. Multivariate testing, on the other hand, involves testing different combinations of webpage elements to identify the most effective layout and design. With VWO, designers and developers can easily create variations of webpages by making changes to elements such as headlines, images, call-to-action buttons, and more. These variations can be tested simultaneously, and VWO uses advanced algorithms to ensure random and equal distribution of the variations to different users. The tool tracks user interactions and provides detailed analytics to measure the performance of each variation.

Validately

Validately is a comprehensive platform designed to support and streamline the process of conducting research and gathering user feedback for Information Architecture (IA) projects. It offers a range of tools and features that enable IA professionals to effectively validate and refine their information structures, navigation systems, and user workflows. The platform allows IA practitioners to create and conduct various types of research studies, such as usability tests, card sorting exercises, tree testing, and surveys. These studies can be customized to gather specific insights and feedback related to the IA being developed. Validately simplifies the process of recruiting participants for these studies by providing access to a panel of pre-screened participants, making it easier to reach the target user demographics. One of the key features of Validately is its remote usability testing functionality, which enables IA professionals to observe and analyze how users interact with their information architectures in real-time. This feature eliminates the need for in-person testing, allowing for more efficient and cost-effective research. IA practitioners can remotely set up tasks and scenarios for participants to complete, and then watch and record their interactions, allowing them to identify potential usability issues and gather qualitative feedback. In addition to remote usability testing, Validately also offers features such as moderated and unmoderated studies, as well as a collaborative and powerful dashboard for analyzing and visualizing research data. This allows IA professionals to gain deep insights into user behavior and preferences, helping them make informed decisions about the design and structure of their information architectures. Overall, Validately is a valuable tool for IA professionals, providing them with the necessary tools and features to conduct comprehensive research, gather user feedback, and refine their information architectures. By streamlining the research process and offering powerful analysis capabilities, Validately enhances the efficiency and effectiveness of IA projects, enabling practitioners to create user-centered and intuitive information architectures.

Vectr

Information Architecture (IA) is the discipline that focuses on organizing, structuring, and labeling digital information to enhance its usability and findability. It involves the design and implementation of a framework that allows users to navigate and interact with information effectively. At the core of IA is the understanding of how users perceive and interact with information. It considers the users' mental models and information needs, aiming to create a structure that aligns with these expectations. By organizing information in a logical and intuitive manner, IA helps users quickly locate relevant content and understand the relationships between different pieces of information.

Version Control For IA

Version control for Information Architecture (IA) refers to the process and tools used to manage and track changes made to the structure, organization, and content of an information architecture system or framework. IA involves the design and organization of information, content, and navigation in digital platforms and systems. It is crucial in ensuring that users can easily find and access the relevant information they need to achieve their goals. However, as digital platforms and systems evolve and grow, it becomes necessary to make changes to the IA. Version control allows for the systematic management of these changes, ensuring consistency, accuracy, and efficiency throughout the IA development and maintenance process.

Virtual Reality (VR) IA

Virtual Reality (VR) is a simulated experience that can be similar to or completely different from the real world. It is typically created using computer technology and is presented to the user in a way that they can perceive and interact with it as if it were a real experience. VR often involves the use of a head-mounted display (HMD) or a similar device that allows the user to see a digital environment that is overlaid or replaces their actual surroundings. This immersive display provides a sense of presence, making the user feel as though they are physically present in the virtual world. The field of Information Architecture (IA) focuses on organizing, structuring, and labeling information in a way that makes it easy for users to find and navigate. In the context of VR, IA is concerned with the organization and structure of virtual environments to ensure that users can effectively interact with and comprehend the information presented to them. One of the main goals of IA in VR is to create a seamless and intuitive user experience. This involves designing the virtual environment in a way that allows users to easily navigate through the space, locate relevant information, and interact with virtual objects or elements. IA in VR also involves considering the user's spatial awareness and the unique challenges and opportunities that arise in a virtual setting. This includes understanding how users perceive and orient themselves within the virtual environment and designing the information layout accordingly. Additionally, IA in VR includes the organization and structuring of virtual content. This can involve creating hierarchical menus, spatially arranging objects or elements, or implementing interactive search functions to help users locate specific information or resources within the virtual space.

Visme

Visme is a web-based tool that allows users to create visually appealing presentations, infographics, reports, and other types of visual content. It provides a user-friendly interface with a wide range of templates, graphics, and design options to help users effectively communicate their ideas and information. In the context of Information Architecture (IA), Visme can be used as a tool to organize and present information in a structured and intuitive manner. IA is the practice of organizing and structuring content in a way that allows users to easily find and understand information. It involves designing the navigation, categorization, and hierarchy of information to create a user-friendly and efficient user experience. Visme offers several features that can assist in the implementation of effective IA. Users can easily create hierarchical structures within their visual content, such as creating categories and subcategories, to clearly organize and present information. The tool also provides the ability to add links, interactive elements, and multimedia to enhance the user experience and engagement. Additionally, Visme allows users to customize the visual appearance of their content to align with their brand or design preferences. This can help in creating a consistent user interface and visual language, which is an important aspect of IA. By maintaining consistency in design elements, such as colors, fonts, and layouts, users can easily navigate through the content and quickly understand the relationships between different pieces of information. In conclusion, Visme is a versatile tool that can be utilized in the field of Information Architecture to create visually appealing and structured visual content. Its user-friendly interface, templates, and design options facilitate the organization and presentation of information in a way that enhances user experience and understanding. By leveraging the features of Visme, users can effectively communicate their ideas and information to their target audience.

Visual Hierarchy

Visual Hierarchy refers to the organization and arrangement of content on a webpage or any other visual interface, with the goal of guiding users through the information in a logical and intuitive way. It is a fundamental concept in Information Architecture (IA) that helps users understand the relative importance and relationships between different elements of the interface. In the context of IA, visual hierarchy is achieved through the careful use of various design principles, such as size, color, contrast, alignment, and placement. By applying these principles, designers can manipulate the visual weight of different elements, making some more dominant and attention-grabbing, while others become more subordinate and supportive. One of the most common techniques used to establish visual hierarchy is through size. Larger elements tend to draw more attention, making them appear more important. By making the most significant elements larger and standout, designers can guide users' attention towards specific areas or actions on the page. Color and contrast can also play a significant role in creating visual hierarchy. By using bold and contrasting colors for important elements, such as buttons or call-to-action items, designers can make them visually distinct and easily identifiable. This helps users quickly recognize the most critical actions or information on a page. Alignment and placement are other essential aspects of visual hierarchy. Elements that are aligned consistently and positioned strategically create a sense of order and structure. For instance, navigation menus are typically placed at the top or left-hand side of a webpage, making them easily noticeable and accessible. Overall, visual hierarchy ensures that users can efficiently scan and comprehend the content hierarchy on a webpage, allowing them to make informed decisions and find the information they need. By leveraging design principles effectively, designers can create visually appealing and intuitive interfaces that enhance the user experience and facilitate the achievement of their goals.

Voice Interface IA

A voice interface IA refers to the design and organization of information within a voice-based user interface. It encompasses the structuring and labeling of voice commands, responses, and prompts to provide a seamless and intuitive user experience. When designing a voice interface IA, it is important to consider the unique characteristics and limitations of voice-based interactions. Unlike traditional graphical user interfaces, voice interfaces rely solely on auditory and sometimes visual cues to convey information. A key aspect of voice interface IA is the organization and categorization of commands. This involves grouping related commands together and creating a hierarchical structure that allows users to easily navigate and access the desired functionality. Effective labeling is also crucial in order to ensure that users can easily understand and remember the available commands. Additionally, voice interface IA involves the design of appropriate responses and prompts. Responses should be concise and clear, providing users with the necessary information without overwhelming them. Prompts, on the other hand, should guide users and clearly indicate the available options or next steps. Furthermore, voice interface IA considers the context in which the interactions occur. It takes into account factors such as user goals, preferences, and previous interactions to provide personalized and relevant information. Contextual cues can help users understand the current state of the system and enable more efficient and effective interactions. In conclusion, a voice interface IA focuses on the design and organization of information within a voice-based user interface. It involves structuring and labeling commands, designing clear responses and prompts, and considering the context of interactions to create a seamless and intuitive user experience.

Voice User Interface (VUI)

A Voice User Interface (VUI) in the context of Information Architecture (IA) refers to the design and interaction techniques employed to create a user-friendly and intuitive voice-controlled system. It is a method of interacting with digital devices and services using spoken commands and responses. VUIs play a crucial role in IA by providing alternative modes of interaction beyond traditional graphical user interfaces (GUIs) and touch-based interfaces. They enable users to interact with applications, websites, and other digital resources using their voice, allowing for hands-free and eyes-free interaction.

WC Product Table

The WC Product Table is an Information Architecture (IA) component that is used to display and organize product information in a structured and efficient manner. It is commonly used in e-commerce websites and applications to enhance the user experience by providing a clear and concise overview of available products. The WC Product Table is designed to present product data in a tabular format, allowing users to easily compare and filter products based on specific attributes such as price, size, color, and availability. The table typically consists of columns that represent these attributes, with each row representing an individual product. By utilizing the WC Product Table, users can quickly scan and locate the desired product without the need to navigate through multiple pages or perform extensive searches. The table can be easily customized to include only the necessary columns and attributes, which helps to reduce clutter and improve the overall usability of the interface. In addition to displaying product information, the WC Product Table often includes interactive features such as sorting and filtering options. These features enable users to quickly find products that meet their specific requirements, enhancing the efficiency of the shopping experience. The WC Product Table is typically powered by a content management system (CMS) or e-commerce platform that manages the product data, including details such as pricing, inventory levels, and product images. It is important for the IA to ensure seamless integration between the WC Product Table and the underlying data source, guaranteeing accurate and up-to-date product information. In conclusion, the WC Product Table is an essential component of IA in e-commerce websites and applications. It organizes product information in a tabular format, allowing users to compare and filter products based on specific attributes. The table is customizable and often includes interactive features such as sorting and filtering options, enhancing the user experience. Seamless integration with the underlying data source is crucial to ensure accurate and up-to-date product information.

WP Onepager

An onepager in the context of Information Architecture (IA) refers to a single HTML document or webpage that contains all the necessary content and sections within a single view. It is designed to provide a concise and focused user experience by presenting all the essential information on a single page, eliminating the need for users to navigate through multiple pages for accessing different sections or content. The purpose of a onepager is to simplify the information presentation and streamline the user journey by condensing the content into a single, easily scannable page. This approach is particularly useful for websites or applications that have a limited amount of content, enabling users to quickly access the desired information without the need for excessive clicking or scrolling.

WP Page Builder Framework

The WP Page Builder Framework is an Information Architecture (IA) tool designed to provide a flexible and customizable foundation for building WordPress websites. It serves as a framework that enables developers and designers to create and organize the structure, layout, and navigation of a website, ensuring a seamless user experience. By implementing the WP Page Builder Framework, users can easily optimize the architecture and organization of their website's content, allowing for efficient information retrieval and clear navigation for visitors. The framework offers a range of features and functionalities that support effective IA, including: 1. Customizability: The WP Page Builder Framework empowers users to tailor the IA of their websites to fit their specific needs, preferences, and branding. Users can customize various aspects of their website, such as the layout, color scheme, typography, and menu navigation, ensuring consistency and coherence throughout the site. 2. Responsiveness: With the increasing prevalence of mobile devices, ensuring a responsive website design has become a crucial aspect of IA. The WP Page Builder Framework is built with a mobile-first approach, ensuring that websites created with the framework are optimized for a seamless user experience across different devices and screen sizes. 3. Performance: The performance of a website plays a significant role in user satisfaction and engagement. The WP Page Builder Framework prioritizes speed and performance, providing users with an optimized code structure and lightweight design. This ensures that websites built with the framework load quickly and smoothly, enhancing the user experience. 4. Integration with Page Builders: The WP Page Builder Framework seamlessly integrates with popular page builders, such as Elementor and Beaver Builder, enhancing the flexibility and capabilities of website creation. Users can harness the power of these page builders alongside the framework to design and develop visually stunning and interactive websites. In conclusion, the WP Page Builder Framework is a powerful IA tool that empowers users to create well-structured, customizable, and user-friendly WordPress websites. By utilizing this framework, users can optimize the architecture and organization of their sites, providing visitors with a seamless and engaging browsing experience.

WP Page Builder Premium

The WP Page Builder Premium is a tool used in the field of Information Architecture (IA) that enables users to create websites with ease and efficiency. It is a premium version of the WP Page Builder, offering additional advanced features and functionalities. Information Architecture refers to the way information is organized, structured, and presented on a website to enhance user experience and facilitate easy navigation. It involves the design and organization of content, user interfaces, and interaction patterns. WP Page Builder Premium plays a crucial role in IA by providing a user-friendly interface for designing and creating websites. It allows users to construct the layout, structure, and presentation of the website using a drag-and-drop system, eliminating the need for coding knowledge or technical expertise. This tool offers a wide range of pre-designed templates, blocks, and modules that can be customized according to the specific requirements of the website. It provides various content elements such as text boxes, images, videos, buttons, and forms that can be easily added or rearranged on the website's pages. WP Page Builder Premium also offers advanced features like animation effects, parallax scrolling, responsive design, and integration with popular plugins. These features enable users to create visually appealing and interactive websites that adapt to different screen sizes and devices. In addition, WP Page Builder Premium allows users to optimize the website's performance by optimizing the code, compressing image files, and implementing caching techniques. This ensures that the website loads quickly and efficiently, providing a seamless user experience. In conclusion, WP Page Builder Premium is a valuable tool in the field of Information Architecture. It simplifies the process of website creation, enabling users to design visually appealing and well-structured websites without the need for extensive coding knowledge.

WP Page Builder Pro

WP Page Builder Pro is a feature-rich plugin that facilitates the creation and customization of web pages without the need for extensive coding or technical knowledge. In the context of Information Architecture (IA), WP Page Builder Pro enables the efficient organization and presentation of information on a website. The plugin streamlines the IA process by providing a user-friendly interface and an array of pre-designed elements and templates. This allows users to easily design and structure the content of their web pages, ensuring a logical flow of information. With WP Page Builder Pro, website owners can effectively arrange and present their content in a visually appealing and user-friendly manner. The plugin offers a vast range of customization options, allowing users to tailor the look and feel of their web pages to align with their brand identity or desired aesthetic. Users can modify colors, fonts, layouts, and styles effortlessly, ensuring consistency and coherence throughout the website. Additionally, WP Page Builder Pro supports responsive design, ensuring that web pages are optimized for various devices and screen sizes. With WP Page Builder Pro, website owners can effortlessly integrate various multimedia elements to enhance their user experience. They can easily embed images, videos, sliders, and other interactive elements into their web pages, adding depth and interactivity to the content. From an IA perspective, WP Page Builder Pro excels in providing a platform for the creation of a well-organized and intuitive website structure. The plugin supports the creation of multi-level menus and navigation systems, allowing users to create clear pathways for users to navigate through the website. This comprehensible navigation system helps users easily find the information they seek, enhancing the user experience and reducing bounce rates. In conclusion, WP Page Builder Pro is a comprehensive plugin that empowers website owners to efficiently implement IA principles in their web design. It simplifies the process of organizing and presenting information and offers a wide range of customization options to ensure an engaging and visually appealing user experience.

WP Page Builder

WP Page Builder is an Information Architecture (IA) tool that allows users to create and design web pages using a visual drag-and-drop interface. With WP Page Builder, users can easily construct and organize the content and layout of their website without needing to have any prior coding or design knowledge. WP Page Builder simplifies the process of building web pages by providing a user-friendly interface where users can choose from a variety of pre-designed elements, such as text blocks, images, videos, and buttons, and easily arrange them on the page. These elements are represented by modules that users can simply drag and drop onto the desired location on the page, allowing for quick and intuitive page creation. Users can also customize the appearance and behavior of these modules by adjusting various settings, including font styles, colors, alignments, and animations. This level of customization allows users to create unique and visually appealing web pages that align with their brand or personal preferences. One of the key benefits of using WP Page Builder is its ability to provide a responsive design. With this tool, users can preview how their web pages will appear on different devices and screen sizes, and make adjustments accordingly. This ensures that the website looks and functions effectively across various platforms, enhancing user experience. In addition, WP Page Builder integrates seamlessly with WordPress, making it easy to install and use for any WordPress-based website. It utilizes the core functionalities of WordPress, such as the built-in media manager and theme customizer, allowing for a consistent and cohesive website building experience. In sum, WP Page Builder is a powerful and user-friendly IA tool that enables users to easily create and customize web pages using a drag-and-drop interface. With its responsive design capabilities and seamless integration with WordPress, WP Page Builder provides a convenient and efficient solution for building visually stunning and functional websites.

WPBakery Page Builder (Formerly Visual Composer)

WPBakery Page Builder (formerly Visual Composer) is a powerful drag and drop page builder plugin for WordPress that allows users to create and customize websites without any coding knowledge. With its user-friendly interface and extensive range of pre-designed elements, this tool simplifies the process of building and managing websites. When it comes to Information Architecture (IA), WPBakery Page Builder helps organizations and individuals organize and structure the content of their websites in a logical and intuitive way. By providing a visual interface to design and arrange different elements on the page, it allows users to create a coherent and user-friendly information structure.

Web Accessibility Standards

Web Accessibility Standards, in the context of Information Architecture, refer to guidelines and best practices that aim to ensure that websites and web applications are accessible and usable by all individuals, regardless of their abilities or disabilities. These standards are crucial in creating an inclusive and equal online experience for everyone, including people with visual, auditory, cognitive, physical, or neurological impairments. By following web accessibility standards, Information Architects can design and structure websites in a way that accommodates diverse users and provides equal access to information and functionality.

Web Design Patterns

Web design patterns in the context of Information Architecture (IA) refer to recurring solutions or best practices used in designing and organizing web interfaces for effective information presentation and navigation. These patterns help designers create intuitive and user-friendly websites by utilizing established design principles and techniques. One commonly used web design pattern is the navigation pattern. This pattern focuses on creating a clear and accessible navigation structure for users to easily find and access different sections of a website. The navigation pattern often includes a menu or a navigation bar that is consistent across all pages, allowing users to understand and navigate through the website without confusion. Another web design pattern is the grid pattern, which involves aligning and organizing content using a grid system. This pattern helps to maintain a consistent layout and structure throughout the website, making it easier for users to scan and locate information. The grid pattern also aids in responsive design, ensuring that the website adapts well to different screen sizes and devices. The card pattern is another widely used web design pattern that arranges content in modular cards. Each card represents a distinct piece of information or functionality, allowing users to easily scan and interact with the content. This pattern is particularly useful when presenting multiple pieces of content or when designing a mobile-friendly interface. The search and filter pattern is a useful design pattern for websites with extensive amounts of information. It allows users to search for specific content or filter information based on certain criteria. This pattern helps users quickly find relevant information, especially in large databases or e-commerce websites with numerous products. Lastly, the breadcrumb pattern provides users with a visual trail of their current location within a website's hierarchical structure. This pattern is typically displayed as a series of links, representing the user's path from the homepage to their current page. Breadcrumbs simplify the navigation process and help users understand the website's organization. In conclusion, web design patterns in the context of Information Architecture are recurring solutions or best practices used to create intuitive and user-friendly web interfaces. These patterns, such as navigation, grid, card, search and filter, and breadcrumb patterns, help designers effectively organize and present information, ensuring a seamless user experience on websites.

Webflow

Webflow is a web design and development platform that allows users to create and publish websites without the need for coding knowledge. It provides a visual interface that enables users to design and customize their websites using a drag-and-drop system. With Webflow, users can create responsive and interactive websites that are optimized for various devices and screen sizes. As it pertains to Information Architecture (IA), Webflow offers a range of features and tools that facilitate the organization and structure of information within a website. IA involves the design and structure of content, user flows, and navigation systems to ensure that users can easily find and access the information they are looking for. With Webflow, users can create a hierarchical structure for their website's content, arrange it into different sections and pages, and establish relationships between different pieces of information. This allows for a logical organization of content, making it easier for users to navigate and understand the website's structure. Webflow also provides options for creating intuitive navigation systems, such as menus and breadcrumbs, that help users navigate through the website and understand their current location within the site. Users can define the main navigation menu, submenus, and links to ensure that visitors can easily find the information they need. Overall, Webflow's IA capabilities enable users to design and build websites that are organized, user-friendly, and optimized for efficient information retrieval. By providing a range of tools for content organization and navigation design, Webflow empowers users to create intuitive and engaging user experiences without the need for advanced coding skills.

Website Architecture

We can define website architecture as the structural design of a website, encompassing the organization, navigation, and hierarchy of the site's content and pages. It is a fundamental aspect of information architecture (IA) that focuses on how the information is organized and presented to the users. The website architecture serves as the blueprint for the site, outlining the relationships between different pages, sections, and elements. It ensures that the content is logically organized and easily accessible, allowing users to navigate the site intuitively and find the information they need.

Website Taxonomy

A website taxonomy, in the context of Information Architecture (IA), refers to the hierarchical structure or classification system used to organize and categorize the contents of a website. It provides a way to logically group and organize information, making it easier for users to navigate, find, and understand the content on a website. Website taxonomy is based on the principles of information organization and categorization. It involves the creation of a systematic and consistent classification scheme that reflects the nature and relationships between different content elements within the website. This classification scheme is typically represented as a tree-like structure, with parent categories at the top level and subcategories below them.

Whimsical

Whimsical in the context of Information Architecture (IA) refers to a style or approach that incorporates elements of playfulness, creativity, and non-conventionality into the design and organization of information. Unlike traditional or strictly structured IA approaches that focus on efficiency and functionality, a whimsical approach introduces a sense of wonder, surprise, and delight for users. It deviates from rigid hierarchical structures and linear navigation systems, offering a more engaging and interactive experience.

Wireframe Annotations

Wireframe annotations are textual notes or labels added to a wireframe to provide additional context, explanations, or instructions for the elements and interactions depicted in the wireframe. These annotations help to guide and inform the development team, stakeholders, or clients about the intended functionality, design choices, and content of the final product.The purpose of wireframe annotations within the context of Information Architecture (IA) is to communicate the designer's intentions and decisions regarding the structure, organization, and behavior of the user interface (UI). They serve as a crucial tool for documenting and conveying the IA strategy and enable effective collaboration and understanding among the project team.

Wireframe Prototyping

Wireframe prototyping in the context of Information Architecture (IA) refers to the process of creating a visual representation or schematic of a website or application. It is a low-fidelity representation of the user interface (UI) that outlines the basic structure and functionality of the system, focusing on the arrangement of elements and the flow of interactions. Wireframes are typically created in the early stages of the design process and serve as a blueprint or guide for the development team. They are an essential tool in IA as they allow designers to plan and communicate the organization and hierarchy of content, features, and navigation within a digital product. Wireframes are often created using simple shapes, lines, and placeholders rather than detailed graphics or actual content. This intentionally minimalistic approach helps to avoid distractions and allows the focus to remain on the overall layout and structure. By abstracting visual design elements, wireframes ensure that feedback and discussions during the early stages of the design process are centered around the fundamental information architecture principles rather than aesthetic preferences. Wireframe prototyping can be done using a variety of tools, ranging from pen and paper to specialized software. Many designers prefer to start with rough, hand-drawn sketches before refining the wireframes using digital tools. The choice of tools may depend on factors such as the complexity of the project, the level of collaboration needed, and the available resources. The benefits of wireframe prototyping in IA are numerous. Firstly, wireframes provide a tangible representation of the planned structure, enabling designers to visualize and evaluate the overall user experience. They help identify potential issues with navigation, content hierarchy, and interactions early on, reducing the need for costly revisions later in the development process. Additionally, wireframes serve as a valuable communication tool between designers, developers, and stakeholders. They facilitate discussions and align expectations by providing a clear understanding of the intended functionality and interface. Wireframes can also be shared with end-users to gather early feedback, ensuring that the resulting design meets their needs and expectations. In conclusion, wireframe prototyping is an integral part of the Information Architecture process. Through the creation of low-fidelity representations of the UI, it allows designers to plan and communicate the structure and functionality of a website or application. By focusing on the organization and flow of information, wireframes enable effective collaboration, early issue identification, and user-centered design.

Wireframe Testing

Wireframe testing refers to the process of evaluating and assessing the usability and effectiveness of a wireframe in the context of Information Architecture (IA). Wireframes are skeletal representations or blueprints that outline the structure, layout, and functionality of a digital product or webpage, without concerning itself with visual design elements. They act as a visual guide to help designers, stakeholders, and developers understand the information hierarchy and overall flow of the user interface. Wireframe testing, therefore, focuses on ensuring that the wireframes effectively serve their intended purpose and meet the needs of the users. The primary objective of wireframe testing is to gather feedback and insights from users in order to refine and optimize the wireframes. By testing the wireframes early on in the design process, potential usability issues, navigation problems, or content gaps can be identified and addressed before moving into the more expensive and time-consuming stages of visual design and development. During wireframe testing, users are typically presented with the wireframes and are asked to perform specific tasks or scenarios. The goal is to observe how users interact with the wireframes, identify any areas of confusion or difficulty, and collect feedback on the overall user experience. This can be done through methods such as user interviews, surveys, or usability testing sessions. The feedback obtained from wireframe testing is crucial in shaping the final design of the digital product. It helps designers make informed decisions about the placement of content, navigation elements, and interactive features. Additionally, wireframe testing allows stakeholders and clients to have a concrete understanding of the proposed solution and provide valuable input to ensure that the final product meets their requirements and expectations. In conclusion, wireframe testing plays a vital role in the Information Architecture process by evaluating the effectiveness and usability of wireframes. By gathering user feedback early on, designers can identify and address potential problems, resulting in a more user-centered and optimized digital product.

Wireframe.Cc

A wireframe is a visual representation of a web page or application that helps in the planning and design process of a project. It is typically used in the field of Information Architecture (IA) to outline the structure and layout of the user interface. Wireframes are created early in the design process to provide a low-fidelity blueprint of the final product. They focus on the layout and functionality rather than the visual design elements such as colors and typography. The purpose of wireframes is to communicate the intended user flow, content organization, and navigation structure to both designers and stakeholders. They serve as a foundation for the development of the website or application by ensuring that all the necessary elements are accounted for and positioned appropriately. Wireframes can be hand-drawn sketches, digital illustrations, or interactive prototypes. Regardless of the format, they typically consist of simple shapes, placeholders for text and images, and annotations to provide additional context. Wireframing is an essential step in the IA process as it allows designers to iterate and refine the structure of the interface before committing to the visual design. It helps identify and address usability issues, such as confusing navigation paths or missing content, early on, saving time and effort in the later stages of development. Overall, wireframes provide a clear and organized representation of the project's information hierarchy and user experience. They enable effective collaboration between the design team, developers, and stakeholders, promoting a shared understanding of the project goals and ensuring a user-centered design approach.

WireframeSketcher

WireframeSketcher is an essential tool used in the field of Information Architecture (IA) that enables designers to create and present visual representations of website or application interfaces. It is a software application that assists in the initial stages of the design process, helping designers to conceptualize the layout and structure of a digital product. In the context of IA, a wireframe can be defined as a simplified and schematic visual representation of a user interface. It focuses on the skeletal framework of the interface, omitting specific colors, graphics, and detailed typography. Wireframes primarily aim to illustrate the structure and functionality of the interface, providing a clear and concise view of the user flow and interactions. WireframeSketcher, specifically designed for wireframe creation, offers a range of features and capabilities that make it a valuable tool for IA professionals. Its user-friendly interface allows designers to easily drag and drop pre-designed elements, such as buttons, menus, and forms, onto the canvas. These elements can be customized and rearranged to create different page layouts and user flows. The software also includes a rich library of UI components and widgets, ensuring that designers have access to a comprehensive set of elements to accurately represent their ideas. Annotations and notes can be added to wireframes, enhancing communication and collaboration between designers, developers, and stakeholders during the design process. WireframeSketcher supports the creation of both low-fidelity and high-fidelity wireframes. Low-fidelity wireframes are quick and basic representations that focus on the broad structure and layout of the interface, while high-fidelity wireframes include more visual details and resemble the final product more closely. Overall, WireframeSketcher is a versatile and powerful tool in the field of IA, enabling designers to create effective wireframes that align with user needs and business goals. By visualizing and validating the structure and functionality of a digital product at an early stage, it facilitates the iterative design process, saving time and resources in the long run.

Wireframes

A wireframe, in the context of Information Architecture (IA), is a schematic representation of a webpage or user interface that illustrates the basic structure and layout of its elements. It is a visual guide that allows designers and developers to plan the organization and placement of content, features, and functionalities before the actual design and development process begins. Wireframes typically consist of simple, low-fidelity sketches or digital diagrams that use basic shapes, lines, and labels to represent different components of a webpage. They focus on the arrangement of elements rather than detailed aesthetics, making them an essential tool for defining the information hierarchy and user flow within a digital interface. By creating wireframes, IA professionals can: - Identify and prioritize content: Wireframes help in identifying the key content elements that need to be displayed on a webpage. They provide a clear overview of how different types of content (e.g., text, images, videos) will be organized and which ones should receive more prominence. - Improve usability and navigation: Wireframes allow designers to define the placement of navigation menus, search bars, buttons, and other interactive elements. They enable designers to test different navigational structures and find the most intuitive and user-friendly options. - Facilitate communication and collaboration: Wireframes serve as a common language between designers, developers, and stakeholders. They provide a visual reference for discussing and aligning on the overall layout, functionality, and user experience of a digital product. - Streamline development time and cost: Wireframes act as blueprints for the design and development teams. By visualizing the interface early in the process, potential issues and improvements can be identified and addressed before investing significant time and resources. - Aid in user testing and feedback: Before investing in full-fledged design and development, wireframes can be used to gather user feedback and validate the usability and effectiveness of the proposed interface. This iterative approach allows for early iteration and refinement.

Wirify

Wirify is a tool used in the field of Information Architecture (IA) to visually represent the structure and organization of a website or digital application. It generates a simplified diagram that captures the hierarchy of pages, menus, and other content elements, allowing IA professionals to analyze and improve the overall user experience. Through a process known as wireframing, Wirify extracts the essential components of a web page's layout and arranges them in a systematic and logical manner. It focuses on capturing the relationships between various elements rather than the visual design or aesthetics of the website. This is particularly useful during the early stages of website development when the focus is on user flows and navigation patterns.

WooCommerce Bookings

WooCommerce Bookings is a plugin for the WooCommerce e-commerce platform that allows businesses to offer bookable products or services on their website. It provides a flexible and customizable solution for managing and selling appointments, reservations, or any time-based offerings. This plugin enables businesses to define available dates, times, and durations for their bookable products or services. Customers visiting the website can view the availability and make bookings according to their preferences. WooCommerce Bookings seamlessly integrates with the existing functionalities of WooCommerce, such as inventory management, pricing, and order processing. With the help of WooCommerce Bookings, businesses can streamline their booking processes, reducing the need for manual intervention and minimizing errors. The plugin offers features like automated notifications and reminders to keep both businesses and customers informed about bookings and schedule changes. The flexibility of WooCommerce Bookings allows businesses to adapt the plugin to various use cases. It supports different booking types, including single or multiple-day bookings, time slots, custom durations, and recurring bookings. It also provides options for managing capacity, allowing businesses to limit the number of bookings per time slot or resource. WooCommerce Bookings provides a user-friendly interface for businesses to manage their bookings efficiently. It offers a centralized booking calendar, where businesses can view and update bookings easily. The plugin also provides reporting and analytics features, enabling businesses to track and analyze their booking performance. In summary, WooCommerce Bookings is a powerful plugin that extends the functionality of the WooCommerce platform to accommodate bookable products or services. It offers businesses the ability to define availability, manage bookings, and provide a seamless booking experience for customers.

WooCommerce Custom Fields

WooCommerce Custom Fields in the context of Information Architecture (IA) refer to additional data fields that can be added to product pages in an e-commerce store built using WooCommerce, a popular WordPress plugin for online selling. These custom fields provide a way to store and display extra information about products, supplementing the default fields such as title, price, and description. Custom fields allow website owners to easily extend the product data stored in their WooCommerce store. This additional information can include product specifications, dimensions, weight, color variations, and more. By incorporating custom fields, store owners can create a more detailed and comprehensive product catalog, providing potential buyers with the necessary information to make informed purchasing decisions.

WooCommerce Customizer

WooCommerce Customizer is an information architecture (IA) tool used to modify and customize the appearance and functionality of an online store powered by the WooCommerce plugin. It provides a user-friendly interface to make changes to various elements, such as layouts, colors, fonts, and more, without the need for coding knowledge. With WooCommerce Customizer, website owners have the ability to tailor their online store to meet their specific branding and design preferences. The tool offers a range of customization options, including the ability to change the site logo, select different color schemes, and adjust the layout of product pages. These modifications can enhance the user experience, reinforce brand identity, and align the online store with the overall visual design of the website. From an IA perspective, WooCommerce Customizer plays a crucial role in structuring and organizing an e-commerce website. It allows store owners to optimize the information hierarchy, ensuring that key elements are easily accessible and well-organized. For example, through the Customizer, website owners can decide where to display product categories, product search functionality, and various call-to-action buttons such as "Add to Cart" or "Checkout." Additionally, WooCommerce Customizer supports the creation of a seamless and intuitive browsing experience. It enables the configuration of navigation menus, sidebars, and footer areas, ensuring customers can easily find the information they need and navigate between different sections of the online store. By offering these customizable elements, the IA of the WooCommerce-powered website can be tailored to facilitate effective user journeys and encourage conversions.

WooCommerce Memberships

WooCommerce Memberships is a plugin designed for the WordPress platform that enables website owners to implement membership functionality into their online stores. It provides a comprehensive set of features and tools for managing memberships, including the ability to restrict content access, offer special discounts, and create exclusive membership plans. The plugin leverages the power of WooCommerce, a popular eCommerce framework, to seamlessly integrate membership capabilities into existing online stores. It enhances the user experience by allowing customers to sign up for various membership plans, granting them access to restricted content, products, and discounts based on their membership levels.

WooCommerce Multilingual

WooCommerce Multilingual is a plugin that enables the translation and multilingual functionality of a WooCommerce-powered website. It is specifically designed to work in combination with the popular WooCommerce plugin, providing a seamless integration for online stores that require multiple languages. From an Information Architecture (IA) perspective, WooCommerce Multilingual plays a crucial role in structuring and organizing the content of a multilingual website. By allowing users to translate their product pages, categories, tags, and other essential components of their online store, it ensures that the information is accessible and comprehensible to users of different languages.

WooCommerce PDF Invoices & Packing Slips

WooCommerce PDF Invoices & Packing Slips is a plugin that enhances the functionality of the WooCommerce platform by providing the ability to generate and manage PDF invoices and packing slips for online store transactions. This plugin is a valuable tool in simplifying the order fulfillment process and improving the customer experience in e-commerce. Within the context of Information Architecture (IA), WooCommerce PDF Invoices & Packing Slips can be classified as a content management component. It facilitates the organization and presentation of transaction-related information, specifically invoices and packing slips, in a standardized and easily accessible format. This component contributes to the overall structure and navigation of an e-commerce website, ensuring that essential documentation is readily available to both business owners and customers.

WooCommerce PDF Product Vouchers

A WooCommerce PDF Product Voucher is a digital document that serves as a voucher or coupon for a specific product in an online store powered by WooCommerce, a popular e-commerce platform. It is designed to provide customers with a printable or downloadable file that contains the necessary details and instructions for redeeming a product or service in a physical or virtual store. As part of the Information Architecture (IA) of an online store, the WooCommerce PDF Product Voucher represents a specific type of content, with its own unique attributes and functionality. It can be categorized as a digital product, distinct from physical goods or other types of digital content available in the store. Its purpose is to facilitate the sale and delivery of intangible products or services, allowing customers to purchase, gift, or redeem them through a voucher system.

WooCommerce Shipping

WooCommerce Shipping is a component of the WooCommerce plugin for WordPress, designed to handle the management and automation of online store shipping processes. As part of the Information Architecture (IA), WooCommerce Shipping provides a structured framework for organizing and presenting information related to shipping options and rates to customers. Within the IA of a WooCommerce site, shipping information is crucial in providing a seamless and efficient online shopping experience. WooCommerce Shipping allows store owners to configure and display various shipping methods and costs, based on factors such as destination, weight, or dimensions. By organizing this information in a structured manner, users can easily understand and select the most suitable shipping option for their orders.

WooCommerce Subscriptions

WooCommerce Subscriptions is a powerful plugin offered by WooCommerce, a popular e-commerce platform built on WordPress. The plugin is designed to enable businesses to sell products or services on a recurring basis, creating a seamless subscription-based business model. With WooCommerce Subscriptions, website owners can easily set up and manage subscription products, allowing customers to subscribe to receive regular deliveries of physical or virtual goods, access exclusive content, or benefit from ongoing services. Whether it's a monthly box subscription, online courses, software licenses, or membership fees, this plugin streamlines the process of generating recurring revenue for businesses.

Woopra

Woopra is an advanced web analytics tool that provides valuable insights and data on website visitors in the context of Information Architecture (IA). Woopra's primary function within IA is to collect, analyze, and interpret data regarding user interactions with a website. This tool allows IA professionals to understand how visitors are navigating through the website, what actions they are taking, and how they are engaging with different elements of the site.

XMind Zen

XMind Zen is an advanced information architecture (IA) tool that facilitates the organization, visualization, and analysis of complex information and ideas. It is designed to help individuals and teams gain clarity and insight by creating clear visual representations of their thoughts, concepts, and data. At its core, XMind Zen enables users to create mind maps, which are hierarchical diagrams that represent the structure and relationships of various ideas or topics. Mind maps are widely used in IA as they allow for the clear and logical organization of information. With XMind Zen, users can easily create, edit, and rearrange nodes within the mind map, facilitating the exploration and refinement of ideas. In addition to mind maps, XMind Zen also offers other IA tools such as concept maps, which focus on exploring relationships between concepts, and org charts, which visualize hierarchical structures within an organization. These tools provide users with multiple perspectives for examining and understanding complex information. XMind Zen's features go beyond just creating visual diagrams. It offers various annotation options, allowing users to add additional context, explanations, or descriptions to their ideas. Furthermore, the software supports the integration of multimedia elements, such as images, videos, and attachments, enhancing the overall presentation and clarity of the information being represented. Collaboration is another key aspect of XMind Zen. It provides users with the ability to share and collaborate on mind maps and other visualizations in real-time, either within a team or with external stakeholders. This capability enhances the efficiency and effectiveness of collaborative IA processes, promoting a shared understanding and alignment among team members. In summary, XMind Zen is a powerful IA tool that helps users organize, visualize, and analyze complex information and ideas. Through its mind mapping, concept mapping, and org chart features, it supports the logical structuring and exploration of information. With annotation options, multimedia integration, and collaboration capabilities, it facilitates a comprehensive and collaborative approach to IA.

Xmind

Xmind is a software application specifically designed for creating and organizing information through the use of visual diagrams. Within the context of Information Architecture (IA), Xmind helps professionals design efficient and user-friendly website structures, navigation systems, and content categorization. Information Architecture refers to the art and science of organizing and structuring information to enable effective discovery, understanding, and retrieval. It involves designing intuitive and logical systems that facilitate easy access and navigation for users. Xmind plays a pivotal role in this process by providing a visual representation of complex information and allowing architects to conceptualize and refine the information structure.

Xtensio

Information architecture (IA) refers to the organization of information in a systematic and logical manner to enhance the usability and accessibility of a website, application, or system. It involves the strategic planning and structuring of content, navigation, and functionality to facilitate efficient and effective user experiences.IA focuses on organizing information in a way that ensures users can easily find what they are looking for, understand the relationships between different pieces of information, and complete their tasks with minimal cognitive effort. It aims to create clear pathways for users to navigate through a website or application, enabling them to locate relevant information quickly and intuitively.

YITH WooCommerce Ajax Product Filter

The YITH WooCommerce Ajax Product Filter is an information architecture component that enables users to refine and narrow down their search results within an e-commerce website that utilizes the WooCommerce platform. This filter operates dynamically, using JavaScript and Ajax technology to update the displayed products on the page without requiring a full page reload. By using the YITH WooCommerce Ajax Product Filter, users can easily navigate through the product catalog by selecting specific criteria or attributes such as price ranges, colors, sizes, and categories. This allows them to quickly find the products that best match their preferences and requirements, saving time and effort.

Zeplin

Zeplin is a web-based collaboration tool designed specifically for the field of Information

Architecture (IA). It aims to facilitate the communication and seamless collaboration between designers and developers, by providing a platform where they can easily share design files, assets, and specifications. Zeplin acts as a bridge between the design and development phases of a project, allowing designers to upload their design files, such as Sketch or Adobe XD, to the platform. These files are then automatically processed by Zeplin, which generates interactive and organized style guides, as well as design specifications. Once the design files are uploaded, developers can access them through Zeplin's user-friendly interface. They can inspect and explore every element of the design, including colors, fonts, measurements, and assets. Zeplin provides developers with all the necessary information and resources they need to implement the design accurately and efficiently. One of Zeplin's key features is its ability to generate automatically generated CSS code snippets. These snippets can be easily copied and pasted directly into the developer's codebase, saving them valuable time and effort in writing repetitive CSS code. Additionally, Zeplin supports other popular programming languages, such as Swift for iOS development and Java for Android development, making it adaptable to various platforms. Moreover, Zeplin allows for effective collaboration and communication between designers and developers. Designers can leave comments and annotations on specific design elements for clarification or feedback. Developers can also leave comments and ask questions directly within the platform, reducing the need for lengthy email threads or meetings. In conclusion, Zeplin is a powerful tool in the field of Information Architecture that streamlines the design-to-development process. Its collaborative features and automated specifications make it an efficient platform for designers and developers to work together seamlessly.

Zion Builder

Zion Builder is a software application designed to facilitate the creation and management of Information Architecture (IA) within a digital environment. IA refers to the organization, structure, and labeling of information resources to enhance the usability and accessibility of digital products, systems, and websites. With Zion Builder, users can efficiently create and modify IA elements such as navigation menus, sitemaps, taxonomies, and categorization schemes. It provides a user-friendly interface that allows for easy drag-and-drop functionality, enabling users to arrange and link various information components according to their desired structure and hierarchy. Zion Builder offers features that simplify the IA design process. It includes a wide range of pre-designed templates and elements that can be customized to suit specific project requirements. Users can select from different navigation styles, color schemes, and typography options to create visually appealing and coherent IA designs. The software also emphasizes collaboration and team-based workflows. It allows multiple users to collaborate on IA projects simultaneously, making it ideal for teams working on complex digital products or websites. Features like version control and real-time editing ensure that all team members have access to the latest changes and updates. Zion Builder incorporates best practices in IA, ensuring that created structures are intuitive and user-friendly. It enables users to conduct user testing and gather feedback, which can be used to refine the IA design and improve the overall user experience. The software also supports the integration of analytics tools, allowing for data-driven decision making in IA design. In summary, Zion Builder is a powerful tool for creating and managing Information Architecture in a digital environment. With its intuitive interface, customizable templates, and collaboration features, it simplifies the IA design process and helps create well-organized and user-friendly digital products and websites.

IPlotz

iPlotz is a software tool designed to assist in the creation and visualization of Information Architecture (IA). Information Architecture refers to the structural design and organization of information systems, websites, and other digital products. It involves the arrangement and categorization of information to enhance user experience and facilitate effective information retrieval. iPlotz allows users to create wireframes, designs, and IA diagrams to plan and communicate their ideas visually. With iPlotz, users can easily create and manipulate different components of IA, such as site maps, navigation systems, and taxonomies. The software provides a user-friendly interface for creating and editing these components, enabling users to quickly design and iterate their IA concepts.

www.ingramcontent.com/pod-product-compliance
Lightning Source LLC
LaVergne TN
LVHW041205050326
832903LV00020B/474